# MARCANTONIO FLAMINIO
Poet, Humanist and Reformer

# MARCANTONIO FLAMINIO

*Poet, Humanist and Reformer*

by
CAROL MADDISON

CHAPEL HILL: University of North Carolina Press
LONDON: Routledge & Kegan Paul

*First published 1965
in the United States of America
by University of North Carolina Press
and in Great Britain
by Routledge & Kegan Paul Limited*

© *Carol Maddison 1965*

*No part of this book may be reproduced
in any form without permission from
the publisher, except for the quotation
of brief passages in criticism.*

*Printed in Great Britain*

# CONTENTS

| | | |
|---|---|---|
| | INTRODUCTION | *page* vii |
| 1 | YOUTH | 1 |
| 2 | FIRST FREEDOM | 8 |
| 3 | HIGHER STUDIES | 24 |
| 4 | ROME IN THE 1520's | 38 |
| 5 | IN GIBERTI'S HOUSEHOLD | 73 |
| 6 | INDEPENDENCE AND PASTORALS | 88 |
| 7 | NAPLES AND THE REFORM | 105 |
| 8 | VITERBO AND CARDINAL POLE | 119 |
| 9 | TRENT | 154 |
| 10 | ROME TWENTY YEARS AFTER | 171 |
| | BIBLIOGRAPHY | 207 |
| | INDEX | 215 |

This work has been published with the help of a grant from the Humanities Research Council of Canada using funds provided by the Canada Council.

# INTRODUCTION

NO period in world history is so brilliant, so exciting, and so important as the first half of the sixteenth century, and few lives have been better timed to illustrate the impact of that period on a young man of talent but no fortune than that of Marcantonio Flaminio (1498–1550), poet, humanist, and reformer. Flaminio was received at the court of Leo X and in the highest circles in Italy, and he was a privileged spectator of the brilliance, debauchery, and infatuate folly of the last days of Renaissance Rome. He saw the old order overturned in the sack of 1527, and he participated in the reconstruction and revaluation of religious policy that led to the summoning of a council at Trent in the 1540's.

Flaminio was the finest lyric poet of this second great age of Latin literature. He wrote with equal sensitivity and sincerity in both the classical and Christian traditions. His pastoral epigrams helped to establish a new literary genre in Latin and Italian, while his hymns to the pagan gods and his odes helped to shape the modern Italian ode. His book of religious lyrics, written as he lay desperately ill, revives the spirit of primitive Christianity, the simple, ardent faith of the early Church and foreshadows the new great age of religious poetry. However, his earlier translations of the Psalms, some of the first in Renaissance Latin, disconcert the modern reader with their mannered charm. In a period of great letter writers Flaminio's letters in Latin verse and Italian prose are outstanding for their ease and limpidity, while some of them are important for their discussions of educational or literary theory and others are precious documents in the history of Italian reform thought. The political ideas ascribed to Flaminio by Vida in his *De Republica* show him to have been one of the precursors of Rousseau.

But, apart from his poetry and letters, Flaminio is remembered as the co-author and publisher of the most popular and most dangerous devotional work in sixteenth-century Italy, *The Benefit of Christ Crucified*. This work sold forty thousand copies, a record for the time, before it was condemned by the Inquisition, put on the Index, and destroyed. For three hundred years

INTRODUCTION

it was believed to have been lost. Then, in the middle of the nineteenth century, a copy was found in St. John's College Library, Cambridge, and the tract was republished in London. The *Beneficio di Cristo* perhaps owes its survival to the fact that it was the favourite reading of King Edward VI.

Flaminio's connections with England were always close. In the early 1540's Flaminio became an ardent believer in justification by faith alone and frequented Valdes' circle in Naples, where he met Bernardino Ochino and Peter Martyr Vermigli, who both fled to England when the persecutions began. Vermigli became professor of theology at Oxford and helped Cranmer prepare the Book of Common Prayer, while Ochino became a canon of Canterbury. Then Flaminio was taken into the household of the great English cardinal, Reginald Pole, who tried to save a man of such potentially dangerous literary abilities from defecting to the enemy. But Pole was already compromised with the Inquisition and this act was later considered to be equivocal and constituted one of the main charges made against him by the Inquisition.

The *Beneficio di Cristo* was translated into English by Nicholas Ferrar in 1638 and published on George Herbert's advice. In the eighteenth century Alexander Pope edited a selection of Flaminio's poetry. Oddly enough, Flaminio seems to have been quickly adopted as a school author in England. A word-for-word translation of his lyrics, that is virtually a crib, has survived from the reign of Charles II, while as late as 1792 an edition of Flaminio's poetry was published for use in Winchester School. The last English edition of his poems was published in 1829.

Flaminio died, probably of malaria, in 1550 at the end of the conclave at which his friend, Pole, was almost elected pope. He was buried in the church of St. Thomas of Canterbury attached to the English College in the Via di Monserrato in Rome.

Since the triumph of romanticism, humanist poetry has been neglected, and Flaminio and the other great humanist poets have been virtually forgotten. The aim of this book is to reintroduce a fine lyric poet and, through an account of his life, to illuminate another facet of the past. With Flaminio we can look at Renaissance Rome, and at Italy in the ferment of religious reform, and see how these events touched the day-to-day living of an educated and thinking man.

*Chapter 1*

# YOUTH

MARCANTONIO FLAMINIO was born in Serravalle, now Vittorio Veneto, in the early months of 1498.[1] His father, Giovanni Antonio Flaminio, was a distinguished humanist who had just been recalled to Serravalle to teach. His mother, Veturia, came from a substantial local family.

Flaminio was a name which the father had received in humanist circles in Venice. His real name was Zarrabini and the

[1] There is some uncertainty about the date of Flaminio's birth because of conflicting statements made by himself and his father. His father, in a letter dated April 26, 1514 (Fr. Domenico Giuseppe Capponi, *Joannis Antonii Flaminii Forocorneliensis Epistolae Familiares*, Bologna, 1744, II, 5, and G. A. Flaminio, *Silvarum II, Epigrammatum III*, Bologna, 1515, sig. Aii$^v$–Aiii$^v$) says that Marcantonio has just passed his sixteenth birthday, but Marcantonio himself, in the dedication of his *Carmina* (Fano, 1515) dated September 11, 1515, says that he is barely eighteen. Is this a young man stretching his age? If his father were right he would be seventeen and a half in September, 1515. But why, then, if he were trying to pretend that he were a bit older, did Marcantonio use the word "scarcely" or "barely", which gives the impression that he is making the most of his youth?

There is a third statement about Flaminio's age. His nephew, Cesare Flaminio, in a letter prefixed to the Lyons edition of Marcantonio Flaminio's poems and dated October 13, 1547, says that his uncle had refused permission to publish these poems which were youthful exercises and unbecoming a man who was almost fifty. Putting all these statements together Flaminio must have been born in the winter of 1497–8. Since his father moved to Serravalle in 1498 and since Flaminio was born in Serravalle, I decided to take 1498 as the date of his birth, although it is possible that his mother preceded his father to Serravalle for her confinement and that Flaminio was therefore born there in 1497.

family came from Cotignola in Romagna, like the Sforzas. Various members of the Zarrabini family had served on embassies for Francesco Sforza, but Marcantonio's grandfather, Lodovico, was a distinguished soldier who settled in Imola, and it was there, in about the year 1464, that the poet's father, Giovanni Antonio Zarrabini, was born.[2] Luckily for us Giovanni Antonio was a great letter writer and from his letters we can reconstruct his son's background and at the same time get a fair picture of the precariousness of even middle-class existence in the most advanced country of the world five hundred years ago.

When he lost all but his life in the Austrian attack on Venice in 1509, Giovanni Antonio Flaminio, as he then was called, wrote a long letter to a boyhood friend, now a powerful cardinal, asking for help. In that letter he told Cardinal Rafaele Riario of the varying fortunes of the past thirty years:[3] After leaving the school at Imola in his middle teens, Giovanni Antonio was sent to Bologna to study under the great humanist Filippo Beroaldo, Sr. But the plague broke out. Rather than return home, Giovanni Antonio, now sixteen, decided to go to Venice. Despite the protests of his parents, who felt that he was too young and too delicate to set out alone, he made his way to the coast and thence, by sea, to Venice. The Venetians were friendly and helpful, and after a few days Giovanni Antonio found a patron in Benedetto of Platea, a wealthy and learned man, who asked him to tutor his son, nine, his daughter, ten, and his brother's son. He was to receive two pieces of gold a month and his keep. For three years Giovanni Antonio lived with this family, treated more as a son than as an employee. Benedetto gave him books to read at home and sent him to the public lectures in Venice where he studied under the well-known humanists Benedetto da Legnagno, Giorgio Merula, and Giorgio

---

[2] For biographical details about G. A. Flaminio see Ercole Cuccoli, *Marc Antonio Flaminio* (Bologna, 1897), pp. 23 ff; Capponi, *op. cit.*, 'Vita'; F. M. Mancurti, *Flaminiorum Forocorneliensium Carmina* (Padua, 1743), 'Vita.'

[3] Giovanni Antonio Flaminio to Cardinal Rafaele Riario, Capponi, *Ep. Fam.*, pp. 12–17. There is also an account of the early years in Venice in a letter to Filippo Beroaldo, Sr., written about 1482–3, *E.F.*, pp. 136–7. Note: All future references to Giovanni Antonio Flaminio's letters will be to Capponi's edition, unless otherwise noted, and will be given in the text immediately following the letter cited.

Valla of Piacenza. When the historian, Marcantonio Sabellico, returned to Venice in 1484, he and Giovanni Antonio became close friends, and it was perhaps Sabellico, fresh from Pomponio Leto's academy in Rome, who dubbed Giovanni Antonio 'Flaminio', probably because he came from Imola, which was in the old Flaminian province. At any rate, Giovanni Antonio says in his letter to Cardinal Riario that he received the name 'Flaminio' from the Venetian Academy early in his twentieth year, i.e., about 1483. 'The Venetian Academy' was probably a rather pretentious phrase used by Flaminio to give the humanist circle in Venice the status of the Roman and Neapolitan Academies.

Giovanni Antonio Flaminio did well in Venice. He grew strong, and his reputation as a scholar and Latin stylist spread. When he was twenty-one, i.e., about 1485, he received an offer of one hundred gold pieces, the highest salary they had ever paid a professor, to go to Serravalle (Vittorio Veneto), a rich and prosperous town in the territory of Treviso, to teach. In Serravalle Flaminio made an advantageous match with the daughter of one of the first families. But in the fourth year after he had gone to Serravalle, and in the first year of his marriage, Flaminio received an offer to teach the children of the patrician families of Venice and Padua at Montagnana near Padua.

Flaminio spent nine years at Montagnana (1489–98) and during that time established himself as a scholar of national repute. He corresponded with Pomponio Leto, Pico della Mirandola, and Poliziano. He borrowed and lent manuscripts in the great, corporate, humanist effort to establish and print definitive texts of the classical authors. He sent his agent to Venice to hunt out rare codices and to the Vatican library to do research on a projected history of the Roman people up to the end of the fifteenth century (*E.F.*, pp. 120–1 and 1–3).

But the air at Montagnana was bad for his wife. Flaminio received a tempting offer from Vicenza, but, fearing that if he accepted it the people at Montagnana would say that the story about his wife's health was made up, he returned to Serravalle, to the joy of the townsfolk. Shortly after her return, Veturia gave birth to her fourth child and third son, Marcantonio Flaminio. A few months later his two elder brothers, Giulio and Fausto, died, leaving Marcantonio the humanist's only son.

The Flaminios settled in Serravalle. The father built a substantial house and, in 1503, received the gift of adjoining land from his wife's uncle, who was angered by his daughter's marriage to a groom (*E.F.*, pp. 178–80). Here, in this bright and industrious outpost at the foot of the Dolomites, Marcantonio Flaminio enjoyed a happy childhood.[4] He studied with the other boys in his father's house, played with the other boys in the streets—for his father, like many of the great Renaissance educators, believed in the importance of sport in the development of the complete man[5]—watched the fullers and armourers at work on the banks of the Mischio, and followed the stream up through the town walls to the wooded hills that lay just outside. Serravalle is a wholesome spot and Marcantonio was not yet troubled with ill health.

Meantime the father's reputation grew. He became sufficiently influential to believe that he might be able to save Imola from Cesare Borgia by pleading on its behalf (*E.F.*, pp. 4–5); he received civic honours from the people of Serravalle (1502); and he prospered materially.

For more than a decade the armies of Louis XII (1498–1515) and Julius II (1503–13) kept central and northern Italy in an uproar, but during all this time the 'Serenissima' Republic of Venice, at the height of her power, remained virtually untouched. Then, between October and December, 1508, the various conflicting powers in Italy, the French, the Austrians, and the Pope, came together in the League of Cambrai, to encompass the destruction of Venice. In 1509 Venetian territory was invaded. The Austrian armies, descending through the Dolomites, fell on Serravalle and devastated the town, raping,

---

[4] See Marcantonio Flaminio's epistle to Francesco Robortelli, then merely a young man from Serravalle who was going to teach Greek and Latin in Venice, *Flaminiorum Carmina*, VI, 29. Here Flaminio describes his own youth in Serravalle. Mancurti's edition of Flaminio's poems is the standard one. It is the edition referred to throughout this book, unless otherwise noted. It is sometimes referred to as the Cominian edition since it was published by the famous Paduan publisher, Comini.

Other details about Serravalle are taken from G. A. Flaminio's letter about the flood, *E.F.*, pp. 95–8.

[5] See G. A. Flaminio, *De Educatione et Institutione Liberorum* (Bologna, 1524), published by G. B. Gerini in *Gli Scrittori Pedagogici del secolo xvi* (Torino, 1897) and *E.F.*, pp. 294–300.

plundering, and burning. The elder Flaminio lost everything, including most of his books and his writings.

Collecting the remains of his property, with his wife and daughter and eleven-year-old son, he returned to his native Imola after an absence of more than twenty-five years. It was on this occasion that he wrote the account of his life and fortunes to Cardinal Riario.

Riario responded with the utmost generosity. He sent Flaminio fifty pieces of gold by banker's order and instructed his agent to send him fifteen cartloads of wood and as much wine and wheat as he and his family needed for a year. He told him to ask his agent if he wanted anything else. 'Use my goods as yours. Send me some of your writings sometimes and, if you come to Rome, you will not regret it.' (*E.F.*, p. 18.)

Giovanni Antonio Flaminio found his father, Lodovico, still alive, his mother well, and a host of friends and relatives to welcome him. In his ebullient, energetic way he sought to repair his fortunes. He got a three-year contract from the citizens of Imola to establish a school—at a higher salary than had ever been offered before! (Flaminio, like all humanists, was much given to boasting and was by no means indifferent to money)—and he was chosen to address Julius II on behalf of the city of Imola when the belligerent pope paused there. Flaminio made a rousing speech to Julius, urging him to drive the foreigners out of Italy. The pope was pleased; he sent Flaminio fifty pieces of gold and a bishop who urged him to come to Rome. Flaminio declined gratefully on the grounds of his contract with Imola, his wife's worsening health, which made travel a source of much suffering, and his need for quiet and tranquillity for his history of the Roman people. He put his duty as a husband and his literary work before all else (*E.F.*, pp. 6–8; 10–12; 20–1).

In the early spring of 1513 Julius II died. In the conclave on March 11 of that year the thirty-seven-year-old Cardinal Giovanni de' Medici was elected pope and assumed the name of Leo X. Paolo Giovio, Bishop of Nocera, in his life of Leo X (1551), says that the older cardinals rallied to the candidate of the younger ones because of the nobility of his birth, the dignity of his manners, his exquisite literary taste, and his extraordinarily easy-going nature. They did not look for spiritual qualities in the new pope. They wanted a man who could command the support of princes, who would be popular with the Roman mob, and who was wealthy and learned. Giovanni de' Medici was aided in his election to the throne of St. Peter by an ulcer from which he had been suffering, which broke during the conclave and filled the council chamber with such a stench of death that his ambitious colleagues felt that they were electing only an interim pope.[6]

On the pope's coronation a piece of tow is burnt, while a priest utters these words, 'Pater sancte, sic transit gloria mundi'.[7] Leo took this admonition to heart, and seemed bent on enjoying as much transitory glory as he could. A few days after his coronation, in April, 1513, Leo X rode to San Giovanni Laterano on the same horse that he had ridden the year before at the battle of Ravenna and the crowd went wild with joy. He scattered gold and silver coins, and it is said that he spent 100,000 gold ducats that day, 'more than a pope has since spent in a year'.[8] Rome felt that the golden age had returned.

Leo was always liberal. He had a purple purse filled with gold daily for distribution. He dined publicly, and spectators enjoyed his bounty, especially those who had put on old clothes. Leo patronized poets, painters, and scholars, and, despite his worldliness, gave monthly subsidies to the cloistered.[9] Indeed, with a catholicity of taste and intellectual interest, he patronized theological studies, and religious poetry and painting, as well as humanist works. He suggested the theme of the *Christiad* to Girolamo Vida and was delighted with Sannazaro's *De Partu Virginis*.

Leo hunted on horseback for days at a time at Cerveteri and at the villa Magliana, down the Tiber, described by Leandro Alberti as a 'very beautiful and delightful place where the popes take pleasure'.[10] He fished at Lake Bolsena and he liked comedies—he had Machiavelli's *Mandragola* performed—and music and jolly companions. After supper he kept six or seven

---

[6] *Pauli Jovii Novocomensis Episcopi Nucerini de Vita Leonis Decimi Pontificis Maximi Libri Quatuor* (Florence, 1551), p. 65.

[7] W. Roscoe, *The Life and Pontificate of Leo X* (Liverpool, 1805).

[8] A. Ciccarelli, *Le Vite de' Pontifici* (Rome, 1587), fol. 224ᵛ.

[9] Giovio, p. 96.

[10] L. Alberti, *Descriptio Italiae* (Bologna, 1550), fol. 75ᵛ. 'Magliana' is now a stop on the Roman 'Metropolitana'.

cardinals with him to play cards and he threw handfuls of florins to the spectators. He was a practical joker.[11] He had great fun with a white elephant which the Portuguese ambassador brought him in March, 1514.[12]

But Leo had his other side. Though he was not a religious man, he exhibited personal integrity in the administration of the Church, he encouraged the propagation of the faith in the New World and in Russia, he founded churches, he tried to end the Syrian and Ethiopian schisms, and he gave benefices only to the able. However, he bestowed ecclesiastical rank according to genius not piety, and his profligacy led him to raise revenue by questionable methods, which were soon to bring the wrath of Luther upon him. Leo even sold the statues of the twelve apostles which had been presented to him by the Teutonic Order.[13]

[11] C. Cantù, *Eretici d'Italia* (Torino, 1866), I, pp. 501–3.
[12] For stories about the elephant see Tidelfo Nardella, *La Seconda Roma* (Milan, 1927), p. 601. This elephant also appears in all the joke books of the period.
[13] Cantù, *op. cit.* I, pp. 510–11.

*Chapter 2*

# FIRST FREEDOM

THE magnificence of the Medici court and the wars that continued to disrupt the life of northern Italy tended to make Rome the mecca of talented young Italians. And so, with some misgiving, the moral schoolmaster Flaminio sent his most brilliant pupil and only son to Leo X in the spring of 1514. Marcantonio was by that time sixteen years of age, an accomplished scholar, and something of a poet.

With the excited good wishes of all in Imola, in the hopefulness of the new season, Marcantonio Flaminio set out for Rome on a borrowed horse towards the end of April, 1514. In his baggage he carried various literary works of his father's to offer in return for patronage. For Cardinal Marco Cornaro of Venice, who was to get him an audience with the pope, he had his father's two books of miscellaneous poetry (*silvae*) and three of epigrams, which were published in Bologna in the following year. For Leo himself he brought a four-hundred-verse epistle urging the pope to make war on the Turks, the elder Flaminio's favourite policy which he continued to press on Adrian VI, Clement VII, and Paul III, and a eulogy of the pope for his exploits at the battle of Ravenna on Easter Sunday, 1512.[1] Flaminio also brought his own present to the pope, his *Mis-*

[1] For the elder Flaminio's letters to Cardinal Marco Cornaro, Imola, April 26, 1514, and Leo X, Imola, April 27, 1514, see GAF, *Silvae*, sig. Aii<sup>v</sup>–Aiii<sup>v</sup> and Aiv<sup>r</sup>–Av<sup>r</sup>.

*cellaneous Notes* (*Annotationum Silvae*), described by Gradenigo as being a collection of extremely erudite and beautifully written notes on or emendations of various passages of the classical authors.[2]

Flaminio was cordially received in Rome by Cardinal Cornaro and was introduced by him to the cardinals of Ferrara and Aragon who took him to see Leo X at the villa Magliana. The pope read Giovanni Antonio's four-hundred-verse epistle without stopping and then read the eulogy aloud. Then he began perusing Marcantonio's work. Amazed at his meticulous scholarship, the pope began questioning the youth. When he found that he could speak as well as he could write, that he had a quick wit and a ready answer on a wide variety of subjects, Leo quoted Apollo's words at the first exploit of the young Ascanius, 'Macte nova virtute, puer; sic itur ad astra,' 'Keep up the good work, boy; that's the way to immortality.' 'Continue what you have been doing and in a short time you will get a great name for yourself and you will be an ornament not only to your father and your family but to the whole of Italy.' Then he asked the humanist and poet, Rafaele Brandolini, who was then living at his court, to look after the boy and he told Flaminio that he would remember him in Rome.[3]

Meanwhile his father fretted anxiously in Imola. He had not had any news and it was the first time that he had been separated from his son for even a day:

> Tell me how easy or difficult was your approach to the cardinals, whom you met, what conversations you had, how you were treated—everything. And how did you attempt to approach the pope? Give me all the details, big and little.... When you are far away and very eager things even seem important that to others appear not worth mentioning.... As to the horse, what are you going to do? I see that my sister's son is not going to be patient much longer. Therefore it is up to you to make an effort, if you think that you will not be coming back by the first, or at the latest the thirteenth of June, to send back the horse as quickly as possible. ... Everyone has high, even fantastic hopes, for you. Therefore

[2] Cuccoli, p. 29.

[3] See GAF's letters to Leo X, *E.F.*, pp. 51–2 and p. 66, his letter to his son, pp. 208–9, and the letters exchanged by GAF and the cardinal of Aragon, pp. 72 and 73. See also Cuccoli, pp. 30–1.

you must exert yourself with all your strength to live up to and, if possible, to surpass them. This journey of yours will bring you much glory if you do not fail yourself.     *E.F.*, pp. 206–7

By the end of May the elder Flaminio had had his letter, and a request that his son be allowed to stay on in Rome. Writing to the pope on the thirty-first of May Flaminio asked to have his son back. He had lost his wife the summer before and Marcantonio was the only one of his four children who remained to comfort him—the daughter was presumably married by then—and he was too delicate to remain far from home (*E.F.*, pp. 51–2).

But Giovanni Antonio was prevailed upon to change his mind in the interests of his son's career. Writing a little later to Matteo Carranto of Stignola he says that he had not intended that Marcantonio should stay long in Rome but that the situation had taken on a momentum of its own. He thanks him for his friendly advice to recall his son, but Rome is where the arts flourish most in Italy and where one can learn best. 'From my long experience of teaching boys I know that if a boy is not upright by nature his father's instructions and diligence will not have much result (*E.F.*, pp. 233–5).

However, Flaminio took the precaution of writing to Antonio Padulense, the Apostolic Secretary, with whom Marcantonio was then staying, to ask him to be a father to the boy and to keep him from depraved company (*E.F.*, pp. 215–6), a request that was not so easy to fulfil at the court of Leo X. For, while Leo liked poets and scholars, he particularly enjoyed the company of courtesans and clowns. His favourite was Fra Mariano, a bearded Dominican in his middle fifties from the convent of San Marco in Florence and a faithful servant of the Medici. He had been Lorenzo the Magnificent's barber. He became Giovanni de' Medici's fool.[4] In 1513 he made everyone laugh at a dinner party presided over by the courtesan Albina by leaping on the table and running from one end of it to the other hitting cardinals and bishops! Such was the taste of the time. In 1514, on the very day of Bramante's death, Leo gave his sinecure ('piombatore') to Fra Mariano and, surprisingly enough, Mariano kept it, even after Leo's death, until his own death in 1531.

[4] Giovanni de' Medici became Leo X.

Fra Mariano was a Rabelaisian glutton. It was said that he could eat twenty capons and suck four hundred eggs at a sitting and that he once ate a camel-hair coat because it was oily and dirty.[5]

Other buffoons at the court of Leo X were Proto da Lucca, Julius II's clown; Andrea Veneziano, a libertine painter and a lewd fellow who was killed by the Spaniards in the sack of Rome; Romanello, a Jewish comedian; Ceccotto, a Genoese tailer renowned as an astrologer, who had a shop at the end of the Piazza San Pietro; 'the brother who ate berettas'; 'Butta là,' 'Throw it there'; and sundry parasites of higher rank. Leo had his fools to dine with him and, although he was a fairly abstemious fellow himself, through the influence of the fools, who invented such dishes as sausages made of peacock meat, he spent half the revenues of Spoleto, Romagna, and the Marche on his table.

And then there were the courtesans. Women were barred from ecclesiastical circles in Rome and yet needed by a society which was devoted to the fullest possible enjoyment of life. To grace their dinner tables, and to have stimulating and refined companionship, the cardinals called in the courtesans, who performed functions somewhat similar to those of the geishas in traditional Japanese society. The courtesans were young, beautiful, brilliantly attired, and extraordinarily well educated. They knew Cicero and Petrarch, Vergil, Horace, and Ovid, Boccaccio, and the romances, and one Jewish girl, Nicolosa, even read the psalms in Hebrew—whether or not to her clients, we do not know. The courtesans were witty and cultivated conversationalists—indeed Montaigne said that one paid as much for the conversation as for the 'negociation entière'— they composed verses, played musical instruments, sang, danced, and were highly skilled in the art of pleasing all manner of men. Their fees were extremely high, twenty-five, thirty, forty, even one hundred gold pieces a night—Tullia

---

[5] For Leo X's parasites see Arturo Graf, *Attraverso il Cinquecento* (Torino, 1888), 'Un Buffone di Leone X', pp. 369–94; A. Ferrajoli, *Il Ruolo della Corte di Leone X*, 1514–16 (Rome, 1911); and G. A. Cesareo, 'Buffoni, parassiti e cortigiane alla Corte di Leone X', *Nuova Rivista Storica*, VIII (Milan, 1923), 79–82. For Fra Mariano Fetti see also Pio Paschini, *Roma nel Rinascimento* (Bologna, 1940), p. 441.

d'Aragona received that in Rome from a German[6]—but they sought out the company of humanists over and above what could possibly have been profitable to them. At no other period in history, except possibly in the first century B.C., did men of letters enjoy such a privileged position. Some of the courtesans were highly thought of by such people as Michelangelo and Vittoria Colonna. Some of them genuinely loved their lovers, and, in December, 1522, the daughter of the famous courtesan Imperia tried to kill herself to avoid having to submit to the desires of Cardinal Petrucci.

In this carnival atmosphere Flaminio settled down to the study of Greek. His teacher, Giovanni Battista Pio, wrote to his father on July 1, 1514, to say that Marcantonio had a good place in Rome, where he could devote all his time to literature and to the study of Greek. He, Pio, would look after him, but his father should not be parsimonious with him, but send him money to buy Greek books (*E.F.*, pp. 221–2). Flaminio also studied at this time with Filippo Beroaldo, Jr. (1472–1518), the historian of Julius II and of the Bentivoglios of Bologna, a member of the Roman Academy, the director of the Vatican library, and a humanist dear to the heart of Leo X for his contrived Latin verses about the leading courtesans and comedians of the Roman court.

But from his father's letters it appears that Flaminio found little time to write home: 'I know that nothing can be more welcome to the absent, nothing more pleasing, than to receive lots of letters from the family, especially since you have now begun to travel abroad for the first time. But please remember your duty to write to *me*. You know I have scarcely time to breathe, and yet I answer your every wish.' (*E.F.*, pp. 209–10). The last statement implies that the father got some letters, the usual requests for money and help that students send home from university. However, he finally received the sort of letter he wanted, enclosing some poems which proved that his son was profiting from his sojourn in Rome and his association with great men. His father was delighted:

[6] Graf, pp. 251–2. The best spenders were the French, then the Germans. The worst were the Spaniards. Among the Italians the Venetians were most generous. The Neapolitans paid with caresses and sighs. The account of the courtesans is based on Graf.

FIRST FREEDOM

I like what you are writing now. The subject matter is rich. It gives you scope to exercise your talents. But ration your strength. There is danger that you may wear yourself out too quickly and leave nothing lasting. Eternal glory is what you want. Everything else is frivolous, momentary, and empty, because in the hands of fortune.... I am near the end of my tragedy, *Priam*, on the last act. I sent you the beginning. I have had a hard time writing this. There have been many obstacles in the way, but I have persisted. *E.F.*, pp. 211–13

What were the poems to which his father referred? When we look through Marcantonio Flaminio's published works, even the volume published in Fano in the following year,[7] we find very little that can definitely be ascribed to this period, and less that could answer his father's description. There are a couple of epigrams translated from the Greek (II, 30 and 32), a Horatian ode on Beroaldo's histories (I, 28), and a hymn to Bacchus (I, 14). It must have been to the latter that his father referred, seeing in this poem, despite its subject, the humanist tradition and, in particular, the imitation of Catullus (63), rather than the influence of the court of Leo X.

Flaminio's hymn to Bacchus, written in the difficult galliambic metre, is an extraordinary *tour de force* for one so young. In fact, Flaminio has succeeded in the dithyramb better than any other neoclassicist. That he is on the whole convincing rather than frigid may be due to the fact that his picture of what it is like to be carried away by Dionysiac enthusiasm is based on sound classical scholarship and expressed in concrete fact and that, far from trying to whip himself into a state of simulated frenzy with a lot of pretentious bombast as others do, he always remains an observer of the bacchanal. Indeed, halfway through the poem he prays Bacchus to spare him the violent excitement of the Dionysiac and to allow his new priest to perform the sacred rites in peaceful coverts, or, if he must suffer the excesses of poetic rapture and dedication to Dionysus, at least to spare him enslavement to a mistress. Catullus, too, in the hymn on Attis and Cybele (63), to which Flaminio is indebted, had begged to be spared the frenzy which led to self-

[7] *Michael Tarchaniotae Marulli Neniae ... M. Antonii Flaminii Adulescentis Amoenissimi Carminum Libellus* (Fano, 1515).

13

mutilation—rather a more serious thing!—but this only in a three-line appendage to a ninety-verse poem, whereas the theme of calm dedication occupies half of Flaminio's twenty-six verses.

The dithyramb is Flaminio's statement of his consecration to poetry. The ode to the younger Filippo Beroaldo marks out his particular field as the lyric. The poem is conventional and traditional. Horace and many humanists before Flaminio had written similar odes. But it is significant and points to a high sense of purpose, undoubtedly inculcated by his eager father, that Flaminio's earliest poems which have survived show such a clear sense of direction. It is not surprising that he should feel that his career lay with literature. Considering his background and the age, that was the only possible career for him. There lay the ready road to success, power, ease, and immortality. But that he should know from the very beginning that the lyric was what he could write shows a realistic critical sense, at least on the part of the father, and a mature acceptance of the facts on the part of the son. Flaminio never allowed himself to be seduced by grandiose dreams of epic or tragedy.

Flaminio's ode is a competent imitation of the ancients, in this case Horace: 'Beroaldo may write serious historical works. Venus does not permit Flaminio. Beroaldo will describe battles he has never seen. Flaminio tries with his lyre to forget those that he has had with his mistress.' There is a curious reflection of the atmosphere in which Flaminio lived in the fictitious name chosen for the mistress, 'Hierophila', 'Lover of sacred things'. Is this the girl, elsewhere called 'Leucippe' (II, 12), who, despite a throng of passionate suitors, became a nun?

Later in 1514 Flaminio went to Naples, where he was warmly received by Sannazaro. They soon became friends and Sannazaro had a lasting influence on his poetry. Flaminio wrote him an epigram complimenting him on his piscatory eclogues (II, 20).

Back in Rome Flaminio met Count Baldassare Castiglione, Urbino's ambassador to the court of Leo X. Castiglione took him into his suite and brought him back to Urbino with him in the late autumn. Flaminio's father wrote Castiglione that he was very pleased that Castiglione had taken Marcantonio into his house as a son. He was also relieved because he had heard that his son had left Rome, but he did not know where he had gone. He had had no letters (*E.F.*, pp. 252-3).

To his son Giovanni Antonio wrote:

> I have been very miserable because of your long silence. I was very worried about you because you are not usually remiss in writing. Therefore I thought there must be some reason. But from your letter I have learnt that you have written often and also that you enjoyed good fortune. With what joy and gladness I read of your health, your success, what you have been doing, where you have been!...
>
> I have sent the works you presented to the pope and to Cardinal Cornaro to the printer in Bologna, because lots of people have been asking impatiently for them. I had delayed so that your notes could be collected and published with them. But when I saw that your work required more time and labour, and when friends in Bologna and the printer were ready to see my poems through, I thought I should not let the opportunity slip. I have written some more recent things to go with them.
>
> Today I am writing to Castiglione to thank him.
>
> *E.F.*, pp. 203-4

In November the elder Flaminio wrote Castiglione that he had sent him two letters, but had had no reply:

> The bearer of this letter is coming back to me; so he can bring your reply. No excuses! I want to know how my son is doing, whether you are satisfied with him, whether he lives up to your expectations, with whom he likes to spend his time—with decent people, I think, because that is the way he was brought up from infancy, and your care and education have followed. But in these depraved times one does not know. He cannot easily avoid associations with courtiers, who are for the most part very corrupt. If he escapes unscathed he will be very fortunate.
>
> *E.F.*, pp. 249-50

It would appear from the subsequent correspondence that the author of *The Courtier* was spared this letter, which apparently went astray.[8]

The court of Francesco Maria della Rovere, Duke of Urbino, was one of the most brilliant of a brilliant age. Perhaps there was less lively conversation then than there had been in the days

---

[8] See *E.F.*, pp. 205-6 and 254-5.

of *The Courtier*, almost ten years before, when the former duchess, Elisabetta Gonzaga, held her salon, while the crippled Duke Guidobaldo rested, but the court was still the most cultivated in Italy, and the Renaissance palace the handsomest. Looking down on smiling slopes planted with vines and fruit trees and olives, in a rich and pleasant part of the Apennines, the castle of Urbino was a triumph of military expediency and rational harmony. The great duke, Frederick II, had built himself a panelled study, one of the finest examples of Italian marquetry, between the two frontal towers, commanding a long view over the mountains. Underneath it, on the way to the banquet hall, was a shrine to the Muses, complete with an altar where offerings were made. Until the seventeenth century, when a commission of cardinals formally desecrated the fane, the Muses were literally worshipped in Urbino.

The rooms of the ducal castle were light and spacious. The walls were hung with silks, and with cloth of gold and silver. There were many paintings—it was here that Raphael began his career—and antique statues in bronze and marble. The doors were inlaid, some from designs by Botticelli. Musical instruments were everywhere.

In this bright and happy palace music, comedy, and ballet flourished. There is an interesting letter from Castiglione to Count Lodovico Canossa, a member of the court in the old days, later apostolic nuncio to France, Bishop of Bayeux, and ambassador of the French king to the Republic of Venice, in which Castiglione describes the sets, the dancing, and the general spectacle of the latest musical production.[9] An example of one of these entertainments, Castiglione's pastoral *Tirsi*, composed with Cesare Gonzaga, his cousin, has survived.[10]

We learn from the elder Flaminio's correspondence that Guido Postumo, an old friend of his from Montagnana days, who had been kind to Marcantonio in Rome, was in Urbino early in 1515. It must have been then that Marcantonio Flaminio wrote the two odes to him which were published in the Fano edition of that year. These odes, again heavily Horatian,

[9] D. Atanagi, *De le lettere facete et piacevoli di diversi grandi uomini* (Venice, 1565), pp. 179–86.
[10] Published in *Lettere di Negozii del Conte Baldasar Castiglione*, ed. Pierantonio Serassi (Padua, 1769), II, pp. 206—17.

develop further the theme of love, which was an undernote in the Roman poems.

One of them[11] is an expansive account of Guido's love affair with one Ianthis, which concludes with a rueful reference to Flaminio's own experience with Cynara. It is full of Horatian commonplaces and echoes the 'Pyrrha' ode (I, 5) and the famous dialogue between jealous lovers (III, 11). The second ode to Postumo continues the tale of Flaminio's unhappy love:

> Now, Posthumus, spring raises his flowery locks
> From Chloris' rosy bosom, and zephyrs
> Drive the cold away, and shaggy
> Earth shakes off the snow.
>
> And singing sailors dare skim with their sails
> On the polished marble of the Adriatic,
> And the Sardinian spreads his nets for the eager
> Fish with no fear for the threats
>
> Of winter. Now grass clothes the green
> Fields and big buds swell the vine
> Shoot's skin. Now birds soften the air
> With their songs.
>
> (But I weep day and night and get no
> comfort from wine or sleep or music.)
>
> But, alas, my wretched mind feasts on anxiety
> And my heart drinks tears and my rest is a worn-out
> Body lying on the iron earth,
> And my song is a tearful
>
> Lament and the name of my mistress. So
> I will never know spring, so the sun will never
> Shine bright for me. So, for me, winter
> Is without end
>
> > Jam ver floricomum, POSTHUME, verticem
> > Profert puniceo Chloridis ex sinu,
> > Jam pellunt Zephyri frigus, et horrida
> > Tellus exuitur nives.

[11] 1515 ed., sig. c iv$^v$–d$^v$. This poem was omitted from the Cominian edition.

> Cantantes Hadriae marmora navitae
> Audent velivolis currere puppibus:
> Nec tendens avidis retia piscibus
> Hibernas metuit minas
>
> Sardus: jam virides gramina vestiunt
> Campos, et tumidis palmes agit graves
> Gemmas corticibus: jam volucres suis
> Mulcent aëra cantibus. . . .
>
> Sed curae, heu! miseri sunt animi dapes,
> Sed cordis lacrimae pocula, sed quies
> Confectum rigidae corpus humi jacens,
> Sed carmen mihi flebiles
>
> Questus, et dominae nomina: sic mihi
> Numquam veris eunt tempora: sic mihi
> Soles non aliquo tempore candidi:
> Sic mi perpetua est hiems.           II, 33

Two other odes in the same vein must have been written about this same time, 'Flora stop looking at me' and 'To Lygda', 'What is the source of this big misunderstanding.'[12]

These early poems are a respectable achievement for a youth who has just turned seventeen. They show the effects of drilling in the favourite Renaissance style-forming exercise of double translation. Flaminio has made the texts of Vergil, Horace, and Catullus his own. As was the aim of the method, classical phrases and classical images supply the poet with conceits and even with many of his ideas. But these poems of Flaminio's are not just a patchwork of handy phrases from the *gradus* strung together as an exercise in verse composition. Flaminio has shaped his poetic reminiscences into poems that are clearly his own. They have a carefully balanced structure which owes more to the sonnet than to the classical ode, an easy rhythm, descriptions of nature that reveal the poet's emotional submergence in the vital processes around him, and a colouring of Petrarchan romanticism. They exhibit careful training, a fine

---

[12] For the first see Giov. Ant. Taygeto, *Carmina Praestantium Poetarum* (Brescia, 1565), fol. 48ᵛ. For the second see the 1515 edn., sig. d iiiʳ⁻ᵛ.

musical ear, and extraordinary flair. Originality was to come later.

His father's view of his son's latest achievement, however, was somewhat different:

*Imola, March 15, 1515*

How glad I was to get your letter after the long delay! Now all annoyance and indignation are gone. I had blamed Castiglione, too. . . .

I have sent your odes to Phileroti [Achille Bocchi]. I like them, everything about them, that is, but the subject matter. It is all right for them to be somewhat gay and jolly, but I should prefer them to be more modest, savouring pleasure less. For you who, as long as you were under your father's supervision and in his care, were brought up as purely as a vestal, must make a tremendous effort to avoid giving the impression that, in the few months in which you have been away from me, you have abandoned the manners of a virgin for those of a whore. I know that very many young people scorn advice of this sort and that people who give it seem ridiculous (so great has been the decline in morality and decency), but it does not suit someone who has been educated as you have been to make a fool of himself with a crowd of depraved young people.

I am sorry to hear of Guido Postumo's illness.

*E.F.* pp. 195–7

In a letter of March 18 Giovanni Antonio thanks his son for his letter:

I read Castiglione's *sylva* with the greatest pleasure. I would never believe that it was struck off in the heat of the moment and not well thought out and criticized. I would be very pleased to have another of his poems, one which is more representative of the author's work.

I have read your more recent odes[13] and sent them to Phileroti so that they could be published with my books. They should bring you no small credit.

I am glad that Guido Postumo is getting better.

*E.F.*, pp. 197–8

On April 13 Giovanni Antonio wrote again, and here we

---

[13] The poems to which his father could possibly have been referring are the Horatian ode to Litavio Speranzo of Fano; the ode on Alessandro Orlogi's laurel tree; the ode on his father's poems; the ode on Bocchi's elm; and the ode on the death of Bocchi's mother.

have the first reference to Marcantonio's stomach trouble: 'I have nothing to write you, but Cornelio is going there, therefore I am sending a few words. I hope you will succeed in overcoming your disease. I believe that all else will go well with you if you only drive the disease from that part of your body' (*E.F.*, p. 198). He goes on to ask again for poems from Postumo and Castiglione and for all his son's news. On the sixth, thirteenth, and fifteenth of May Giovanni Antonio answers letters his son has written him about the meaning of various words and the allegory of the myth of Phaeton (*E.F.*, pp. 199; 200; 201-2).

In the early summer of 1515 Marcantonio Flaminio went to Mantua, Castiglione's home town, either with Castiglione or on a mission for him, and stopped over for some time with his father on the way back. His father, who had been having a lot of trouble with his publisher in Bologna—letter after letter refers to incomprehensible delays—sent his son to straighten out some misunderstanding about the epigrams, which were printing (*E.F.*, pp. 391-2). By August 13 Marcantonio was back in Urbino 'perhaps later than Castiglione had expected but sooner than his affectionate father desired' (*E.F.*, p. 259).

Giovanni Antonio continued to have trouble with his book. In December he was still urging Leandro Alberti to find out what the printer was doing (*E.F.*, p. 395). Marcantonio, however, had better luck. His first collection of poetry, which the Bolognese nobleman Achille Bocchi (Phileroti) had urged him to publish, appeared quickly and without difficulty in Fano in September, 1515. I quote his prefatory letter to Achille Bocchi:

> You have made a gain. I am sending you the book you wanted to see in print and with it Marullus' *Neniae* which I edited for you. But I ask you to be as liberal as I am, and to send me your Democritus, which I expect will make me laugh so long that I will forget all the miseries and grief that I suffer through my love for Lygda.

One of the poems in this first volume is an eclogue called 'Thyrsis' which Flaminio, in a special dedicatory letter to Alessandro Muzzoli of Bologna, says that he wrote in these last days on his return from Mantua to Urbino. This speaks for speedy publication.

The 1515 poems include the praise of Mantua, and the

eclogue 'Thyrsis,' both about Castiglione; Horatian odes to Cornelio Balbo of Bologna and Litavio Speranzo of Fano, who appears actually to have seen the work through the press; an ode on a laurel tree belonging to Alessandro Orlogi; an ode on his father's poems, which were due to appear; Marullus' epitaph; three poems to his patron, Achille Bocchi; and a Catullan love lyric. The edition of a posthumous work of Marullus shows Flaminio's claims as a scholar.

Among the poems to Achille Bocchi is one which is a little jewel. This shows what Flaminio was capable of as a lyric poet. Here are economy, delicacy, and due measure. It is an ode to Diana (I, 34) on Bocchi's dedication of an elm to her on which he will hang up the spoils of the chase. It follows the form of an inscription, the first stanza tells to whom the dedication is made, the second names the donor and the object, the third tells what purpose it is to serve.

> Maiden, tamer of the wild beasts of the woods,
> Who, in the company of the quiver-bearing nymphs,
> Range Cynthius' hill and the forest
> Of black Erymanthus,
>
> Bocchi, the glory of the two tongues,
> Skilled at starting the wandering deer,
> Dedicates to you this elm
> In the midst of his estate,
>
> From which the lynxes will hang, brought down
> By his swift shaft, and the timorous does,
> And, consecrated to you, the antlers
> Of the long-lived stag.

Virgo syluestrum domitrix ferarum,
Quae pharetratis comitata Nymphis,
Cynthium collem peragras, nigrique
Siluam Erymanthi,

Bocchius, linguae decus utriusque,
Doctus errantes agitare cervos,
Hanc tibi villa media locatam
Dedicat ulmum.

Unde veloci domitae sagitta
Pendeant lynces, timidique damae,
Atque vivacis tibi consecrata
Cornua cervi.                                    I, 43

The ode on the death of Bocchi's mother (I, 43) is a work of piety—Flaminio was not good at obituaries. The other poem to Bocchi (II, 29) is a piece of Catullan wit on his sending him his volume of poems.

The last poem, and one which Flaminio must have written on his return to Urbino just before his book went to press, is a Catullan love lyric, 'To Septimilla',[14]

>Please, my dear Septimilla,
>Where is the sweetness, where is
>The passion which you showed for me previously
>When you called me your delight,
>And your hope and comfort,
>Swearing that there was nothing in the whole world
>More lovely or more elegant than I?
>See, now, your Flaminio is returning
>To Urbino, my dear Septimilla,
>And with him he is bringing many thousands
>Of kisses and with them that incomparable
>Plaything which you always yearned
>To hold in your hands and to toy with.
>Say sweet things to me, make love
>To me passionately, my dear Septimilla,
>For I have always loved you more than life
>Itself and I will love you without cease
>Until death shrouded in darkness
>Devours me in his dreadful maw.

>Amabo, mea chara Septimilla,
>Ubi blanditiae, libidinesque
>Quas in me facere antea solebas?
>Cum me delitias tuas, tuamque
>Spem et solatiolum tuum uocabas
>Adiurans nihil esse in orbe toto
>Me venustius, elegantiusue.

[14] *Michael Tarchaniotae Marulli Neniae. Eiusdem Epigrammata nunquam alias impressa. M. Antonii Flaminii Adulescentis Amoenissimi Carminum Libellus* (Fano, 1515), sig. e^v–e ii^r.

En nunc Flaminius tuus rediens[15]
Urbinum mea chara Septimilla
Secum millia multa basiorum,
Secum illum quoque passerem elegantem[16]
Ferens, quem in manibus tuis tenere
Qui cum ludere saepe gestiebas.
Dic mi blanditias, libidinesque
In me fac mea vita Septimilla,
Nam te plus oculis meis amaui
Semper, assidueque amare pergam,
Donec mors tenebris operta nostrum
Funesto caput ore deuorabit.

After this pleasant diversion with Septimilla Flaminio was immediately recalled by his father, who wrote Castiglione,

> I had expected him back [from Rome] soon and had planned to send him to Bologna in the autumn to study. He had spent enough time on the liberal arts, which are ornamental rather than useful for earning a living. But the boy was attracted by the brilliant appearance of the city [of Rome] and by all the learned men who were there and asked my permission to stay longer. At first I was disturbed, but on reflection I realized that he would gain much from some months in such a city in the company of such brilliant men. And he did. Then you took him away with you. I was very glad at that, in contrast to my original attitude towards his staying on in Rome. I know that Marcantonio has gained a lot from you in learning and manners, but now I think it is time he applied himself to more serious studies and I would be very pleased if you would be the apparent author of a decision to send him to Bologna now.  *E.F.*, pp. 259–61

At the same time the father apparently asked the Bolognese nobleman, Francesco Bentivoglio, if he would look after Marcantonio in Bologna; for we have a letter from Giovanni Antonio to Bentivoglio thanking him for offering to take Marcantonio into his house (*E.F.*, pp. 141–2).

Castiglione responded swiftly to the father's request. There is a letter from Giovanni Antonio dated September 26 [1515] thanking Castiglione for returning his son (*E.F.*, pp. 262–3).

---

[15] The hasty composition is revealed in the false quantity in 'rĕdĭens' The metre requires ᴗ — ᴗ.

[16] *Sensus obscoenus.*

*Chapter 3*

# HIGHER STUDIES

'BOLOGNA teaches, the mother of universities' is the proud boast of the old coins and seals of Bologna.[1] It was here that Giovanni Antonio had started his higher studies. It was here that he sent his son. In the autumn of 1515 Marcantonio Flaminio settled in the Bentivoglio household in Bologna and began the study of philosophy with Pomponazzi, who enjoyed great notoriety for his book denying the philosophical proof of the immortality of the soul.

Soon the city was the scene of great events. Leo X was making peace with Francis I and meeting the twenty-one-year-old conqueror of Milan in Bologna,[2] the second city of the papal domains. The pope entered his northern capital on December 7, in cold pomp, before a sullen crowd. On Tuesday the eleventh the king arrived. All the cardinals with their trains went to meet him, and the procession entered the city with the papal guard on horseback and the Swiss guard on foot, with trumpets and drums leading the way. They were followed by the king's heralds, their trumpets hung with golden fleurs-de-lis on an azure ground, and by the king escorted by two cardinals. The meeting lasted six days and was followed by the treaties of Noyon and London, of August and October, 1516, which

[1] G. Giordani, *Della venuta e dimora in Bologna di Clemente VII*... (Bologna, 1842), 'notes', p. 48, no. 193.

[2] For descriptions of the meeting between Leo X and Francis I see Roscoe, III, 50–97 and Giordani, 'notes', p. 9.

secured the peace of Europe for a few years by recognizing the *status quo* in Italy, i.e., Francis in Milan, Charles V in Naples, and the Venetians in Verona.

When Flaminio had been barely three months in Bologna he was offered a lucrative post in the office of the papal secretary by the secretary himself, Sadoleto. But his father refused to allow him to accept it. He wanted his son to get a solid education (*E.F.*, pp. 139–40).

Henceforth we hear little of Flaminio for five-and-a-half years, from the end of 1515 until the summer of 1521. An occasional letter or reference here or there reveals him for a moment engaged in some ordinary activity, and then there is silence.

Almost all that we know about the Bologna period is that in the beginning of 1516 Flaminio wrote a saint's life for the Dominican scholar, Leandro Alberti;[3] that he made two life-long friends at university, Lodovico Beccadelli and Count Nicolò d'Arco; and that he swam in the river Reno in the summer.[4] There are, however, two extant descriptions of

[3] 'The Life of the Blessed Maurice of Hungary', L. Alberti, *De Viris Illustribus Ordinis Praedicatorum* (Bologna, 1517), fol. 217ᵛ–220ᵛ.

[4] See 'Nymphae, quae parui colitis vaga flumina Rheni'. The poem appears in Janus Gruter, *Delitiae CC Italorum Poetarum* (Frankfurt, 1608), IV, 31–2, under the name of Antonio Mario of Imola. Cuccoli has proved, pp. 161–3, that the Antonio Mario poems were by Flaminio. However, the explanation that he gives for some of Flaminio's poems appearing under the name of Antonio Mario, namely, that these are early poems, that this was Flaminio's baptismal name, and that he adopted the humanist 'Marcantonio' later, is implausible. Flaminio is already referred to as Marcantonio by his father as early as 1513 (GAF, *E.F.*, pp. 444–6) and he was well known in humanist circles as Marcantonio from 1514 onwards, while all the 'Antonio Mario' poems must, on internal evidence, have been written after that date.

Moreover, Marcantonio was quite a popular given name in the period—I counted some two dozen well-known men by that name in the course of my reading, including his father's old friend, the historian Marcantonio Sabellico, who gave the family their humanist surname 'Flaminio'. Furthermore, Marcantonio is a likely Christian name for a child born in the Republic of Venice, for St. Mark is the patron of Venice, and St. Anthony of Padua, in whose territory his father was teaching just before Flaminio's birth. Antonio was also his father's second name. Thus there seem to have been many motives for the father to call his son Marcantonio: that combination of names was both humanist and Christian, and it enabled the father to name his son after an old friend and a distinguished scholar, as well as

Flaminio in 1516 which show him to have been a worthy provincial, shy, quiet, considerate, and unassuming, but bright. In a dialogue which forms part of his *Illustrious Men* Leandro Alberti refers to Flaminio as a very modest and very learned young man, full of good qualities, whom he loves very dearly, as a son, because of his frank and upright nature. 'Who could help liking him, since he is both good-looking and intelligent? He shines in conversation, in poetry, in music, and now he is applying himself to the study of philosophy.'[5] While, in a letter to Giovanni Antonio Flaminio, dated November 10, Marcantonio's old mentor in Rome, Giovanni Battista Pio, refers to his affection for Marcantonio, a young man of mature intelligence and one of nature's favourite children. 'I can think of innumerable examples of his dutifulness and thoughtfulness towards me, but he suffers from a rather provincial shyness, as one might expect. He hardly ever comes to visit me and when he does he is timid, as though he had to look Augustus in the eye and were offering a green shoot to an elephant. Tell him to be more at his ease' (*E.F.*, p. 479).

Flaminio did not stay long in Bologna. After his taste of life in the universal city the university city was dull. By 1519 we find him back in Rome as a student of literature and philosophy and a bosom friend of the charming but dissolute poet, Francesco Maria Molza. Giraldi, writing at this time, describes Flaminio and Molza as two furious scribblers of great promise, ardently devoted to poetry. He adds that Molza was even more ardently devoted to women and was known to many people only by his mistress's name.[6]

This was the time of the Longolio case and one 'Flaminio' offered to read his defence. In the light of the subsequent close friendship between Marcantonio Flaminio and the Belgian, Christophe de Longueil (Cristoforo Longolio, as he was known in Italy), it was thought that this Flaminio was our poet, but as Cuccoli has pointed out, it is more likely that it was Flaminio

---

[5] Alberti, fol. 153ʳ.
[6] Pierantonio Serassi, *Poesie di Francesco Maria Molza* (Milan, 1808), 'Vita', pp. 23–4, quotes L. G. Giraldi, *De Poetis nostrorum temporum*, II (Basle, 1580), p. 396.

---

after himself. There were no equally obvious reasons for the father to have called the son Antonio Mario.

Tomarozzo, an admirer of Longueil's style, whose father, Giulio, had put Longueil up when he came to Rome.[7]

According to Giraldi, Flaminio suffered severely from stomach trouble at this time.[8]

After the controversy over his admission to Roman citizenship Longueil went to France, then, in the autumn of 1519, to Venice, where he was the guest of Bembo until the spring of 1520. Early in April of that year Bembo left for Rome, and, in the middle of April, Longueil went to Padua to study. There he was received into the household of the wealthy young Genoese aristocrat, Stefano Sauli, who already had Marcantonio Flaminio with him. For a little more than a year they all studied, played ball, joked, laughed, and discussed literature together.

What brought Flaminio to Padua we do not know. Presumably he had met Sauli, who nominally occupied a post in the papal court, in Rome and the latter, as was customary for wealthy young men of the time, had taken the poor student into his household to profit from his conversation. At any rate Flaminio was enrolled in the University of Padua for the year 1520. He studied literature with the humanist, Romolo Amaseo, Aristotelian philosophy with Marcantonio Passero, and law with the great jurist, Parisio.[9] A fellow student was Reginald Pole, cousin of Henry VIII, and later Flaminio's patron and protector.

We hear little about Flaminio for that year, except that he was in Venice in the summer. Perhaps while he was there he visited his father, who had returned to Serravalle for the third time in 1517 and was now preparing to leave it again. We have an interesting letter written on July 25, 1520, by the elder Flaminio to Cardinal Grimani, Bishop of Ceneda, the diocese which included Serravalle (the two neighbouring towns now form Vittorio Veneto), telling him that he was leaving Serravalle about the middle of August to settle in Bologna. But the real purpose of the letter was to inform the cardinal of the shocking conditions that existed in the convent in Serravalle about which no one else would tell him. The immorality of the clergy

---

[7] Cuccoli, pp. 48–9. See Sadoleto's letter to Longolio, Rome, September 8, 1519, Jacobo Sadoleto, *Epistolae Familiares* (Rome, 1760), I, 43.

[8] Cuccoli, pp. 47–8.  [9] *Ibid.*, p. 50.

and nuns there was so flagrant that the mass had fallen into contempt because of the behaviour of the priests, and popular indignation ran high. Some of the nuns lived like prostitutes. The people were so horrified that it was a wonder they did not attack the convent and burn it down. For the few good ones life with the others was a torment, they were constantly submitted to indignities, and there were brawls at morning and evening prayers (*E.F.*, pp. 42–5).

The winter of 1520–1 ended as it had begun in the north of Italy, with heavy rains and flooded fields. To this there was added the danger of marching armies, French, Swiss, Spanish, Venetian, and sundry Italian. On February 8, 1521, Marcantonio Flaminio went to Venice, probably on business for his patron, Stefano Sauli. He was back in Padua by the fourteenth. The next month it was Longueil's turn to go, and then it appears that Stefano Sauli went to Rome, if the setting of Bartolomeo Ricci's dialogue, *De Judicio*, in which Giulio Camillo, Marcantonio Flaminio, and Sebastiano Delio appear discussing literature, is at all exact.[10]

Sauli was back in Padua by the beginning of May, when he received distressing news. His brother, Giovanni, was seriously ill. Sauli set out for Genoa on May 4 taking Marcantonio with him.[11] Longueil, left alone in Padua, became a member of the household of Reginald Pole, who was to take in his friend Flaminio just twenty years later.

On June 12 Longueil wrote Sauli and Flaminio that he missed the gaiety of their company and the pleasantness of their conversation, which were everything to him. He hoped for their early return. From this letter we get an interesting sidelight on the period. Longueil tells his friends that he has been asked by the Germans to defend Luther, and by the pope to attack him. He does not know what to do. He does not want people to think that he has sold himself to the stronger side if he helps the pope![12]

Three days later Longueil heard of the death of Giovanni Sauli and wrote straightaway to both Stefano Sauli and Flaminio. He wrote Stefano Sauli a letter of condolence. In his

---

[10] See Cristoforo Longolio, *Epistolarum Libri IV* (Paris, 1526), fol. 240ᵛ–241ʳ; 241ʳ–242ʳ; 170ʳ; and B. Ricci, *De Iudicio* (Ferrara, 1562), sig. Bʳ.

[11] Longolio, fol. 170ʳ⁻ᵛ.

[12] *Ibid.*, fol. 199ʳ–200ʳ.

letter to Flaminio we find the first reference to Flaminio's curious inhibition about writing in Latin:

> P. Alcyonio said that he would not go without letters for you and Stefano Sauli. Therefore I wrote in haste and invited him to dinner, but he forgot both the dinner, the letters, and my good opinion of him—you know what he is like. Therefore I hope you will complain to him.... If you feel reluctant to write to me in Latin—for I know that you are never satisfied with your performance in that language—then I will allow you to write in Italian....[13]

The poets Giulio Camillo and Sebastiano Delio were with Flaminio in Sauli's villa near Genoa in 1521 and the four spent a happy literary summer there reading, writing, and discussing literature and philosophy. Towards sunset they would go to the water's edge and sit on rocks, and fish, watching the boats sailing on the reddening sea. In an epistle in hendecasyllabics (V, 28)—for, if Flaminio could not write Longueil in Latin prose, he could in poetry—Flaminio describes their life there, and invites Longueil to join them, if it appeals to him. But Longueil was busy with Bembo and Navagero perfecting his Ciceronian style in Venice.

In this letter to Longueil we have the first reference to Flaminio's *lusus pastorales*, his pastoral epigrams modelled on Navagero's. Flaminio writes, 'Now I am amusing myself with the kind of poetry that the Arcadians sang in the dark ravines of Mount Lycaeus before a fierce race from the land of the wild Scythians sent Menalcas and Tityros fleeing far.'

With a reasonable degree of confidence it is possible to assign eleven of the *lusus pastorales*, all from book III of the definitive edition of Flaminio's works, to this summer. These poems are all either about a girl called 'Ligurina' or are related to the poems about Ligurina. Since Ligurina is not a conventional classical[14] or pastoral name, and since its meaning is 'the girl from Liguria', the name for the Genoese coast, which Flaminio visited only on this occasion, it seems highly unlikely that Flaminio wrote these poems at any other time.

Like a sonnet sequence, these little lyrics perpetuate various

---

[13] *Ibid.*, fol. 203ᵛ–204ᵛ.
[14] There is, however, a Ligurinus in Hor., *Odes*, IV, 1.

moments and moods in a love relationship, telling the tale of a summer romance:

> Now the blazing sun burns the fields in the heat of noon.
>   Lead your snow-white flock to the valley, Ligurina.
> Here the birds sing, here the brightest of springs leaps
>   From the cave, here the shadow falls from the serried
> Oaks, where the bees buzz happily among the flowers,
>   And zephyr murmurs sweetly.
> Here, beautiful one, my flute will tell your praises.
>   You sing of the sweet thefts of love in the woods.

> Jam rapidus torret mediis Sol aestibus agros;
>   Ad vallem niveum duc, Ligurina, gregem.
> Hic avium cantus, hic fons nitidissimus antro
>   Prosilit, hic densis quercubus umbra cadit:
> Et circum flores examina laeta susurrant,
>   Et Zephyri blando murmurat aura sono.
> Hic laudes, formosa, tuas mea fistula dicit:
>   Tu Dryadum calamo dulcia furta canes.
>                                             III, 8

> It is rising. The evening star, cruel to our love,
>   Now bids us fold our well-fed flocks.
> Ligurina, my darling, I am forced to leave you,
>   But I shall stay with you in mind and heart,
> And when Aurora drives the night away
>   And in the yellow light of morning leads the sheep to
>     the woods,
> Let us bring our herds together again here, my love,
>   And let sweet love again join me here to you.

> Nascitur, et nostro Vesper crudelis amori
>   Jam caulis saturas ducere mandat oves.
> Deliciae Ligurina meae, te linquere cogor,
>   Sed tecum remanet mens, animusque meus.
> Quod superest, ubi jam tenebris Aurora fugatis
>   In silvam croceo mane reducet oves,
> Hic illas, mea vita, iterum cogamus in unum,
>   Hic iterum dulcis me tibi jungat amor.
>                                             III, 9

> Mighty Ceres and Pan be my witness and holy
>   Venus who makes fast the faith of lovers,

## HIGHER STUDIES

No day, Ligurina, will see the end of my love for you,
  Not if one of the race of Dryads should seek me.
As the east wind lashes the cliff with its terrible blasts,
  But the cliff does not crumble under the hammering blows,
So my mountain-like faith will remain immovable,
  And my heart will always obey you alone.
God grant that we may live happily, loving one another,
  And that one hour may bury us in a single grave.

    Esto magna Ceres, et Pan mihi testis; amantum
      Et quae firma facit foedera, sancta Venus;
    Nulla dies, Ligurina, tuo me solvet amore,
      Non si me Dryadum sanguinis una petat.
    Ut rupem hanc validis impellunt flatibus Euri,
      Sed nullo rupes verbere pulsa labat,
    Sic semper mea magna fides immota manebit,
      Et mea mens uni serviet usque tibi.
    Dii faciunt, in amore pares vivamus, et uno
      Ambos una tegat funeris hora loco.
                              III, 10

Where you said that you would go when your mother went to the city,
  There I will go first, my sweetheart, in secrecy,
And until you come the short hour will seem longer than
  The lengthy year. Therefore, if you care anything about me,
Avoid all delay, and do not be afraid. Venus
  Herself will be your companion and guide on the road to love.

        Quo te venturam dixti, cum mater ad urbem
          Iverit, huc furtim, lux mea, primus eo.
        Dumque venis, longo brevis hora videbitur anno
          Longior. Ulla igitur si tibi cura mei,
        Tolle moras omnes, timor omnis et absit; amanti
          Et comes, atque viae dux erit ipsa Venus.
                              III, 11

If Ligurina does not trifle with my passion today,
  If today she comes into my arms,
In my joy I will build an altar to you, Cytherea,
  Of green sod in this mossy cave,

In my joy I will pour out three bowls of foaming fresh milk
  And as many bowls of wine.
Then your altar, heavily perfumed with all kinds of flowers,
  Will be dyed with the blood of a chosen
Sheep. Ligurina will dance. My flute, my sweet-singing
  Flute will sing your praises.
Every year I will perform these solemn sacred rites, holy
  Venus,
  And I will worship you always with high honour.
Goddess, grant that while I entreat and adore your divinity
  My dear girl may rush into my arms.

> Si Ligurina meos hodie non ludit amores,
>   Amplexus hodie si petit illa meos,
> Hoc tibi muscoso laetus Cytherea sub antro
>   Aram de uiridi cespite constituam,
> Laetus ego spumante nouo tria cymbia lacte,
>   Et totidem fundam cymbia plena mero,
> Tum late varijs halantem floribus aram
>   Imbuet effuso lecta cruore bidens.
> Saltabit Ligurina, tuas mea tibia laudes
>   Cantabit, dulces fundere docta modos.
> Haec tibi sancta Venus solennia sacra quotannis
>   Et faciam, et magno semper honore colam.
> Tu fac Diua, tuum supplex dum numen adoro
>   Currat in amplexus cara puella meos.[15]

Six other poems (III, 17–22) are a series of Petrarchan conceits addressed to Lygda and Ligurina. Each one is six verses long and each one follows the same rhetorical pattern. In the first four verses a picture is drawn, in the last two the application is made. A single sample will suffice:

> Have you seen the shining droplets tumble in the white
>   Lilies when the rain falls in a gentle
> Shower? And the dew drip from the red rose-bushes
>   In the welcome, chill breath of the dawning day?
> This is the face, the image of weeping Ligurina.
>   Fierce Love fires me with her tears.

[15] This poem was suppressed by Mancurti but appeared in the last edition of Flaminio's poems published while he was still alive, in *Carmina Quinque Illustrium Poetarum* (Florence, 1549), pp. 234–5, where it followed III, 11. It was also printed in the most complete edition of Flaminio's poems before Mancurti's, in the third edition of *Carm.* 5 (Florence, 1552), p. 264.

Vidisti nitidas per candida lilia guttas
  Ludere, cum tenui decidit imber aqua?
Et rorem de puniceis stillare rosetis,
  Cum spirat nascens frigora blanda dies?
Haec facies, haec est Ligurinae flentis imago;
  Illius lacrimis me ferus urit Amor.

III, 22

These are the works of a mature poet, self-confident and at ease. All of these *lusus* deal with a high moment in the love relationship or toy with some mood. The first five express their themes briefly, economically, and with a deceptive simplicity that is almost colloquial. With a few deft strokes Flaminio makes the lover reveal himself. He is young and innocent, romantic and passionate at the same time, and honest and straightforward in his dealings with Ligurina. She, as is usual in love poetry, comes through only as one who is tender and desirable. Love is egotistical The poet-lover is concerned only with expressing his own passion. The passion, close to nature, has the innocence of Eden about it. It is as fresh as when the world began.

The art of these first five epigrams consists largely in their simplicity and naturalness. There is little ornament in these poems, but the imagery is always harmonious and appropriate.

In contrast the six short epigrams are all ornament. These poems are much more conventional than the others, for these conceits were the stuff of Italian poetry. But again Flaminio has chosen his conventional imagery with sensitivity. The two flowers in the epigram quoted are the conventional symbols of a fair complexion and at the same time flowers which through their form and fragrance and the tactile image of caressing droplets have strong sensuous associations which prepare us emotionally for the marinistic conceit of the final verse. We expect this kind of reverie to lead to passion.

In the *lusus pastorales* the psychology of the lover rings true. That summer in Genoa Flaminio was twenty-three and a student on holiday—but it is always a mistake to attempt to read autobiographical fact into poetry.

Sauli had originally planned to return to Padua in the autumn. But he changed his plans and decided to winter in Genoa, perhaps because of the political situation; for a letter from Longueil to Flaminio dated October 23 [1521] says that they could not go safely to Padua now. All the roads on the other side of the Po were beleaguered by three different armies, and fighting was going on even in Emilia.[16]

At the same time other bad news reached Flaminio. Serravalle suffered its second great disaster in little more than a decade, and the Flaminios further losses. On October 15 thick black clouds rolled over the Alps which separate Italy from Germany. A terrible thunderstorm lasted all day and all night. The next day, Wednesday, about midnight, the Mischio, which runs through the city, usually a shallow, harmless, gently-flowing stream, began to swell. It was soon in flood, swirling with mud and gravel. Then a large part of the mountain which overhangs the lake a mile from the town fell into the lake. The lake had been very deep, but immediately you could walk across it with dry feet. The water from the lake poured down the bed of the Mischio to make a lake of the town. Those who could fled to the nearby mountains. All the buildings were filled with water up to the first-floor level. The force of the river was so great that some boulders which had fallen from the mountains and which could not be moved by fifty oxen were carried into the centre of the town. The walls of Serravalle were completely flattened at the places where the river enters and leaves the town. The garden walls, the famous armament factory, the mills, the fullers' factories, etc., all that was on the river's bank, collapsed. The church of St. Mary, which is built in the centre of the town on arches over the river, was severely damaged. St. Anthony's altar fell into the river and was washed away. The houses were filled with sand and pebbles. Casks of wine swam in the cellars. Horses drowned in the stables.

The women and children wailed. Men clutched each other as though the last day had come. It was worse than when the town was captured and burnt by the enemy. It seemed that there was no possible escape, the water was so deep and wild. Most of the buildings of the town, including the church, were so weakened that they appeared about to fall down. Now disease was rife.[17]

[16] Longolio, fol. 212ᵛ–213ᵛ.
[17] GAF. *E.F.*, pp. 95–8. Flaminio refers to this disaster in the fifth elegy of the second book.

A letter from Longueil to Flaminio, dated January 19 [1522] tells us that Flaminio was ill that winter from working too hard. Longueil advises him to be content with the principles of philosophy. With a little thought he will discover everything else through his natural intelligence. Leave the rest to us who are less gifted but have more strength to stay up late at night studying[18]—Longueil was dead in eight months, Flaminio lived another twenty-eight years.

It must have been at this time that Flaminio had the dream reported by his friend, Fracastoro, the doctor who first described and named syphilis. In *De Intellectione*, composed sometime in the 1540's, Fracastoro writes, in his discussion of extra-sensory perception,

> We all know Marcantonio Flaminio ... an uncommonly good modern poet. Once when he was in Genoa with his benefactor Sauli and was not in the best of health, he was glad to get the loan of a book in Italian. He had been reading it for several days when he rather carelessly left it on top of a couch. Shortly afterwards the man who had lent the book wanted it back but, although they hunted everywhere for it, it was not to be found. Flaminio was very upset about this because of his friend, whose loan he could not return. At length, however, he found the book this way, through a dream. In his dream he saw one of the maids pick up the book from the couch where he had left it. When the girl was putting it on a table, he saw the book fall and one of its covers break. When the maid saw this she was frightened and hid the book.
>
> After his dream, which he told in the morning, they went to look for the book. It was found where he had seen the girl hide it, with the cover broken just as he had seen it. When the girl was questioned ... she told everything just as Flaminio had seen it in his dream[19]

Flaminio describes this illness in a long elegy (II, 5), 'Ergo adeo coeptum peraget Mors impia cursum', written in January, 1522, in which he asks whether Death, after having knocked his house down (the clue to the date) will now carry him away in the flower of youth, when his face is still smooth and his hair

---
[18] Mancurti, p. 313, and S. Verrepaeus, *Selectiores Epistolae Clarorum Virorum* (Dilingae, 1573), pp. 97–9.
[19] G. Fracastoro, *Opera Omnia* (Venice, 1574), p. 142.

still black. He had so many literary plans! But if he must die, he prays to go to the Elysian fields where Tibullus and Catullus are and his Lygda will run up to him and embrace him sweetly and kiss him and make love to him.

From an epigram, 'On the Efficacy of his Mistress's Kisses', published by Jean Gagny, Chancellor of the University of Paris, in *Doctissimorum Nostra Aetate Italorum Epigrammata* (Paris, 1548), fol. 28$^v$, it appears that Flaminio was cured by Lygda or some other in this world.

A third poem, perhaps written about this time, is the first of the big formal odes, 'On Good Health',

> Goddess, the enemy of wasting disease,
> To whom a vigorous mind and solid strength,
> And sweet merriment and the joys
> Of wit are dear,
>
> We sing of you as the parent of pleasure,
> Caressing Venus' fair companion,
> The unique ornament of life and misfortune's
> Sweet assuager.

(Young and old cherish you. Every one desires you for himself and his own. When you are there the family flourishes, the old enjoy the strength of youth, Venus dwells on earth and Bacchus and good Hymen.)

> O you who bring repose to all, O kindly
> Mother of men, O you whom all must worship, for
> What can be pleasing without you, what seem
> To anyone sweet?
>
> Come here and pity my suffering, . . .
>
> At long last come here, good goddess, and warm
> My weak limbs with your health-giving breath.
> Do not let wasting disease consume my youth.
> I do not deserve it.

> Diva funestis inimica morbis,
> Cui vigor mentis, solidumque robur,
> Et joci dulces, animique semper
>    Gaudia cordi:

Te voluptatis canimus parentem,
Candidam blandae Veneris sodalem,
Unicum vitae decus, et malorum
   Dulce levamen; ...

O quies rerum, o hominum benigna
Mater, o cunctis veneranda; namque
Quid potest gratum sine te, quid ulli
   Dulce videri?

Huc ades nostrum miserans laborem, ...

Huc ades tandem, bona diva, et artus
Languidos aura refove salubri,
Ne meam tabes edat immerentis
   Atra juventam.

We get an inkling from this ode what Flaminio was beginning to suffer through ill health.

*Chapter 4*

# ROME IN THE 1520'S

On the night of November 24, 1521, the news reached Leo X at the villa Magliana that the papal forces had overcome the French and entered Milan. The next day the pope rode in triumph to Rome. The weather was raw and cold, and the pope much exposed during the festivities. 'Sic transit gloria mundi.' Leo's brilliant life burnt out like the flax. On December 1 he died of the chill that he had caught at the moment of victory. He was in the forty-sixth year of his age. Only his clown, Fra Mariano, was with him at the end. Horrified when he saw that his master was dying, the worldly monk urged the pope to remember God, 'Raccordatevi di Dio, Santo Padre,' but the pope died without the sacraments.[1] Soon a lampoon, attributed to Sannazaro, was circulating in Rome, 'If perhaps you wonder why Leo could not take the sacraments at his last hour, he had sold them.'[2]

As soon as Flaminio had recovered from his illness he and Sauli went to Rome, in January, 1522,[3] to be there for the coronation of the new pope. The plague was raging, the Tiber in flood, the cardinals had fled, paganism had come to life—an ox was crowned with flowers and sacrificed in the Colosseum—and Rome was full of warring factions.[4] Flaminio describes these conditions in a poem to Apollo found in a manuscript which had belonged to his nephew, Gabriele Flaminio, and

[1] Graf, p. 390.
[2] Quoted by Cantù, I, p. 511.
[3] Longolio, fol. 274r–276r.
[4] Cantù, I, p. 512.

which was published by the eighteenth-century editor of the joint edition of Flaminio's and Fracastoro's poems.[5] The poem can be dated from the reference to the siege of Rhodes. It is illustrative of the spirit of the times that Flaminio addresses his prayer, 'That he free us from the plague' to Apollo, the author of the famous epidemic among the Greek forces at Troy, rather than to the Archangel Michael whose statue stands on top of the Castel Sant'Angelo, sheathing his sword, in commemoration of the vision of St. Gregory the Great during the Roman plague of A.D. 590.

In the hope of healing the Lutheran schism and of conciliating Charles V the conclave had elected Charles's old tutor, Adrian of Utrecht, pope on January 9, 1522.[6] Adrian was not present at the conclave and did not reach Ostia until May. Thus there was a six-month interregnum in Rome which was marked by disorder and disaster.

Rome was a particularly dangerous place at this time for the Sauli family, who apparently risked losing their lives as well as their property. Perhaps this was why Longueil recommended Flaminio to another patron, Mariano Castellano, in a letter written from Padua on February 23:

> He is a youth worthy of all your humanity and liberality. You have treated him with the greatest kindness, but he was not so needy then as now, nor had he then shown such promise of learning. Do not imagine that there is or has been for many centuries anything like him in genius or industry or probity or seriousness. No one today has been more kindly treated by nature or more harshly afflicted by fortune. Do not let a young man of so much

---

[5] G. Fracastoro and M. A. Flaminio, *Carmina* (Verona, 1747), p. 180.
    Hunc tibi, Phoebe pater, lunata fronte juvencum,
      Tybris qua undose largius amne fluit,
    Alcimedon jactata alte post terga securi
      Mactat, et in sacros porrigit exta focos.
    Tu si saevitum est satis, et si caedis abunde est,
      Poenarum exsolvit si tibi Roma satis;
    Illuviem hanc expelle, inimicaque tela reconde,
      Ey melius Turcas mitte perire feros,
    Qui cinxisse Rhodum perstant nunc fortibus armis
      Dilectam, et cives perdere classe tuos.

[6] For accounts of Adrian VI see Leopold von Ranke, *The History of the Popes*, tr. E. Foster (London, 1906), I, pp. 68–74, and Cantù, II, pp. 58–73.

promise and so much virtue, who is also near you, go in want, when he is well on the way to the greatest learning and dignity. He will reach his goal and, if you will aid him a little now, he will carry on our great tradition.[7]

A letter written to Flaminio on March 3 tells how worried Longueil is about Flaminio and Sauli because of the war raging in Rome.[8] A later letter, written to Sauli on May 13, gives a shocking picture of what Longueil knows Rome to be like from experience.:

> ... for I am afraid, my dearest Stefano, that you are not very safe struggling unarmed against armed men when you are in the complete power of your enemies and when murders take place on such a scale. Remember that you are in Rome and, what worries me the most, in a city which today is not only without a ruler, but is actually held now by powerful forces of your adversaries. Undoubtedly things will be better when the pope arrives. ....[9]

Writing to Flaminio the same day Longueil comments on the misfortunes that have befallen their various friends in Rome, including one Lelio [Giraldi?] who is in danger of losing not only his equestrian rank but also his 'equus'. He adds in a postscript that he has just heard from Mariano [Castellano] what has happened to their friend Molza, that he has seven transverse wounds and a constant fever. .... He asks for immediate news of Molza's health. He cannot write more for grief.[10]

Giovanni Antonio Flaminio apparently knew nothing of conditions in Rome. In a letter probably written on May 6 1522, he says that he has been very worried and anxious by his son's long silence. Now he is much relieved. He did not know where he was and this gave rise to the worst suspicions.

> I knew you went to Genoa last year, but after your departure from Padua I received no letters. I wrote to many friends in Venice and Padua and no one had heard from you. You say you wrote often. Now I gather you are in Rome and plan to stay for several months. I would not mind if you could carry on your philosophical studies there. I am amazed that you have written nothing about your studies. You should have, when you know how much your work and well-being mean to me. I am very

[7] Longolio, fol. 245ᵛ.  
[8] *Ibid.*, fol. 247ᵛ–248ᵛ.  
[9] *Ibid.*, fol. 264ᵛ–266ʳ.  
[10] *Ibid.*, fol. 266ʳ–267ᵛ.

worried that you may be abandoning philosophy. It is not strange when you have been away so long that a father should expect an account of what you have been doing.

I have been in Bologna almost two years now and am doing well here. I have no exciting news. I have as many students as I want in the house, ten of the noblest children. I could send you money if you needed it . . . I will leave you a larger estate than I received.

. . . please, son, exert yourself and try with your whole heart and soul to realize the promise of your childhood, the expectations of your adolescence, and the wonderful capacities that your young manhood reveals. Become the man which the whole of Italy, which knows of you both through my efforts and your industry, believes and boasts that you are. Continue the way you have been going. Make your father's prayers and precepts for your studies your own with the heartfelt obedience and constancy that is your duty and I see that nothing will keep you from gaining the immortality that is prophesied. *E.F.*, pp. 191–5

The same month Giovanni Antonio wrote two interesting letters about cattle rustlers in the Bologna area (*E.F.*, pp. 88–9; 90–1). He also sent the usual exhortation to Adrian VI to make war on the Turks (*E.F.*, pp. 105–18).

That aged pontiff had finally reached Ostia and, to the consternation of the Romans, as soon as he disembarked he ordered all the preparations that had been made to receive him to be cancelled. Triumphal arches were for pagans, not for Christians and churchmen. A gloomy pope was the severest blow of all! At least there might have been some merriment to take one's mind off the plague!

Adrian VI lived in Rome as he had lived in his priory in Holland. He had the same servant and the same service. Every night he gave his housekeeper one ducat to buy his food for the next day. He ate so much cheap fish that he drove the price of kippers up. When told that Leo had one hundred palfreys he said that four were more than enough for him. He limited his court expenses to ten ducats a day.

Adrian did not give the Romans the bread and circuses they were accustomed to. He also did not make the sweeping reform of the Church that had been hoped for. He seemed to be stunned into inactivity by the magnitude of his task. He could only tackle superficialities. He made the cardinals promise not to carry arms, not to harbour bandits and rogues in their palaces, and to let the police in to execute warrants. Ecclesiastics were not allowed to grow beards like soldiers and were required to wear their proper habits—it had been their custom to ride about with swords at their sides, in short capes and bearded. Cardinal Giulio de' Medici, later Clement VII, used to go to church in Florence fashionably attired, with a beard half-way down his chest, and accompanied by armed men, not by priests and clerics. Cardinals and prelates regularly came out of church masked and ready to go to parties, weddings or balls.[11]

But a serious movement for reform within the Church, which was eventually to lead to the Council of Trent, had begun in Rome in the last years of Leo X. In 1520 the Oratorio del Divino Amore was founded, a group of sixty clerics and laymen who met on Sunday afternoons in the church of Saints Silvestro and Dorotea in Trastevere to discuss theology and to practise spiritual exercises. A list of current and former members of the group, drawn up in 1524 by the Brescian ecclesiastic, Bartolomeo Stella, later a member of Pole's circle at Viterbo, includes the names of the founder, Gaetano Thiene, who was later canonized; Gianpietro Caraffa, the founder of the strict Theatine order, later Pope Paul IV; and Marcantonio Flaminio, listed as a poet from Serravalle.[12] Famous liberal churchmen like Sadoleto, secretary to Leo X, later Bishop of Carpentras; Giberti, Clement VIII's datary, later Bishop of Verona; and Contarini, the great legate to the Diet of Ratisbon (1541) who almost effected a reconciliation between the Protestants and the Catholics, were not original members of the group. In fact the group did not really become important until after the fall of Rome to the imperial forces in 1527. Then the Oratory of Divine Love moved to the Republic of Venice where it became, under the new pope, Paul III, the kernel of the Counter-Reformation.

The sad reign of Adrian VI lasted little more than a year. On September 14, 1523, the Roman people, who were not allowed to celebrate his arrival, celebrated his departure to his reward. The conclave on November 20 hastened to elect another Medici pope. Their choice fell on Giulio de' Medici, Leo X's

[11] Cantù, II, pp. 67–8.
[12] A. Cistellini, *Figure della Riforma Pretridentina* (Brescia, 1948), pp. 271 and 282–3.

cousin, the illegitimate son of Lorenzo's brother, Giuliano, who was killed in the Pazzi conspiracy of 1477. He began life as a knight of Jerusalem combining the functions of a soldier with those of a priest. Giulio helped his cousin, Giovanni de' Medici, the senior ecclesiastical member of the family, and, when the latter became pope, Giulio became cardinal. In the government of Leo X Cardinal Giulio de' Medici was vice-chancellor. He was also a leader of the papal forces.

On his election Giulio adopted the name of Clement VII. The names of the other Renaissance popes were all names of grandeur, of great princes or leaders, Alexander, Julius, Leo, Adrian, Paul. The one pope who took a milder, Christian name was a weak man with a vacillating policy who brought Rome to disaster.

Clement VII was not a bad man. He did not tolerate simony. He did not distribute benefices by caprice. He maintained regularity. He lived with literary men, philosophers, theologians, and engineers, rather than with entertainers and buffoons. He was generous, like all his family, but, since he did not give away what did not belong to him, he was accused of meanness. However, he believed in his own infallibility. He asked opinions, then did what he wanted to—or too often did nothing at all. His politics consisted in irresolution, his cleverness in variations. He had no judgment. He tried to play France and Austria off against one another and succeeded in antagonizing both of them. He could make himself neither loved nor feared.[13] There is a sonnet by Berni criticizing Clement VII as a man 'full of deference, reflection, and talk, of "furthermore", of "then", of "but", of "if", of "perhaps", of "however", of a lot of words without effect.'[14]

Clement's mainstay was Gianmatteo Giberti,[15] the illegitimate son of a wealthy Genoese merchant, born in Palermo on his father's return from the Orient, about the year 1495. He was left in Palermo until he was eleven or twelve years old, then his father sent him to various universities. He was an excellent scholar. He preferred Greek and Latin literature, but he also

[13] Cantù, II, pp. 74-5.
[14] Quoted by Graf, p. 391.
[15] For an account of Giberti's life see G. B. Pighi, *Gianmatteo Giberti* (Verona, 1900).

studied the sciences, logic, jurisprudence, and later, theology. His father, like Flaminio's father, believed that Rome was the place of opportunity for such a boy. Accordingly he brought him to Rome about 1513. Giberti did not have to go alone as Flaminio did at a more tender age—wealth could do something to mitigate the disadvantages of illegitimacy.

Giberti was a robust young man with flashing eyes and a quick tongue, though what he said always appeared to have been pondered. He early showed signs of resolution, energy, and great enterprise. Cardinal Giulio de' Medici immediately took him into his household and gave him important duties there and in the Roman court. Leo X was also impressed. Therefore, when barely twenty, he became secretary to the vice-chancellor, Giulio de' Medici, and played an important part in Vatican relations with the princes of Europe. Even at this early stage he carried on most of the correspondence about Luther with the nuncio in Germany.

Giberti quickly became very important. Charles V commended himself to him. He became governor of Tivoli. Leo X made him priest, granting a special dispensation because of the irregularity of his birth. As soon as Giberti became a priest he studied theology and lived a Christian life, blameless like a hermit amid the luxury of the Medicis.

On the election of Adrian VI who, because of his advanced years, could not live long, Cardinal Giulio de' Medici sent Giberti canvassing Charles V, Henry VIII, and Francis I to get support for his candidacy at the next conclave. When Giulio was elected, Giberti became datary, the pope's chief minister and confidant. The following year Clement set up a commission to study reform. It met two hours every Sunday, a puny effort on the pope's part, far below the exigencies of the situation—it took the Romans twenty-five years to realize the seriousness of the Lutheran revolt. Giberti was an obvious member of the reform commission and his work there was so highly praised that the pope made him a bishop.

On July 26, 1524, Cardinal Marco Cornaro, Bishop of Verona and the old patron of the Flaminios, died in Venice, where he had taken refuge from the plague that continued to afflict Rome. The church in Verona was in a bad way because the bishop had been constantly absent. Anxious about the growing public immorality, the citizens of Verona wrote Doge Andrea Gritti (Verona was a Venetian possession) on August 1 to ask the pope for a bishop who could reside there half time. The pope picked Giberti, who at first refused, because he felt unworthy. However, he was persuaded, and became Bishop of Verona on August 8. He was then about twenty-nine years old.

In 1524 Giberti also helped Caraffa found the Theatine Order and would have liked to have joined it himself, but he had just been made bishop and the pope needed him to mediate between Charles V and Francis I (October, 1524). Giberti's efforts were in vain and the ensuing war ended with Francis's being taken prisoner at the battle of Pavia on February 24, 1525. The Austrian victory in the north of Italy augured ill for the future of Rome. Giberti, alarmed at the overwhelming power and ambition of Charles, tried to protect the papal states by making a secret treaty with Francis.

As soon as he had become established in Rome, Giberti had gathered literary men about him. Some formed part of his household, others met in his gardens in a kind of literary academy. Giberti was known as the father of the poor and of men of letters.

Literary groups meeting in gardens were a characteristic of Rome throughout this period.[16] Sadoleto had gardens on the Quirinal near the church of Santa Susanna. Beyond them, then in the suburbs, were the gardens of Angelo Colocci, stretching from the Quirinal side of the modern Via del Tritone to beyond the church of Sant'Andrea delle Fratte, i.e., up towards the Piazza di Spagna. An arch of the Aqua Vergine still standing near the church of Sant'Andrea was in his garden. Here he had his fountain. The water then went on to the Trevi fountain. When Pomponio Leto died Colocci invited the members of his academy to his gardens.

In a well-known letter[17] Sadoleto describes the literary set there and their meetings. He tells how 'after a friendly dinner, not characterized by its dainty seasoning so much as by its witty saltiness, they would recite poems or argue, to the very great delight of those of us who heard them, because they

---

[16] See Domenico Gnoli, 'Orti Letterarî nella Roma di Leone X', *Nuova Antologia* (January 16, 1930).

[17] J. Sadoleto, *Opera* (Verona, 1738), I, pp. 117–22.

revealed their genius therein and because what they said was both elegant and humorous.' Sadoleto also tells of meetings in the Circus Maximus and on the banks of the Tiber.

But the most famous gardens of all belonged to Johannes Goritz, a Luxemburger from near Trier, who was papal referendary. Goritz's gardens were near Trajan's Forum, on the slopes of the Capitoline, partly on the site of the modern monument to Victor Emmanuel II. They were adorned with lemon and cedar trees, with antique statues, sarcophagi, and inscriptions. There was a grotto there and, of course, a fountain.

Goritz was not a wealthy man, but he laid his money out carefully to satisfy his artistic tastes. He had a house on the Piazza della Cancelleria[18] in the heart of literary Rome, which then extended from the Campo dei Fiori and the Tor di Sanguigna to the Tiber. His church was Sant'Agostino and there he had Sansovino build an altar to St. Anne with a group of St. Anne, the Virgin, and Christ. This was placed against the third pilaster of the middle aisle and on the column above it he had Raphael paint the prophet Isaiah. When the altar was ready he invited all the poets to the feast of St. Anne (July 26) and then to a banquet afterwards in his gardens. It would appear that Flaminio was one of this group, for he wrote a sapphic ode 'On Goritz's Chapel' (I, 7).

Goritz's celebration of the feast of St. Anne became a regular institution. He had six tables placed near the altar of St. Anne where his poet friends placed their poetic offerings. Poems also appeared in his gardens, fastened to cedar trees and to statues, or lying in the grotto, or by the fountain. Goritz's fellow maecenas, Biagio Pallai, collected some of these in 1524 and had them published under the title *Coryciana*. Poor Goritz! His refined literary life was to end in the sack of Rome, in which he lost all his treasures. He died shortly thereafter, in 1527, on the way back home, possibly in Verona.

Other famous gardens were those behind the Vatican belonging to Biagio Pallai, the Villa Lante on the Gianiculo, still a park and the Mellini gardens on Monte Mario.

Flaminio not only frequented these literary groups. He also knew something about the high-society literary circles graced

---

[18] His house was destroyed to make way for the modern Corso Vittorio Emmanuele II (Gnoli, p. 21).

by the courtesans through his friendship with Molza who was the lover of the famous courtesan, Beatrice Spagnuola.[19]

Courtesans formed an important part of Roman life. When Pius V later tried to drive them out of Rome he found that they, with their hangers-on, numbered 25,000, out of a population estimated at 85,000.[20] Giulia Ferrarese, a well-known courtesan herself and the mother of the most famous of them all, Tullia d'Aragona (d. 1556), said that the 'strada del populo' in Rome, now the Via di Ripetta,[21] was paved by the contributions paid by the prostitutes—Giulia Ferrarese was a witty woman; once when she slightly brushed a gentlewoman in the street and the lady began to abuse her Giulia said, 'St. Mary, forgive me, I realize now that you have more reason to be in this street than I.'[22]

The courtesans were one of the sights of Rome, speeding by in splendid coaches, riding prancing Spanish steeds, or led by grooms on mules that were richly caparisoned and plumed. They were attended by maidservants and pages, and often accompanied by admirers and bravos quick on the draw. They dyed their hair blond and made up in red and white. They were heavily perfumed. Their clothes were of the highest elegance and the greatest luxury. They wore the finest perfumed underwear and dresses of silk, velvet, and the richest gold brocades. Their accessories were showy: the rarest of furs, the most precious Venetian laces, gloves perfumed with Spanish jasmin or carnation, dazzling jewellery—rings, bracelets, necklaces, earrings, and diadems. They were always in the latest fashion. The poorer courtesans rented outfits to go out in. And they went out a lot, not only to parties and receptions, but also to the public and Turkish baths—Giberti's secretary, Francesco Berni, notes that they were outstanding for their cleanliness—and to the principal masses. The churches were one of the chief places where they carried on their trade. Their clients left the mass with them, as du Bellay noted in 1550.

[19] Graf, p. 262.
[20] Graf, pp. 269–70. Aretino called Rome the *terra da donne*, Graf, p. 283. The population estimate is that given by Paolo Giovio in his life of Leo X (1551), p. 95.
[21] P. Paschini, *Roma nel Rinascimento* (Bologna, 1940), p. 436.
[22] Graf, pp. 234–5. The following account of the courtesans is taken from Graf.

## ROME IN THE 1520'S

The houses of the courtesans were fit for princesses. Indeed one of them, Angela Zaffetta, wanted to rent the Loredano palace in Venice. In Rome they often lived next door to prelates. Their walls were hung with arras, brocades, cloth of gold or gilt leather, or painted by the greatest artists of the day. Turkish carpets covered the floors and tables. The curtains were of satin. The large, elaborately carved chairs were upholstered in crimson velvet striped with gold. The beds had the most gorgeous hangings, the finest lawn sheets, and luxurious bed covers. There were carved screens, richly bordered mirrors, caskets and jewel boxes engraved or inset, cupboards full of silver, maiolica, and Venetian glass, paintings, statues, precious vases, elegant arms, lutes, mandolins, books, all sorts of ornaments and antiques, lap-dogs, elegant, beribboned cats, talking parrots, fantastic monkeys, etc. The patios, loggias, and antichambers were full of flowers and exotic plants. The servants were gracious, the cellars were stocked with the best wines, and the larders with the greatest delicacies, so that at any hour of the day it was possible to serve a tasty lunch or an appetizing dinner.

One of the most vigorous poems of the period is *The Ferrarese Courtesan's Boast*,[23] the fifteen-year-old girl's enthusiastic appreciation of the good life that she leads, but there is a companion piece to this poem, *The Courtesan's Lament*, the account of the degradation that followed on syphilis. For two years she let rooms. Then she was driven to washing clothes. For a while she cooked in the taverns. Women like her used to sell candles, but now the brothers do that. Her only resource is begging or stealing. She wears coarse sack, sleeps outdoors, drinks water from the gutters, uses foul-smelling ointment, and goes to the hospital. She wishes she had enough money to buy a glass of poison. The companion of these girls, Flaminio's friend, Molza, died miserably of venereal disease in 1544.

Flaminio is described at this time (*c*. 1523) as being a young man of austere life, as one might expect of a member of the Oratory of Divine Love, with a marvellous facility for writing verse,[24] and most of the poetry that can be ascribed to the years 1522–4 is remarkably facile occasional verse. There is the poem about the sacrifice of the bullock; a poem on Domenico Sauli's

[23] Published by Graf, pp. 355–8. The companion *Lament* is on pp. 358–61.
[24] G. Tiraboschi, *Storia della Letteratura Italiana* (Modena, 1772), IV, p. 247.

dignity in the face of some scurrilous attack by his enemies (V, 29); an epigram on Molza, the Tibullus and Petrarch of his age (II, 19); the ode on Goritz's chapel; a love epigram, 'When Julia looks at me I live';[25] and an early example of what was to become one of Flaminio's favourite themes and an important neoclassical genre, the retirement ode (V, 39). Here Flaminio praises the simple, austere, but tasteful dwelling of an elderly priest living in retirement outside Rome. He finds the life spent among books, paintings, and in a peaceful garden with the companionship of a witty old manservant very attractive. There one has no fears, nor any desires. It is pleasant to come across a picture of the other side of ecclesiastical life, to find that there were still decent people in the Church even in the 1520's.

During this period Flaminio met Giberti. It is not surprising that the two men should be attracted to each other or that the reforming young prelate with a taste for classical literature should take the uncorrupted young poet into his household. By September, 1524, Flaminio was in Giberti's service and visiting Padua where he and his friend, Giulio Camillo, lunched with his old professor, Romolo Amaseo.[26]

This same year the elder Flaminio published an important treatise on education dedicated to Antonio Pucci, Bishop of Pistoia, later cardinal. Pucci rewarded Flaminio with a benefice, the priory of San Prospero, outside Faenza. The Flaminios came to look upon this pleasant piece of property as the family estate.

Marcantonio Flaminio tended to fall ill in the winter. During the winter of 1525-6 his health gave cause for alarm, so that it seemed best that he should leave Rome for some months for a cure in his native mountains. He apparently left the city in January, 1526, for a letter from Giberti to Count Lodovico Canossa, French ambassador in Venice, dated February 3, indicates that Flaminio has been in Venice for several days. Giberti, obviously a considerate patron, writes that he realizes that Flaminio, with the journey he has made, will have incurred great expenses and that he will not be able to wait until the next regular instalment of his pension. Therefore he asks Canossa, if Flaminio is still there, to have him paid fifty ducats in advance.[27]

[25] Published in Paris in 1548 and in Verona in 1747.
[26] Marcantonio Flaminio, *Alcune Lettere* (n.p., n.d.), pp. 25-6.
[27] Pighi quotes the letter, pp. xvii-xviii.

A little later Flaminio seems to have visited Paolo Giustiniano a hermit and philosopher-reformer of the Camaldolese, for Giustiniano wrote him a letter on March 24[28] which reads like the continuation of a conversation. He writes to Flaminio as to one who is dedicated to the study of philosophy and calls him his singular friend in Christ. He urges him to take orders. The highest human felicity is knowing and loving God, words that Flaminio was to echo many times twenty years later.

Meantime, however, Flaminio went on to Serravalle where he regained his health and continued writing the *lusus pastorales* which he had begun in Genoa five summers before. This time a poetic epistle to his former host, Stefano Sauli (II, 1), tells how he is getting on and what he has been doing. Flaminio reassures Sauli about the state of his health. He need no longer worry. After the pestilential air of Rome, Serravalle is wholesome. Now his strength has returned, the emaciation has departed, he has regained some colour, and he can sleep at nights. Life is simple, but satisfying. He eats apples and olives, lives in a tiny house, and wears two layers of clothing to keep out the cold, but he is happier than he was in the palaces of princes in Rome. The second half of the poem tells how Sauli, whose ability and birth made the highest honours possible, shuns these things for a life of scholarly retirement in the countryside, tending his garden and looking after his bees. Flaminio would follow his example.

Flaminio followed his example for the best part of a year and during that time wrote some of his finest poetry. He probably wrote sixteen of the remaining eighteen poems of his first book of *lusus pastorales*[29] at this time, as well as his ode 'To Aurora' and perhaps also the odes to Pan and Diana and the translation of Petrarch's 'Chiare, fresche, e dolci aque'.

The *lusus pastorales* follow the seasons through. 'The winter flees, the tree puts on his glossy foliage, now, Amaryllis, is the time for love' (III, 3). Summer comes and with it a rendezvous:

---

[28] Paolo Giustiniano, *Trattato di Ubidientia . . . con una Pistola del Medesimo a M. Marc' Antonio Flaminio* (Venice, 1535), fol. 73$^r$–104$^v$.

[29] The original 1548 edition contained twenty-nine poems, five of which were censored by Mancurti.

## ROME IN THE 1520'S

Now lovely Lucifer sends the dank shadows flying,
    And the sweet-voiced bird salutes the dawn.
Get up, Amaryllis, drive your white flocks to pasture,
    While the grey dew falls on the cold grass.
I am feeding my goats in a woody valley today,
    For today the broiling heat will be at its height....
There I will wait for you alone, my dearest
    Nymph. If you love me, come alone too.

    Jam fugat humentes formosus Lucifer umbras,
        Et dulci Auroram voce salutat avis;
    Surge, Amarylli, greges niveos in pascua pelle,
        Frigida dum cano gramina rore madent.
    Ipse meas hodie nemorosa in valle capellas
        Pasco, namque hodie maximus aestus erit....
    Illic te maneo solus, carissima Nympha:
        Si tibi sum carus, tu quoque sola veni.   III, 4

But the poet is not faithful to Amaryllis. Soon he is enticing Lygda out of the heat into the shade with him, while the swarthy Nigella continues cutting the grain in the blazing sun (III, 15). Then it is Nigella's turn:

    Unshorn hills and the hills' deep shadows
        Which the rising spring waters placidly,
    If ever you concealed Faunus' tender loves,
        If you delight in the Nymphs' furtive pleasures,
    Be good to me, offer me a safe hiding-place,
        While dear Nigella sits on my lap.[30]

    Intonsi colles, et densae in collibus umbrae,
        Et qui vos placidi fons rigat ortus aqua,
    Si teneros unquam Fauni celastis amores,
        Si vos Nympharum dulcia furta iuuant,
    Este boni, tutasque mihi praebete latebras,
        Dum sedet in gremio cara Nigella meo.

    Oh, what shall I do? I shall die, sweet Nigella,
        If I don't snatch a wee kiss straightaway,...[30]

[30] One of the *lusus* censored by Mancurti. It was published in 1529 in *Actii Synceri Sannazarii Odae. Eiusdem Elegia de Malo Punico. Ioannis Cottae Carmina. M. Antonii Flaminii Carmina* and in *Carmina Quinque Illustrium Poetarum* (1549), p. 231, and (1552), p. 260.

## ROME IN THE 1520'S

Heu quid ago, moritur mi animus mellita Nigella
Ni tibi quamprimum basiolum rapio, ...

> Moon, heaven's beauty, horned queen of the stars,
>   Sliding swiftly across the middle zone of heaven,
> I am hastening to my mistress. No fairer girl
>   Pastured or ever will pasture flock.
> I pray you, radiant goddess, hide your light
>   That no one may be able to catch love's thief.
> So may you shine independently; so may you
>   Go the equal and rival of the great-rayed sun.

> Luna decus caeli, astrorum regina bicornis,
>   Quae medio raptim laberis alta polo,
> Ad dominam propero, qua nec formosior umquam
>   Pavit, nec pascet ulla puella gregem.
> Tu, mea ne quisquem valeat deprendere furta,
>   Conde, precor, lucem, candida diva, tuam.
> Sic tibi sit proprio splendescere lumine: sic par,
>   Et magni radiis aemula Solis eas.           III, 24

Flaminio serenades Pholoë as the cicadas sing; in the autumn he invites her to the fireside to roast chestnuts and sing songs and listen to the old women telling stories (III, 7); he wishes that he could be the rosy wreath he gathers for Thestylis (III, 12); he brings Thestylis presents from the city (III, 13); he begs her to come to a rendezvous to get them (III, 14); he finds Thestylis unfaithful with Thyrsis;[31] he bids the stream water Phyllis' garden (III, 16); and he celebrates the setting of their first embrace in an epigram that Laumonier believes inspired Ronsard's 'A La Fontaine Bellerie',[32]

> Flowing fountains, and vale of the fountains,
>   And forest encircled by pine-bearing peaks,
> Where fair Phyllis gave me her first kisses and I
>   Gained my first crown in the song competition,
> Live happily, and may neither the heavy heat of summer
>   Nor gloomy winter with its cruel cold harm you,
> May the four-footed beast not sully your clear water,
>   Nor the hard axe the woods, nor the fierce wolf the fold,

---

[31] Censored by Mancurti, published in *Carmina Quinque* (1549), pp. 237-7, and (1552), pp. 265-6.
[32] P. Laumonier, *Ronsard Poète Lyrique* (Paris, 1923), p. 271.

## ROME IN THE 1520'S

May the nymphs celebrate the sanctity of the place
In joyful rounds, and Pan prefer it to his Arcadia.[33]

> Irrigui fontes, et fontibus addita vallis,
>    Cinctaque piniferis silua cacuminibus,
> Phyllis ubi formosa dedit mihi basia prima,
>    Primaque cantando parta corona mihi,
> Viuite felices, nec vobis aut grauis aestas,
>    Aut noceat saeuo frigore tristis hiems,
> Nec lympham quadrupes, nec siluam dura bipennis
>    Nec violet teneras hic lupus acer oues,
> Et nymphae laetis celebrent loca sancta choreis,
>    Et Pan Arcadiae praeferat illa suae.

Apart from the two poems about Nigella the only one of these *lusus pastorales* which was published in 1529 was 'Ianthis',

> At last you have come, at last you have come, my only
>    Joy, and you have brought life and light to a wretched
>      woman. . . .
> Without you, dear boy, life was drearier than death
>      itself. . . .
> Now sweet joy has returned to everything with you.
> See, the pine tree hugs you happily in its shade,
> The rushing water greets you, murmuring clearly,
> And the pale apples blush rosy for you.
> Now I will look at your sweet face as much as I want.
> I will no longer be so thin, I will no longer be so pale,
> And I will live long years of happiness with you. . . .
> Whatever you do, beautiful boy, your dear girl will
>    always
> Be with you, she will go as your companion into every
>    land.
> Now I have learnt what it is to wait for a man who is
>    long
> In coming. Even waiting a night a woman grows old.

> Venisti tandem, tandem, mea sola voluptas,
> Venisti, et lucem miserae vitamque tulisti. . . .
> Te sine, care puer, leto mihi tristior ipso. . . .
> Dulcia nunc tecum redierunt gaudia cunctis.

---

[33] Censored by Mancurti, publ. in *Carm.* 5 (1549), p. 237, and (1552), p. 267.

Aspice, te laeta pinus complectitur umbra;
Arguto properans te murmure lympha salutet,
Albaque purpureum tibi ducunt poma colorem;
Ipsa ego nunc dulci saturabo lumina vultu.
Discedet macies, discedet corpore pallor,
Et tecum longos peragam feliciter annos. . . .
Quidquid ages, formose puer, tua cara puella
Tecum semper erit, terras comes ibit in omnes.
Jam didici, quid sit juvenem exspectare morantem;
Exspectans una vel nocte puella senescit.

II, 2

Two more conventional epigrams complete the series, one on the lover outside his mistress's door on a stormy winter night (III, 6), the other on the two lovers' desire to live and die together, like two doves sacrificed on Venus' altar (III, 23).

It is now possible to reach some general conclusions about Flaminio's first book of *lusus pastorales*.

The *lusus pastoralis* or 'pastoral trifle' was a new literary form created by the Venetian humanist and ambassador to Spain and France, Andrea Navagero (1483–1529). Navagero's *lusus pastorales*[34] were, for the most part, a collection of short poems on pastoral themes written, with few exceptions, in elegiac couplets. Many of them were close to the real problems of country life, they prayed gods to aid in the sowing and the threshing (1 and 2), to make the vine flourish (4); they told of a prized dog drowned in a swollen stream (10), and of another's being gored by a wild boar (8); of a shepherd's success in hunting (5); and of a girl whose marriage was arranged by her mother (14). Many of these poems were highly practical, some of them recount complex rural adventures such as appear in Sannazaro's *Arcadia* or in the classical *Daphnis and Chloe*, but compress the whole story into eight or ten lines. There are a dozen such poems averaging a little more than eight verses each.

Another dozen and a half *lusus* deal with love. The shepherd Thyrsis dedicates violets to Venus in gratitude for the three kisses he stole from Leucas behind a hedge (6); Thyrsis will always love the oak and the wood where he first possessed Leucas (7); Thyrsis and Nape dedicate amaranth and lilies to

[34] Navagero's *lusus* are printed in *Opera Omnia* (Padua, 1718).

Venus to make their love lasting and pure (13); the shepherd goes to town to buy Leucippe presents which she can receive among the hazel bushes (12); the poet loves every part of Hyella but her eyes fire his passion most (32); he and Hyella love each other above all else, he prays that this may last (33); day and night mean nothing to him, Hyella brings him his light and dark (38); he sends Hyella his picture for New Year's Day (28); he asks the night to hide his love-making with Hyella (22); Hyella captures Cupid with a garland of roses and lilies—an Anacreontic idyll (21); Almo dies for love of Leucippe (18); the poet tells the story of Echo, then laments his own love (19); Gellia has gone to the country for the summer—does she still remember him? (26); Iolas, the shepherd, wants nothing in the world but to live and die with Amaryllis (27); the poet asks Venus to extend her sway over Lalage (41); the poet possesses the proud Neaera in a dream (29). These poems are rather longer than the first group, averaging twenty-five verses, although the first six are as short as the more general pastorals.

The remaining poems are of a more traditional sort and have no claim to the title *lusus pastorales*. There is a familiar Horatian ode to Bembo on how he wanted to write of wars but love forbade (36); a traditional classical elegy on the power of love, illustrated by the stories of the nightingale and of Orpheus and Eurydice (25); an ode to the dawn (37); epigrams on the laurel and on Pythagoras' portrait (23 and 24); an epitaph on the death of King Louis of Hungary (40); a hymn in glyconic stanzas to the archangel Gabriel (34); a familiar letter in hendecasyllabics to his friends Canale and Bembo discussing their literary work and his passion for Hyella (30); a description of a Paduan village in the springtime (31); and two poems about the wars (20 and 35).

If we deduct the miscellaneous poetry, then, the *lusus pastoralis* created by Navagero is found to be a fairly short poem in elegiac couplets on pastoral themes or on love in a pastoral setting.

It is the latter type of poem that inspired Flaminio. Following Navagero's lead Flaminio wrote a series of poems that were closer to popular poetry, to the madrigal, the *pastourelle*, or the sonnet, than to anything in classical literature, although all these poems were given the polish and ease of classical Latin.

They were like the popular poetry in their exclusive concern with love, in their brevity, simplicity, and innocence of tone. They average eight to ten verses, too, the length of the madrigal, and, like the madrigal, they are written from the viewpoint of one who is normally a city-dweller, enjoying and idealizing the countryside in the good weather. Nature and topography are described with a sensitive and sensuous eye, but only as a setting for love. The one element of pastoral realism that intrudes in Flaminio's poems is the possibility for isolated encounters that the shepherd's life affords.

The imagery is the straightforward, conventional imagery of medieval poetry, largely concerned with the beauties of spring and the horrors of winter. There is little suggestive imagery and no wit except in the short conceited poems, and then it is not subtle or metaphysical, but consists of the conventional sort of Ovidian and Petrarchan amorous conceit.

The *lusus* maintain a kind of decorum. Since they are almost all poems of direct address, and since the supposed recipient is a young peasant girl of no education, the language used is virtually colloquial, simple and straightforward with no learned pretensions. The few references to the classical gods are of a very general sort. The tone of the *lusus* is simple and innocent. There is no sophisticated immorality as in Ovid's *Amores*. In this, too, they are modern and not classicizing.

There is little tension in these poems, only two or three create moods of excitement or anxiety. Over most of the poems there hangs a dream-like atmosphere. They are the creations of an imagination absorbed in the contemplation of ideal beauty.

Though the subject matter and mood of Flaminio's *lusus* is limited, Flaminio has created a distinctive genre in Latin literature, a pastoral epigram of madrigal length celebrating some aspect of a love relationship, simple in language, idealistic in tone, and modern in mood. A few of these poems were inspired by classical or Petrarchan models.

On November 10, 1526, Lodovico Canossa wrote to Flaminio inviting him to visit him in his villa at Garziano[35] and Flaminio replied in the now familiar form of a verse epistle in hendecasyllables (V, 43). He accepted for the following day, 'As soon

[35] D. Atanagi, *De Le Lettere di Tredici Huomini Illustri Libri Tredici* (Roma, 1554), pp. 36–7.

as lovely light begins to restore their colours to things'. This conceit from Vergil and St. Jerome appears again in the 'Hymnus in Auroram' published in 1529. For this reason, as well as on internal evidence, I am inclined to assign this hymn to the period of Flaminio's illness in 1526. The 'Hymn to Aurora' is one of Flaminio's great poems and it inspired one of the first odes in Italian, Bernardo Tasso's 'A l'Aurora'. For these reasons I shall quote it virtually in full.

> See, from the farthest east Aurora
> Comes in her dewy four-horse chariot.
> Radiant, she wears gleaming light
>    On her rosy bosom.
>
> Go, paling shadows, back to hell,
> Go, you who bring me the whole night through
> The frightful faces of the dead and
>    Dreadful dreams.
>
> Give the poet his lyre, boy, and scatter
> Flowers while I sing. Good goddess, hail,
> You who make the dusky earth gleam
>    With your shining light.
>
> Here are sweet violets for you, and the crocus,
> Here are baskets of fragrant herbs.
> The soft breeze rises and carries
>    Our perfumes to you. . . .
>
> Who can worthily celebrate your light,
> O mother of kindly day? Who
> Your beauty, O goddess before all
>    Goddesses most beautiful?
>
> When you raise up your rosy cheeks and golden
> Hair in heaven, the tawny stars give way,
> The moon withdraws, vanquished
>    By the blushing beauty.
>
> Without you mortals would lie buried in eternal
> Night; without you things would have
> No colour, and life would not be civilized
>    Through the learned arts.
>
> You shake sluggish sleep from heavy eyes—
> Sleep is the image of death—Calling

## ROME IN THE 1520'S

From the rooftops you send each man
  Happy to his toil.

The hurrying traveller springs onto the road,
The powerful oxen return to the yoke,
The jolly shepherd hastens to the woods,
  Driving his flock.

But the lover weeps as he abandons the couch
Of his beloved girl, and he curses you bitterly
As he is wrenched from the soft embrace
  Of the mistress he has longed for.

Let him love the hiding-places of treacherous night,
May the day be always good to me. Mighty
    goddess,
Grant that I may for long years
  See the shining light.

Ecce ab extremo veniens Eoo
Roscidos Aurora refert quadrigas,
Et sinu lucem roseo nitentem
  Candida portat.

Ite, pallentes tenebrae, sub Orcum,
Ite, quae tota mihi nocte diros
Manium vultus, mihi dira semper
  Somnia fertis.

Da lyram vati, puer; ipse flores
Sparge, dum canto. Bona diva, salve,
Quae tuo furvas radiante terras
  Lumine lustras.

En tibi suaves violas, crocumque,
En odorati calathos amomi:
Surgit, et nostros tibi dulcis aura
  Portat odores. . . .

Quis tuam digne celebrare lucem
Possit, o almae genetrix diei?
Quis tuam formam, o dea ante divas
  Pulchrior omnes?

Ut genas caelo roseas, comamque
Auream profers, tibi fulva cedunt
Astra, decedit rutilante victa
  Luna decore.

## ROME IN THE 1520's

Te sine aeterna jaceant sepulti
Nocte mortales: Sine te nec ullus
Sit color rebus, neque vita doctas
    Culta per artes.

Tu gravem pigris oculis soporem
Excutis; (leti sopor est imago)
Evocans tectis sua quemque laetum ad
    Munia mittis.

Exsilit stratis rapidus viator,
Ad jugum fortes redeunt juvenci,
Laetus in silvas properat citato
    Cum grege pastor.

Ast amans carae thalamum puellae
Deserit flens, et tibi verba dicit
Aspera, amplexu tenerae cupito a-
    vulsus amicae.

Ipse amet noctis latebras dolosae,
Me juvet semper bona lux. Nitentem
Da mihi lucem, dea magna, longos
    Cernere in annos.

                                      I, 5

    This is a splendid ode in the classical tradition. It is also a poem written by a sick man, a man whose nights are tormented and sleepless, who watches eagerly for the first traces of light which will alleviate his suffering, restoring him to the society of his fellow creatures, banishing the dreadful, lonely spectacle of a dead, brown world. He sees each category of society return to life. Only for the lover does day mean death. The strong can afford to suffer like that, but for the sick man light means life, and it is good to him. He prays that he may live to see it for many years. Flaminio is still young and he feels desperately that he needs time to live and to accomplish things. The conclusion of the ode is pathetic.
    Another ode written between 1516 and 1529, possibly about this time, during Flaminio's long sojourn in the countryside, is

the 'Hymn to Pan' (I, 2). Whereas the controlling formal influence in the 'Hymn to Aurora' was Horatian, the dominant influences here are Catullan and Homeric. Catullus has supplied the verse form, the glyconic stanza (see 61), Homer, occasionally bolstered by the Ovid of the *Fasti*, has supplied the lore about Pan. The ode is a texture of classical reminiscences, a possible argument for an earlier dating during this period. The opening, 'I have sung enough of the fierce wars of kings', is a conventional one borrowed from many lyric poets and has no relevance to Flaminio's own history. The following rhetorical question, 'What god shall I celebrate', is borrowed from Pindar, *Olympian* 2. The second strophe is full of Vergilian epithets and borrows a line from Catullus:

> You, guardian of the woolly
> Flock and of the burgeoning woods,
> Who love the black back
> Of Maenalus and the topmost temples
> Of chill Lycaeus?[36]

> An te, lanigeri gregis
> Silvarumque virentium
> Custos, cui nigra Maenali
> Terga, cui gelidi placent
> Summa templa Lycaei?

With the third strophe the echoes of Homer begin. They, along with other classical allusions, will be indicated in the footnotes.

> Nymphs, sing of the half-animal son
> Of Jove, sing of goat-footed
> Pan, the leader of the nimble
> Choral dances with the Dryads
> In the lofty woods.[37]

[36] 'The woolly flock', 'lanigeri gregis', Verg., *Georg.* III, 287; Pan as guardian of sheep, Verg., *Georg.* I, 17; 'the burgeoning woods', 'silvarumque virentium', Cat. 34, 10; 'chill Lycaeus', 'gelidi Lycaei', Verg., *Ecl.* X, 15. In the second and last passages of Vergil cited Maenalus is linked with Lycaeus and in the last passage it is called 'pine-bearing', 'pinifer'. This undoubtedly inspired Flaminio's 'black', 'nigra', for the Italian pine is very dark.

[37] In the 'gradus' 'half-animal', 'semiferus', and 'goat-footed', 'capripes', are two suggested epithets for Pan. The last half of the stanza is inspired by the Homeric Hymn to Pan, ll. 2-4.

Hear how the god shatters the loved silence
With his song that wanders in the night.[38]
See, 'Io', he comes, see he comes,
Shaking the crown of pines
On his wild head.[39]

>Nymphae, semiferam Jovis
>Prolem dicite, dicite
>Pana capripedem, leves
>Suetum cum Dryadis choros
>Silvis ducere in altis.

>En ut grata silentia
>Cantu noctivago deus
>Rumpit. cernite, io, venit,
>En venit capitis feri
>Serta pinea quassans.

Borrowing from Catullus and Horace Flaminio summons pure youths and maidens and banishes the profane.[40] He exorcises grief and summons gaiety.

>O Pan, father of the Naiads,
>With a pack of dogs at your side
>You drive the wild lynxes
>Through the pathless mountains
>And the secret valleys.[41]

>The father of gods and men
>Made you the lord of the woods
>From the place where the rosy day rises
>To where it sets, drowned in the sea's
>Red waves.

---

[38] Inspired by the Homeric Hymn to Pan, ll. 14–16.

[39] Faunus, the Latin equivalent of Pan, is described as wearing pine on his head, Ovid, *Fasti*, III, 84, and *Metam.*, I, 699.

[40] Cat. 34, 1, and Hor. Odes, III, 1, 1.

[41] This stanza is based on the Homeric Hymn, ll. 12–14. In Homer Pan just hunts 'wild beasts', '$\theta\hat{\eta}\rho\alpha\varsigma$', but later on he is described as wearing a lynx skin (ll. 23–4). In Callimachus' 'Hymn to Artemis', ll. 69 ff., Pan cuts up a lynx to give it to the gods. The 'secret valleys', 'vallium reconditarum', echoes Catullus' 'saltuumque reconditorum'.

You give the herds the flowing fountains
They need and the grass they delight in,
You are called the mighty protector
Of sheep, you load their soft fleeces
With glistening wool.[42]

The lambs that you once have looked upon,
Holy one, with your pious gaze,
Will not be carried off from the stable
By the enemy wolf nor harmed
By outbreaks of disease.

Blessed are the leaves of the groves
Which have heard you singing your songs
On your sweet flute when dewy
Evening brought forth
The sliding stars.[43]

Then the stars shine brighter,
Conscious of the purity of the night,
Then Zephyr's breath is stilled,
Then the earth spangles the joyful
Lawns with crocus flowers.[44]

Not so sweetly sings the swan,
Dying in the water meadow,
Or the nightingale, when spring
Is in flower, lamenting in the deep
Shadows of the wood.[45]

> O Pan Naïadum pater,
> Qui per devia montium
> Valliumque reconditarum
> Agrestes agitas, canum
> Cinctus agmine, lyncas:

---

[42] Pan as 'the protector of sheep', 'custos ovium', comes from Verg., *Georg.*, I, 7.

[43] 'Dewy evening', 'roscidus vesper', is an Ovidian phrase, *Fasti*, II, 314.

[44] Pan delights in meadows where crocuses bloom in the Homeric Hymn, ll. 25–6, but Flaminio has added the bright, unblinking stars and the hushed breeze and he makes the flowers actually open up for Pan.

[45] The nightingale comes from the Homeric Hymn, ll. 16–8, but Flaminio has added the swan.

Te divum, atque hominum sator
Silvarum dominum dedit
Esse, qua roseus dies
Surgit, quaque cadens rubris
Ponti mergitur undis.

Tu fontes liquidos gregi, et
Laeta pabula sufficis:
Tu custos ovium potens
Dictus, mollia candidis
Exples vellera lanis.

Quos tu, sancte, pio semel
Agnos lumine videris,
Illos nec stabulis lupus
Infestus rapiet, mala
Nec contagia laedent.

Felices nemorum comae,
Quae te, cum vaga roscidus
Vesper sidera protulit,
Dulci carmina fistula
Audivere canentem.

Tunc purae melius nitent
Noctis conscia sidera:
Tunc aurae Zephyri tacent:
Tunc laetas croceis humus
Spargit floribus herbas.

Non tam dulce sonat cadens
Udo in gramine cycnus, aut
Veris tempore floridi
Ales sub silüae querens
Densis Daulias umbris.

Then the Hamadryads dance, Pan leads the song, and Echo moans from the depths of the valleys.[46]

> Soon the wearied bands of Dryads
> Sit by the grassy bank
> Of the river, here where the swaying
> Marjoram breathes abroad
> Its sweet perfume.

[46] Again inspired by the Homeric Hymn, ll. 19–21.

And, while they gather apples red
And sweet, or wash their golden
Hair in the cool stream,
They sing at the same time, in
Their clear voices,

How Maia's brilliant son
Left the glittering stars
And the high halls of heaven
To pasture the snowy sheep
By the wandering streams,[47]

> Mox fessa Dryadum agmina
> Propter gramineam sedent
> Ripam fluminis, hic ubi
> Dulcem mollis amaracus
> Late spirat odorem.
>
> Et dum suave rubentia
> Carpunt mala, vel aureos
> Crines frigidulis aquis
> Immergunt, liquida simul
> Voce carmina dicunt.
>
> Ut fulgentia sidera
> Et magnos superûm domos
> Linquens, ad vaga flumina
> Paverit niveas oves
> Majae clara propago,

on Cyllene's slope and, reclining on Dryope's soft bosom, preferred the leafy grove to heaven. Nine months passed, and Dryope brought forth her child. The Dryads fled, his mother ran away in terror, for the boy was from the waist down a stinking goat and two horns protruded from his flaming forehead.

> Then his father carried him hidden
> In a white fleece and came
> To the threshold of mighty Jove.
> Straightaway the ruler of boundless
> Olympus laughed.

[47] The account of the birth of Pan is taken from the Homeric Hymn, ll. 27-45, but it is less factual than in Homer, though more richly pictorial. Here we see the contrast between a genuine hymn and the romantic re-creation of paganism.

The gods above laughed, but Venus
Held the boy to her bosom and fed
Her gaze on the lovable monstrosity
And bestowed her treasured kisses
On his swollen brow.

Hail, ruler of the Naiads,
Hail, and drive away weeping
Disease and wretched famine
To the most distant homes of the Arabs
And the fierce Turks.

Tunc illum genitor ferens
Albis pellibus abditum,
Ad magni solium Jovis
Venit: nec mora, risit immensi rector Olympi:

Riserunt superi: at Venus
In sinu puerum tenens,
Visus pascit amabili
Monstro, grataque turgidae
Libat oscula fronti.

Salva, o Naïadum potens,
Salve, et hinc lacrimabiles
Morbos, et miseram famem in
Extremas Arabum domos,
Et feros age Turcas.

    This type of ode, this modern re-creation of the beauties of pagan religion with mythology used to form gorgeous tableaux in the manner of the Renaissance painters, was to have a strong influence on Ronsard. The sensuous beauty of women washing in rivers and pools is a common theme in late medieval and Renaissance Italian poetry and in romance.

    Flaminio was fundamentally an occasional poet and he excelled in capturing the mood and emotion of the moment. Thus he was extremely successful in the verse epistle which, coming from his pen, was simple and natural and not formal and artificial. He made the verse epistle seem the normal way of corresponding with a friend. But he was a classicist, too, and in his classical set pieces he was studied, elaborate, and pictorial, although he was always guided by a sense of form, both poetic and graphic, with the result that his odes were never overcluttered with description, nor his pictures blurred by a profusion of sensuous detail.

We find this kind of pictorial classicism in the epyllion, 'Hercules and Hylas' (II, 6), published in 1529. The Alexandrian epyllion appealed to Renaissance poets as classical mythology appealed to Renaissance painters. They both offered the sixteenth-century artist new subject matter and new scenes of beauty to portray within the discipline of classical form. They presented a new humanity, more beautiful in this world, enjoying a wider variety of joys and pains, than the old god-centred man who knew only the happiness of infancy in his mother's arms and who looked forward only to the cross. For the poet who was attracted by art for art's sake the epyllion exercised a fascination.

'Hercules and Hylas' is a carefully constructed and studied work. It is given apparent immediacy by introductory and concluding quatrains in which the poet gives advice to his friend suffering through his love for Lycinna. The epyllion is an exemplum, the story of how even the mighty Hercules, who bore heaven upon his shoulders and braved the gates of hell itself, loved and suffered for a beautiful youth called Hylas.

Hercules and Hylas were inseparable. Hylas accompanied Hercules on all his labours. Thus he sailed with the Argonauts when the rising Pleiades warned men that the seas were safe for sailing. They put to shore in Mysia on the Hellespont. While the others slept in the deep perfumed grass Hylas went in search of water. He found a fountain shaded by a poplar—the natural image—and by myrtles and roses—the symbolic imagery, the emblems of the goddess Venus. In this lush and fatal setting the grass ominously bloomed with narcissi, crocuses, and hyacinths, whose petals were marked with the signs of grief, all flowers that grew from the victims of love. And there was the amaranth, symbol of immortality. In the centre of the fountain the nymphs played naked, their hair flying across their rosy countenances. They looked at the beautiful youth and desired him. When he stepped into the fountain, they snatched him and pulled him under the water. Like a falling star in the night sky he shone, and then was extinguished—a Homeric image that Milton was to use to a much more powerful effect in *Paradise Lost*.[48]

In this poem Flaminio is never diffuse. Now the skipper shouts, 'Unfurl the sails, the wind is with us.' Hercules calls for Hylas up and down the beach. A nice use of anaphora and a clever juxtaposition of words conveys his mounting panic.

Flaminio had apparently once been impressed by the sight of a dumb beast wild with grief at being separated from its loved one. He had already used this theme in the *lusus pastorales*. He introduces it now in an epic simile. Hercules like a cow whose heifer has been sacrificed on the smoking altar—a sight that Flaminio had probably seen in Rome in the interregnum between Leo X and Adrian VI—now charges through the forests crying aloud in the hope that he may again set eyes upon his beloved. The call 'Hyla' again picks up the anaphora, knitting the story together. The bereaved Hercules grieves and weeps and thinks of suicide, while Jason sails away to Colchis.

It was perhaps encouraged by Flaminio's success in the epyllion that Ronsard wrote 'La Defloration De Lede' and 'Le Ravissement de Cephale'.

Sometime about this time, Flaminio wrote his fourth hymn, 'To Diana' (I, 4), in glyconic stanzas like his hymn 'To Pan', but in stanzas of four rather than five verses like Catullus' own hymn to Diana (34).

In Flaminio's hymns the ancient gods are adapted to modern culture. Gone is most of the mythology, the complicated cult associations, the often strange formalities, and the practical purpose—genuine hymns and prayers are always intended to get something out of the gods. Instead, the gods are celebrated as nature spirits and the emphasis is shifted to their sensuous beauty. Here Diana is the moon goddess, the patron of hunters, the protectress of the countryside, the ruler of the female fertility cycle. Maidens worship her. The silvery magic of her beauty is described as she rises out of the ocean. The poem is almost as short as Catullus' hymn to Diana (twenty-eight as against twenty-four verses) and it covers the same ground, but

[48] Flaminio's use here of Apollonius' conceit of the nymphs pulling Hylas into the water to make love to him may have inspired his admirer Bernardo Tasso in his ode on the death of a friend's brother by drowning, B. Tasso, *Rime II* (Bergamo, 1749), p. 250.

with its barking dogs, singing arrows, shimmering sea, woodland dances, gold and purple flowers, dewy fields of growing grain, and women in childbirth it is a much more romantic poem than Catullus'. It shows how classical form and compression can be adapted to modern emotional needs by a choice of exact yet suggestive images which work upon our feelings. The reference to the purity of the night when the woodland spirits dance links this poem temporally and conceptually with the hymn 'To Pan'.

Another ode in the same four-verse glyconic stanza also published in 1529 is 'O Fons Melioli sacer' (I, 6), Flaminio's extraordinarily successful translation of Petrarch's most famous *canzone*, on the fountain of Vaucluse, 'Chiare, fresche, e dolci acque.' Flaminio's translation is expansionary, but it has succeeded in capturing the lingering mood of sensuous reverie in a setting of Botticelli-like prettiness which is the chief characteristic of Petrarch's poem. It has not in the same way succeeded in transmitting the nuances of acute feeling that rise from time to time through the reverie, and it seems less factual and more remote, though at times the Latin is, in fact, more concrete. But one cannot expect a translation to equal one of the great masterpieces of one of the world's greatest lyric poets.

Flaminio could not realize his dream to live out his life in the country. As he tells us in a poem published in 1529 and for some reason thereafter suppressed and ignored, even by his eighteenth-century editor and his nineteenth-century biographer,[49] Giberti summoned him, and he came. This poem,

[49] Abibo Sylvae, nam Gibertus acciuit
Carissimae Sylvae mihi, tamen uerum
Fatebimur, multo ille carior uobis.
Quod si Giberto in hac recondita ualle,
Saltuque uestro nos dei frui uellent,
Si nunc legendo, nunc iocando securam
Quiete vitam degeremus in dulci,
O quid hilarius, quid beatius nobis?
Sed hunc tenet, tenuitque semper inuitum
Orbis regendi cura, maximi Patris
Amor, bonorum supplices preces, at me
Tam longe abesse tam diu nefas, quare
Valete Sylvae, iam ualete Conualles:

'Abibo Sylvae, nam Gibertus acciuit', served as an introduction to 'Formosa silva, vosque lucidi fontes' (I, 10) which was reprinted in all the collections of Flaminio's poetry and in the standard edition, and it explains the circumstances of his farewell to his native place. The two poems are written in the same choliambic metre. Putting together the information gleaned from these two poems with what we obtain from the anxious epistle to Raimondo della Torre, 'Venimus, bone TURRIANE, ad Urbem' (V, 34), we can establish that the two poems about leaving his beloved forest refer to Serravalle,[50] that the time is when Giberti is still datary, and, more specifically, when the hostile Austrian armies are already advancing on Rome.

In these circumstances the ode to his native place, independently a work of perfect art and of great rhythmical and conceptual beauty, takes on a depth of meaning. It is the sadness lying behind the love, the poignancy, the sense of possible finality, which has enabled the poet to create a lasting monument to the life which he loves. He looks at it above the turmoil of everyday events and sees in it only the things of permanent and universal value, and, as he surveys his life, his mind fills with classical reminiscences of pastoral beauty which give his poem a timeless quality.

> Beautiful woods, and you gleaming fountains,
> And the holy places of the radiant nymphs,
> How blessed I would think myself, how beloved of the
>     gods
> If I could live and die in your bosom!

[50] The topographical details in these two poems refer clearly to Serravalle, the woods, the hidden valley, the mountain glen, the ravines, 'conualles', of 'Abibo Sylvae', and the woods, the fountains, the mountain, the solitary retreat of 'Formosa silva'. This could not have been Bardolino or San Prospero or even, I think, the Val di Lavino, Flaminio's other places of refuge. Moreover 'Abibo Sylvae' tells us clearly that Giberti is still datary. Therefore the place must be Serravalle and the date 1526-7.

'Formosa silva' follows. For some reason Flaminio apparently decided to suppress this poem. It was not republished in the Lyons edition of 1548 and hence was not in the manuscript of his poems that Flaminio had given to della Torre. It was also not published in the Paris edition of 1548 or in any of the editions of *Carm. 5* before the eighteenth century. Then it was republished in the edition of *Carm. 5*, Bergoma, 1753.

Now harsh necessity forces me to go
To a far-off place and to exhaust my weak
Being in foreign toil.
But you, Diana, guardian of this mountain,
If I have often sung your praises on
My sweet flute and crowned your altar with flowers,
Grant, goddess, that I may return to your solitudes
    swiftly.
But, if I return or if the Fates forbid,
As long as I retain consciousness I will remember you,
Beautiful woods and you gleaming fountains
And the holy places of the radiant nymphs.

> Formosa silva, vosque lucidi fontes,
> Et candidarum templa sancta Nympharum,
> Quam me beatum, quamque dîs putem acceptum,
> Si vivere, et mori in sinu queam vestro!
> Nunc me necessitas acerba longinquas
> Adire terras cogit, et peregrinis
> Corpusculum laboribus fatigare.
> At tu Diana, montis istius custos,
> Si saepe dulci fistula tuas laudes
> Cantavi, et aram floribus coronavi,
> Da cito, dea, ad tuos redire secessus.
> Sed seu redibo, seu negaverint Parcae,
> Dum meminero mei, tui memor vivam,
> Formosa silva, vosque lucidi fontes,
> Et candidarum templa sancta Nympharum.
>
> I, 10

Flaminio's ode is simple, and the structure is marked. In two verses Flaminio expresses his vision of the country that he loves, two more verses tell that he would like to live and die there. A first tercet tells that he is forced to go far away, a second calls on his patron goddess. A solitary, key verse expresses his prayer, that he may be allowed to return swiftly. The last four verses balance the first four in reverse order: as long as he is alive, he will remember his native land. The language is simple, the outline is clean and spare, the emotion is sincere. 'Formosa silva' is one of Flaminio's masterpieces in the elegiac mood.

Totally different is the hurried and anxious epistle to Raimondo della Torre, patriarch of Aquileia:

My dear della Torre, I have reached the city
Safe and sound without suffering any hardship
Along the way, but whether I am going
To remain safe and sound in the city in the future
I don't know. Roman territory
Is in the greatest uproar, the barbarian soldier
Approaches. He is ferocious and threatens
Murder and burning and I don't see any way
Out of the tremendous dangers that threaten us.
But nothing is more upsetting nor bothers
Me more than to see your brother's son here.[51] . . .
What makes my grief almost unbearable
Is the thought that I may have been responsible
For his coming here. Good Lord, I beseech you,
May the evils that threaten this boy fall upon
My head. What has he done to deserve this? . . .

> Venimus, bone TURRIANE, ad Urbem
> Salvi, et incolumes, nec ulla passi
> Viae incommoda; verum in Urbe posthac
> Salvi, et incolumes utrum futuri
> Simus, nescio; tremit tumultu
> Tellus Romula maximo: propinquat
> Miles barbarus, et ferox minatur
> Caedem, incendia; nec satis videmus
> Tantorum effugium periculorum.
> Sed cum multa animo meo recursent
> Molestissima, nil ita ad dolorem
> Accidit grave, ut hic videre fratris
> Tui filium. . . .
> Me ne, quod nimis ingravat dolorem,
> Exstitisse profectionis hujus
> Auctorem? bone Juppiter, malorum
> Quidquid huic puero imminet, redundet
> In meum caput, obsecro. quid iste
> Puer commeruit?
>
> V, 34

Giberti's policy had failed and Clement's foolishness brought disaster on Rome. With his own army disbanded, deserted by his vassals the Dukes of Ferrara and Urbino, Clement faced

[51] Francesco della Torre, who joined Giberti's household the following year and to whom Flaminio dedicated the Lyons edition of his poems and the first four books of later editions.

annihilation by the Austrian forces at the beginning of May, 1527. On the night of May 5, 40,000 Germans, Spaniards, and Italians under the command of the Constable of Bourbon were massed on Monte Mario and the Gianiculo. They attacked on the morning of the sixth. The week of rape, slaughter, plunder, and burning that followed has often been described. Rome had not suffered such a murderous attack since the days of the Norman invasions five hundred years before; for added to the brutality of war was the ferocity of religious bigotry. The majority of the soldiers were Lutherans, lusting to strike down the great whore of Babylon. The pope with his court hid in the Castel Sant'Angelo. Somehow or other Flaminio escaped, though how or to where we do not know.

Even when Rome was occupied Giberti tried to initiate some policy which would put the pope in a stronger position for bargaining, but in vain. Finally, on June 6, a pact was concluded. The pope admitted his defeat, ceded certain cities to the emperor, undertook to pay 400,000 ducats, and to remain prisoner in the Castel Sant'Angelo with his cardinals until 150,000 of them were paid. Then he would go to Gaeta until the emperor's pleasure be known. He had to give six hostages, among them Giberti.[52]

Until the end of November Giberti was held prisoner by the imperial forces in the Palazzo della Cancelleria. From time to time the soldiers took the prisoners out and tortured them for money. Giberti handed his diocese over to Caraffa for administration, and wrote letters of good heart from prison to such friends as Vittoria Colonna. Then, on November 29, he put a closely worked out plan into operation. He got the guard drunk, then with his fellow prisoners escaped by climbing up ropes attached to a chimney of a house belonging to the Colonnas. He soon found his way over the rooftops to a friendly house in the neighbourhood, where he hid. Later he escaped on foot in disguise to the camp of the Duke of Urbino. Thence he went to Orvieto, where he met the pope between the tenth and fifteenth of December and asked for permission to retire to his diocese. The permission was granted.[53]

[52] Pighi, p. 38.   [53] Pighi, pp. 39–40.

*Chapter 5*

# IN GIBERTI'S HOUSEHOLD

THE collapse of Rome sent many a humanist bishop on the road to his diocese. Sadoleto departed twenty days before the sack, to spend the rest of his life in Carpentras. In February, 1528, Giberti made his solemn entry into Verona, and a new way of life for him and his entourage began.

In the Venetian gothic palace by the Adige, at the flank of the great, marble, Romanesque cathedral, Giberti practised in his own household the reforms that he later applied to the clergy of his diocese and which in many cases formed the basis of the reforms adopted by the Council of Trent. Giberti's house was like a monastery of the most rigid observance. Even the servants had to be of exemplary life. In the morning a period of meditation was followed by communal prayers and mass. Frequent communication was obligatory. There were two meals a day, barely half an hour long, the more elaborate of which consisted of three courses, and this only out of consideration for the bishop's high-ranking guests. The meals were accompanied by the reading of sacred books, which the bishop afterwards discussed with his friends. The household assembled again in the evening for the penitential psalms and the office. Sleep was limited to seven hours a day, hard work was the rule, and leisure condemned.

Giberti's domestic circle was brilliant. In addition to Flaminio, his household consisted of Galeazzo Florimonte, later bishop of Sessa, tutor to the young heir of Milan, and finally bishop of Aquino, a great wit and the inspiration of della Casa's *Galateo*; the famous satirical and comic poet, Francesco Berni, who died poisoned, apparently by Cardinal Cibo, because he refused to poison Cardinal Giovanni Salviati;[1] Adamo Fumano, a Greek and Latin poet, later Cardinal Pole's chancellor when he went to England as papal legate on the accession of Queen Mary; Matteo Bardolini, a mathematician; and Francesco della Torre, Giberti's secretary for eighteen years, a man of taste, learning, and influence, to whom Flaminio dedicated the collection of his poems which appeared in Lyons in 1548. The great humanist physician, Girolamo Fracastoro, was a frequent visitor and a particular friend of Flaminio's.

Giberti had an excellent library containing very rare codices, many of them Greek and many of them unpublished. For this reason he summoned the printers, the da Sabbio brothers, from Venice to set up a press in his palace. He had Greek characters struck there, made Bernardino Donato, professor at Padua, his editor, and published sacred Greek texts and sometimes translations.[2]

Giberti had always been devoted to his pastoral duties, so that even today he is remembered in Verona as the great bishop. When Clement VII refused to allow him to abandon the post of datary to go to his diocese, Giberti sent investigating officers to Verona, and, on their reports, began a vigorous reform of local corruption; when he was in prison, he gave over the administration of his diocese to the ardent reformer, Gianpietro Caraffa, founder of the rigorous Theatine Order and later head of the Inquisition; and, when he was finally allowed to retire to Verona, his efforts were tireless in extirpating abuses,[3] in reviving religious enthusiasm, and in promoting preaching throughout his diocese, although he was unable to preach him-

---

[1] G. Toffanin, *Il Cinquecento*, 4th edn. (Milan, 1950), p. 369.
[2] Cuccoli, p. 58.
[3] See Flaminio's letters to Contarini describing some of the bishop's struggles, G. Biadego, 'Marcantonio Flaminio ai servizi di Gianmatteo Giberti Vescovo di Verona', *Atti del Reale Istituto Veneto*, LXV, 2 (1905–6), 220–22, 227.

self because of the weakness of his voice. Giberti was inclined to be severe. He had a cold manner and was harshly outspoken about faults both in himself and in others, yet he would sometimes go down on his knees, tears streaming down his face, to plead with the hardened sinner or the defector to return to the ways of God.

Flaminio spent fourteen years with Giberti, ten of them in Verona. Here his concern with religious problems grew and he became acutely aware of the need for reform. At the same time his studies became more serious and philosophic. Life at Giberti's, however, was a bit too rigorous, both for his tastes and for his constitution, as he later admitted to his old friend, Galeazzo Florimonte.[4] Both of these men apparently felt like becoming epicures after they left Giberti's, although this phase did not last long with Flaminio!

The harsh climate of the water-ringed city within sight of the Alps, and the austerities of the bishop's palace in Verona, quickly took their toll on Flaminio's health so that, by the end of October, 1528, his doctor, Fracastoro,[5] ordered him to a more temperate place for the winter. Francesco della Torre, writing to Bembo on October 26, said that Flaminio had gone to the Friuli area for the winter.[6] It was hoped that the milder climate would restore him.

Against his will Giberti was still called on by Clement VII and the Roman curia in times of crisis. He was summoned to Viterbo in September, 1528, when relations with France became strained. He was summoned again, to Rome, in February,

---

[4] See D. Atanagi, *De Le Lettere Facete, Et Piacevoli di Diversi Grandi Huomini, et Chiari Ingegni* (Venice, 1561), I, pp. 304–6. This letter to Carlo Gualteruzzi dated Sessa, November 11, 1538, is listed as being by 'incerto autore', but it is obviously by Flaminio. All the biographical facts fit his life exactly and all the people referred to are his friends. Flaminio, did, however, love Verona. See I, 31.

[5] Flaminio wrote two poems to Fracastoro at this time about his health, V, 49, and 'FRACASTORI venerande, anima mihi carior ipsa' published in *Doctissimorum*, fol. 29ᵛ–30ᵛ.

[6] D. Atanagi, *Delle Lettere da Diversi Re, et Principi et Cardinali, et altri huomini dotti a Mons. P. Bembum* (Venice, 1560), fol. 56ʳ⁻ᵛ. Della Torre refers to the Friuli area as Flaminio's 'patria', therefore was it really to Serravalle that he went? Della Torre must have been mistaken either about Flaminio's place of origin or about the location of Serravalle.

1529, when the pope fell ill and his life was in danger, and he was forced by crowding events to stay on in Rome until April 26, 1529.[7]

In June, 1529, Charles V called a general Diet in Barcelona to form a league against the Turks.[8] Princes and ambassadors came from every part of his vast empire. A general treaty was signed in Barcelona on June 29, while on June 30 an alliance was proclaimed in Bologna between Charles V and his brother, King Ferdinand of Hungary, and Clement VII. To cap his policy Charles V was now determined to be crowned Holy Roman Emperor by the pope, the honour which Francis I had contested so bitterly with him for so long.

The devastations of the invasion of Italy had been followed by those of the plague, and the country was now poor and hungry. There was great suffering in all the Italian cities. Bologna was reduced to famine. The prior of the Dominicans there sold a large piece of property belonging to his Order to buy bread for the poor while a preacher in San Petronio persuaded the rich to sell their jewels and gold and silver plate to buy food for the starving. In these conditions, even Charles's court tried to persuade him to abandon his plan and the papal emissaries applied all the pressure they could; for the pope was terrified of Charles's reappearance in Italy. But all efforts were in vain. Charles never abandoned a favourite policy.

So, on the morning of August 1, Charles pretended that he wanted to sail with Andrea Doria on the smooth sea off Barcelona. As soon as he was a little way from shore, he gave orders for a general embarkation and headed towards Genoa. He reached Genoa on the twelfth of August with twenty-eight galleys, seventy barques, and other ships carrying infantry and cavalry. Apprised of Charles's embarkation, Clement ordered Giberti to Genoa to meet him, sending at the same time, from Rome, Cardinals Ercole Gonzaga, Alessandro Farnese (later Paul III), Francesco Quignones, and Ippolito de' Medici, who was accompanied by his brother, Duke Alessandro, betrothed

[7] Pighi, p. 41.
[8] The following account of the coronation of Charles V as Holy Roman Emperor is taken from G. Giordani,'*Della Venuta e Dimora in Bologna del Sommo Pontifice Clemente VII per la Coronazione di Carlo V Imperatore* (Bologna, 1842).

by the Treaty of Barcelona to the Emperor's illegitimate daughter, Marguerita d'Austria.

The papal emissaries tried to detain Charles in Genoa, but Charles wanted to go into Italy. Promising that he would do no violence to the papal states, Charles departed for Piacenza early in September. His desire would have to be acceded to now. The pope had to meet him and crown him. But where? He dared not let him get so far inside Italy as Rome, especially since the Colonnas were pro-Imperial and might surrender the city to Charles as his capital. The second greatest city in the papal domains, Bologna, was therefore chosen as the meeting place for the pope and emperor. The time was fixed for November. Bologna was the city where Leo X and Francis I had reached agreement in December, 1515, and it had the advantage of being in the north. Giberti went with the emperor to Piacenza, while the pope sent Cardinal Innocenzo Cibo, legate of Bologna, to his legation to prepare for the reception of the two courts, and the princes, ambassadors, and nobles who would be coming to the coronation.

We do not know whether Flaminio accompanied Giberti to Genoa and Piacenza, but he was invited to the coronation in Bologna and must have been a close witness of the colourful ceremonial there, of the splendidly costumed processions, of the various triumphal arches and allegorical decorations, and of the rich entertainments which lasted for four months while the peace of Italy was being negotiated and a policy was worked out against the Turks who had just been thrown back from Vienna and were now besieging Budapest.

For the coronation festivities Veronica Gambara, the poetess and sister of the governor of Bologna, had taken over the *palazzo Marsili*, down the street from the *palazzo pubblico* of Bologna where the pope and emperor were staying. Here she lived in the grand style, like a princess, and filled her house with literary people and artists. Among her guests were Bembo, Molza, Trissino, Bernardo Cappello, Francesco Berni, Giulio Camillo, Claudio Tolemei, Achille Bocchi, and the two Flaminios. She entertained people of the highest rank, and of every profession. It was perhaps here that Flaminio met one of the men close to Charles V, Don Luis d'Ávila y Zuniga, a native of Plasencia in Estremadura, a distinguished diplomat, brave general, and honoured historian, whom he celebrated in a Horatian ode, 'Amice magni Caesaris Auila'.[9]

In December, 1529, a collection of Flaminio's poetry appeared in Venice with poems of Sannazaro and Cotta, a passionate young love poet from Verona who had died of the plague in 1510 when only thirty years of age.[10] This was the last humanist poetry that Flaminio wrote for some seven years.

After the sack of Rome, the fall of Florence to the Hapsburg-bolstered Medici dynasty, and the occupation of Milan by the Spaniards, the intellectual centre of Italy shifted to the still free Republic of Venice. Here, in the 1530's, the reforming Oratory of Divine Love met, in Venice, at the house of Gregorio Cortese, a New Testament scholar and the abbot of San Giorgio Maggiore; in Padua, at Bembo's; and in Treviso, at Luigi Priuli's villa. The group included Giberti; Caraffa, who was working for the reform of the monastic orders in Venice and Verona; Flaminio; Pole, when he could be there; Jacopo Nardi, the exiled Florentine follower of Savonarola; Antonio Brucioli, a publisher of Reform tracts; and the Venetian nobleman, Gaspare Contarini, its head.[11] Contarini had been Venetian ambassador to Charles V from 1521 to 1528 and he appreciated the gravity of the Lutheran revolt and the desperate need for reform within the Church. He was still a Venetian senator at that time and an amateur philosopher and mathematician. It was Paul III who was destined to make him, as well as many another great man, cardinal. The Oratory spent much time discussing Luther's key doctrine of justification on which the orthodox position was as yet undefined.

In 1532 Flaminio urgently asked for admission to Caraffa's newly founded Theatine Order in Venice. He was not accepted because he asked, on medical grounds, for some indulgence from the full rigours of the rule. He offered to do some building for the Order if he were accepted, and he had the support of

[9] For Veronica Gambara see Giordani, pp. 77–8 and notes thereon; for Don Luis d'Ávila, *ibid.*, 'notes', p. 66, # 361; for the poem see Gruter, *Delitiae CC Poetarum Italorum*, IV, 29–30, where it appears under the name of Antonio Mario of Imola. It was also printed by Ubaldini, fol. 22ᵛ–23ʳ, under that name.

[10] Flaminio wrote an epigram on Cotta, preferring him to Catullus, probably about this time (II, 28).

[11] Cuccoli, p. 79.

one of its benefactors, the Venetian nobleman Francesco Capello, but the Theatines felt that a true vocation meant taking up the cross.[12] They belonged to the new order of things and were unwilling to compromise their principles to oblige a gentleman or to grace their brotherhood with a distinguished poet. The Church was gradually to discover in its dealings with the Lutherans that cultivation and learning, elegance and style were no substitute for fervent belief and hard logic. The Theatines realized that the day of the humanist was past and that the only man who counted in religion was the man who was willing to die for it. Though Flaminio was sincere in his religious belief, he did not appreciate the hard necessity for martyrdom. He could imagine death as a surrender to the ecstasy of God's love, but he felt no burning desire to go out and meet it in the harshly practical way of St. Theresa. But then Flaminio was not physically strong and good health is a prime asset to energetic action.

His desire to adopt a religious life frustrated, Flaminio turned more and more to scholarship, to the study of Greek, and later Hebrew, to the study of philosophy, and later theology. It gradually became known that Flaminio was working on a translation of the psalms, which were not yet available in a modern, i.e., humanist Latin, translation. Much interest was aroused in cultivated religious circles and in the autumn of 1533 Bembo asked Flaminio to let him see what he had done. Flaminio, in a letter written to Bembo from Verona on November 12,[13] says that his paraphrase is sound, because it has been checked by Contarini and Cortese, but he feels that the style is inadequate, for it is his first essay at prose writing. Therefore he begs Bembo not to persist in his desire. But if he wants to see the translation despite the imperfections of style, he will send it, because he would rather obey than hide his ineptitude. On November 28 Bembo replied, insisting.[14] He felt that Flaminio was incapable of anything inept, but he would promise not to show his work to anyone else if that were his wish.

In 1534 an event took place which shocked the whole of

[12] D. G. Kaminski, 'Marcantonio Flaminio ed i Chierici Regolari', *Regnum Dei*, II (1946), 8–13.
[13] Atanagi, *Lettere da Diversi . . . a Bembo*, fol. 49$^{r-v}$.
[14] P. Bembo, *Epistolae Italicae* (Venice, 1552), p. 352.

Italy and which hardened Charles V in his determination to make a descent upon the coasts of Africa[15] despite the steadfast refusal of the Venetians, who were traders as well as Christians, to attack the Turkish empire in Egypt. Khaireddin Barbarossa,[16] a Muslim who began his career in the service of the Sultan of Tunis, had captured Algiers, killed the Bey, and placed the city under the sovereignty of the Porte. Selim I made him Viceroy and sent him two thousand janissaries. Barbarossa occupied the fortress built by the Spaniards near Algiers, and, in two or three years, had built a new port there with the labour of thirty thousand Christian slaves. Thence he preyed on all the merchant shipping off the Barbary coast and made landings in Andalusia, whence he rescued seventy thousand Muslims from Catholic persecution. Suleiman II thought him the only one to match Andrea Doria, and so made him admiral of the fleet. Barbarossa in turn offered the Sultan the conquest of Tunis.

In 1534 Barbarossa put to sea with eighty galleons to devastate the coasts of Italy as a preliminary to his attack on Tunis. As a special prize he sought Giulia Gonzaga, reputedly the most beautiful woman in Italy, to offer her to the Sultan for his harem. Barbarossa is described at this time by the gossipy bishop, Paolo Giovio, who knew everything about everyone, as being a man of sixty-five years of age, squarely built and muscular, with heavy, bushy eyebrows, a man who was both prudent and resolute.

At the end of July, 1534, Barbarossa burnt ships that he surprised at Messina, sacked San Lucido in Calabria and put all to the sword, destroyed Cetraro, which belonged to the monks of Monte Cassino, and burnt seven galleons which Toledo, the Viceroy of Naples, had had built there, sailed in front of Naples, to the great terror of the Neapolitans, desolated the Neapolitan island of Procida, and proceeded up the coast to Sperlonga. No more romantic spot for a pirate raid can be imagined. Wild headlands sink into a sapphire sea, stretching bright and jewel-coloured into the distance, and desolate hills clasp secret coves at Sperlonga. Here Tiberius had a villa once, before he with-

[15] Ciccarelli, fol. 237ᵛ–238ʳ.
[16] The account of Barbarossa's raid is taken from B. Amante, *Giulia Gonzaga* (Bologna, 1896), pp. 121–31.

drew to Capri, and the emperor dined in the great cave by the sea which has given the place its name, while across the cliffs straggled the Roman road built by Valerius Flaccus. Over the hills a few miles away, on the Appian road, lay Fondi, and its mistress, Giulia Gonzaga, the twenty-one-year-old widow of the famous soldier, Prospero Colonna.

On August 5 Barbarossa landed at Sperlonga, killed the commandant of the fort and most of its inhabitants, and was guided by a traitor at night over the wooded mountains to Fondi. He entered Fondi just before dawn on August 6. The mayor and the bishop both fled, panic-stricken, offering no resistance. Most of the inhabitants of the town were slaughtered in their sleep. Those who were spared were chained together and marched to Sperlonga where they were embarked for the slave markets of Africa. The town was fired, the cathedral sacked, tombs were opened and the ashes scattered. When the pirates were already in her palace a faithful servant managed to warn Giulia, who escaped from her window in her nightdress and fled on horseback to the woods. Barbarossa searched for Giulia Gonzaga in a neighbouring convent inhabited by twenty very young Benedictine nuns. When she was not to be found his men raped and killed the nuns and burnt the convent.

This horrifying news reached Rome as Clement VII lay dying. Giulia's friend, Cardinal Ippolito de' Medici,[17] raised six thousand men and marched against Barbarossa, who fled. The cardinal found Giulia hiding in a cave and reinstated her in Fondi.

Barbarossa now conquered Tunis, which he made his headquarters, and it was partly to punish him that Charles V attacked Tunis in the following year. The feeling that they had of narrow escape lies behind the delirious welcome that the Neapolitans gave Charles's fleet when it returned triumphant in 1535.

In December, 1535, Giulia moved from Fondi to Naples to

---

[17] Cardinal Ippolito de' Medici was poisoned on August 5, 1535, while he was visiting Fondi and 'died in the arms of the Donna Giulia like a good Christian', Paolo Giovio to Rudolfo Pio, Bishop of Faenza and papal nuncio to France, August 20, 1535, in Atanagi, *Lettere Facete*, pp. 69–74. Flaminio's friend, Molza, and Soranzo, Bishop of Viterbo when Flaminio was there, were with the cardinal.

supervise the education of her husband's four-year-old grandson. She was given permission to live in a convent annexed to the church of San Francesco delle Monache[18] and it was in Naples, in Valdes' religious circle, that Flaminio met her in 1540 and became her friend.

Cardinal Alessandro Farnese[19] had been a favourite in the conclaves which elected Adrian VI and Clement VII. As Clement VII lay dying he said repeatedly that Cardinal Farnese should be the next pope. In the forty years in which he had been cardinal Farnese had always managed to be neutral between France and the Empire, he was liked by both parties, he had no enemies, he lived a good, retired life, and he appeared to be a profound thinker, though he was a choleric man. He was now sixty-seven years of age. He was elected on the first day of the conclave, on October 14, 1534.

Although they originated in Farneto near Orvieto in Tuscany, the Farnese family was considered to be Roman, and Cardinal Alessandro Farnese was at that time building the greatest of the Roman *palazzi* with Sangallo the younger, then Michelangelo as his architects. Thus the Roman people went wild with joy when Farnese was crowned on November 1, the first Roman pope in a century. He took the name of Paul III. Shortly after his coronation, Paul III made two of his grandchildren cardinals. Guido Ascanio Sforza and the pope's namesake, Alessandro Farnese, were sixteen and fifteen years old respectively. Nepotism unfortunately blotted the record of this great pope, as it did those of so many of his predecessors.[20]

While these events, which were destined to change his life, were taking place, Flaminio was still living his semi-monastic, retired, scholarly life in Verona, interrupting it only for visits to friends in Venice or the Bologna area.[21] The winter of 1535–6 Flaminio spent listening to the lectures of the visiting theologian, Jan van Kampen, who discoursed on the major and minor prophets, St. Paul, the canonical epistles, and Genesis;

[18] Amante, p. 150.
[19] The account of the election of Paul III is taken from Ciccarelli, fol. 236$^v$–237$^r$.
[20] The creation of the duchy of Parma for the Farnese family was the worst example of this.
[21] Atanagi, *Lettere . . . a Bembo*, fol. 90$^v$–91$^r$ and Flaminio's epistle to Dandolo, V, 2.

and translating the twelfth book of Aristotle's *Metaphysics*, the fundamental one which treats of God.[22] Flaminio's 'Aristotle' was regarded by his contemporaries as a brilliant translation and a great work and it undoubtedly filled an important need for many generations. It was not, by modern standards, a translation, but the Renaissance theory of translation was different from ours. Then a translation was an adaptation of a work to the translator's audience. Modern relevance was always sought. Flaminio was not concerned, as the present-day translator is, with what Aristotle meant to his fellow Greeks, with Aristotle's position in the history of Greek philosophy, but with what Aristotle meant to the modern thinking man whose world was torn apart by religious controversy, and with Aristotle's place in the greater history of God's revelation of meaning to man, the only thing that really mattered.

On March 8, 1536, Gregorio Cortese, abbot of San Giorgio Maggiore, wrote a letter from Venice to his fellow Venetian, Gaspare Contarini, now cardinal in Rome.[23] After telling Contarini how much he missed him, despite the company of Reginald Pole, who was so much like him, Cortese went on to say,

> Also my household has been increased by the addition of Messer Marcantonio Flaminio who has come from Verona and will spend the whole of Lent with me. He is a very great consolation to me not only during the day but for a good part of the night. We are inseparable.
>
> Flaminio is here to publish his paraphrase of the twelfth book of the *Metaphysics*, work on which has already been started. His Aristotle should be very successful for the beauty and loftiness of the matter and for the style, which is exactly right, straightforward and elegant. I always expected much of the judgment and genius of Messer Marcantonio, but in this he has surpassed even my expectations, especially since this is the first time that he has tried writing in prose. And now his style appears to be the quintessence of excellence, to the point where, in my opinion, he is inferior to no one writing today. And it is so very clear and plain that if the rest of Aristotle were treated in the same way he would easily be accessible to everyone and there would be more learned men.

[22] Biadego, *Atti del Reale Istituto Veneto*, LXV, 2, 222 and 224.
[23] Cortese, *Opera* (Padua, 1774), I, pp. 103-6.

Flaminio wanted to dedicate his Aristotle to Giberti but Giberti insisted that he dedicate it to Paul III. Paul III in return offered Flaminio, through Giberti, the benefice of San Colombano above Bardolino on Lake Garda.[24]

By 1536 Flaminio was reading the works of the reformers. On June 22 Cortese, who still expected that a council on the reform of the Church would be held in Mantua in the following year, wrote to Contarini to ask him to get him the pope's permission to read Lutheran works. He asked for a written permit which he could keep. He had had Clement VII's oral permission, but he was afraid that it might have expired with his death and he would not like to have happen to him what had happened to Messer Marcantonio in Holy Week. He was particularly afraid of Caraffa's knowing about it.[25] Flaminio was apparently already getting into trouble for his interest in reform.

After leaving Cortese's, Reginald Pole, created cardinal by Paul III in December 1535, for his defence of the unity of the Church against his cousin, Henry VIII of England, went to Luigi Priuli's villa at Treviso. Writing to Priuli on June 14[26] Pole said that Flaminio had invited him to Verona to spend a few days with the bishop and that he had decided to accept because summer was at hand and he had not planned on writing this summer, but on thinking, and he could think as well there as elsewhere.

Both Pole and Priuli went to Verona that summer, but his father's death prevented Flaminio from being there with them. A letter written to Contarini from Bologna on July 8, 1536, reveals Flaminio irritated by the legal problems of winding up the estate and by the necessity of being absent in Bologna while his friends were in Verona.[27] Apparently his father did not leave him the comfortable estate that he had expected, but debts and a possible court case! To make matters worse the father's profitable benefice of San Prospero outside Faenza, which the Flaminios regarded as the family estate, was given

[24] Biadego, *Atti del Reale Istituto Veneto*, LXV, 2, 216.
[25] Cortese, *op. cit.* I, pp. 106–8.
[26] Pole, *Epistolae* (Brescia, 1744), I, pp. 424–5.
[27] Biadego, *Atti del Reale Istituto Veneto*, LXV, 2, 225. Flaminio wrote an epigram to his father when he was dying, I, 25.

to another, while the benefice of San Colombano on Garda, which Flaminio had been offered, would require rather than yield an income to maintain it.[28] Flaminio passed a gloomy summer in financial anxiety. However, in the autumn an opportunity to redress his fortunes presented itself.

Paul III had nominated Cortese, Giberti, and Pole as members of a council of nine set up to investigate evils afflicting the Church and to suggest remedies. They were to meet in Rome in the early autumn of 1536. At the beginning of September, Giberti and Pole left Verona together for the conference in Rome[29] and Flaminio accompanied them to try to regain the benefice of San Prospero.

When Flaminio reached Rome towards the end of September, he found preparations afoot for the celebration of the anniversary of Paul III's elevation on October 14. He seized this opportunity to win the favour of the Farneses by writing one of his greatest odes and one of the finest poems ever written on a political event.[30]

One reason for the success of Flaminio's ode on the papacy of Paul III was the sincerity of the emotion. Popular enthusiasm for the pope ran high. His policy kept Italy at peace, human life was secure and property safe from pillage, the battered cities were repaired, a rich harvest was gathered in, and the country prospered. Moreover, while decency and stability were restored to Italian life, Rome was enjoying vicarious glory on the frontiers through the victories of her vassal, the emperor, over

---

[28] *Ibid.*, 224. See also 216.

[29] Cortese, *op. cit.* I, pp. 113-15.

[30] This ode was written for an anniversary of Paul III. Therefore the earliest date for it would be 1535. The poem sounds as though it were written in Rome and it was written long enough after Paul III's accession so that the pope had time to make a mark and reveal a policy, but before the summoning of the Council, the pope's greatest achievement. Since the Council was first called for Mantua in 1537 and was then expected to assemble more or less annually until 1542, it seems highly probable that this ode was written on the occasion of Flaminio's visit to Rome in 1536. He would have arrived at just the right time that year to write it. Flaminio does not seem to have been in Rome again until May 1541—and then only for a matter of days. The next time he was in Rome was in January, 1543, again only for a few days, after the first Council called at Trent had failed—hardly the occasion for such an ode. Also by then the fresh enthusiasm for Paul's reign would have worn off.

the Turks. And then, there were high hopes for the resolution of the religious dispute through the Council which the pope had summoned for the following year. It seemed that a new order had come into being, that the sun had indeed risen on a glorious day.

Moreover the technique of the laureate ode, its pomp and mythological apparatus, were uncommonly appropriate here, for in Rome such things come naturally. They are part of the imperial tradition. But the pictorial style of the ode, its series of grand tableaux, is not only part of the classical tradition, it is also the style of Renaissance painting, and therefore makes this work a harmonious expression of the ethos of the age. Another thing that contributes to the success of the ode is Flaminio's sensible use of mythology and personification. He uses both of these devices sparingly, like a true classicist drawing only on what has survived the test of time and become part of the common heritage of educated people. The echo of Vergil's messianic eclogue, familiar to everyone, was well chosen to express the depth of emotion at the restoration of peace, personal security, and prosperity. Monotony is avoided and drama is introduced by the dawning of the anniversary day about which the poet has been meditating on the bank of the Tiber as the birds sang in the half-light of dawn.

With this lavish laureate ode to offer, Flaminio felt that he could make a strong claim on the Farneses' patronage. He felt that he was justified in asking for the priory of San Prospero. Therefore he approached the pope's favourite grandson, Cardinal Alessandro Farnese, formally, in a Horatian ode to Apollo (I, 22), a work of classical art and tasteful flattery. The ode is composed of five sapphic stanzas: the first describes Apollo; the second tells of the poet's devotion to him; the third, and central one, asks that Farnese give him the benefice, so that he can be free from worry and lead a life of leisure; the fourth tells us why, so that he may praise Farnese; whose glory (stanza 5) will be evergreen like the myrtle. Flaminio was fond of formal balance in his formal odes.

An enthusiastic ode in the more familiar iambic trimeter (I, 17) tells the whole story. On his father's death poor weeping Flaminio was cast out of the family home by a hard-hearted successor. But kindly Farnese has restored it to him. In accents of Catullan joy Flaminio tells how he will again see the little field and the beautiful little villa and the trees that his father had planted. Now he will be able to sleep in his father's bed. 'Fountains rejoice, and limpid streams. Now, soon, the son of your old lord is coming, and he will delight you with his sweet flute' as he sings the praises of famous Farnese, while the Naiads and goat-footed Pan gaze in wonder.

Now at last Flaminio's troubles were over, now at last he had achieved independence—how he had hated the client's life appears in a later letter.[31] Flaminio wrote a gleeful poetic epistle to his friends Stefano Sauli and Ulisse Bassiano (VI, 3) on how he had acquired the benefice and he set out for Faenza as soon as he could, midst a profusion of grateful verses to Farnese.[32]

However, Flaminio did not immediately sever his connection with Giberti. It was almost two years before he definitely quit his household, although he apparently spent less and less time in Verona. Giberti, for his part, spent a considerable portion of 1537 with Pole, who was sent as legate to France and Flanders, investigating abuses in the Church on the spot.

[31] See Flaminio's letter to U. Bassiano, Civitella, July 14, 1549, Atanagi, *Lettere 13*, pp. 349–51.
[32] e.g., II, 4; VI, 1–3, 5–10; I, 29; III, 1–2.

*Chapter 6*

# INDEPENDENCE AND PASTORALS

WHEN he was ill in the autumn of 1528, Flaminio wrote two poetic epistles to his doctor friend, Fracastoro.[1] In what was probably the first of these two letters,[2] since he does not seem to be so ill here and is still able to gossip, Flaminio tells Fracastoro about his unhappy psychological state, particularly about his financial worries. He begins by comparing Fracastoro's knowledge of the sciences with his own ignorance. Like the man in the street he gapes at wonders. Since he does not understand what life is about, he is easily deluded by vain hopes or fears. Sometimes he is happy for no reason, sometimes sad. The thing that frightens him most is poverty.... 'I often tell myself... "Start living content with your lot and stand up to proud fortune, free and unafraid. No one is wretched because he is poor, nor happy because he is rich. Move the sick

---

[1] V, 49, and 'FRACASTORI venerande, anima mihi carior ipsa' from *Doctissimorum*, fol. 29ᵛ–30ᵛ. See *supra*, p. 75. I ascribe these poems to the illness of 1528, his first serious illness after he went to Verona and became a friend of Fracastoro's, because in both these poems he emphasizes his youth, because in his vocabulary he is still a paganizing humanist praying to Apollo, whereas we know that by 1532 he had become devoutly religious, and because he emphasizes his poverty and seems unknown and insecure, which was not the case after his second collection of poems appeared in 1529.

[2] The one in *Doctissimorum*.

Chromilus from his poor bed to a gilded couch with an embroidered coverlet, this will not make the fever leave his ailing body. He will still be irritable, raving, and sleepless. Yet the same man, when he was strong and hunted wild boars in the woods, slept through the winter night peacefully in the deep snow.... The good enjoy poverty, for nature gives man whatever he actually needs to live: water, humble food, and plain clothing... thus in the golden age man lived in peace and tranquillity in the happy countryside and Astraea ruled the fortunate lands, while the father of the gods himself did not disdain to visit humanity nor to lend his presence to country dinners."[3] The spectre of poverty appears again in many of the San Prospero poems (VI, 3, 5, 9, 10). Now at last Flaminio was freed from this dreadful anxiety!

The benefice had been given Flaminio to provide him with the leisure to write and, happily, with his new security he felt the return of poetic inspiration (VI, 2). There was a great, immediate outpouring of poetry in praise of Cardinal Farnese,[4] tasteful and sensitive variations on the same theme, which were probably presented to the young prelate in the form of a booklet straightaway. Then, on his return to San Prospero, Flaminio, in his exhilaration, composed a series of very funny poems about his grapes and a glutton who ate them. There are nine epigrams (I, 46–54) about the voracious Pimmalione Formiano, a comic figure in ancient fashion, enlivening a jolly, Pompeian, harvest frieze. They again show the ingeniousness of Flaminio's invention, how he was able to treat the same theme over and over again with ever fresh variety.[5] The cleverest poem is probably the one in which a vine which Pimmalione had eaten bare addresses the passer-by like the solemn statue on a Roman funerary monument (I, 49). The casting of the material in epitaph form is a delightful comic device. An amusing memo to the chief of police on the dangers of a wine famine (I, 50) also deserves mention.

[3] Cf. the ideas ascribed to Flaminio in Vida's *De Republica*, *infra*, pp. 155–8.

[4] See II, 4; I, 29; VI, 6; VI, 7; VI, 8; III, 2; III, 1. By 1536 Cardinal Farnese was seventeen.

[5] Cf. the Turunda poems, *infra*, p. 172, and the poems on his illness in 1549, *infra*, pp. 185–193.

INDEPENDENCE AND PASTORALS

Now, with the security of San Prospero, Flaminio decided to accept the poor priory of San Colombano because he liked the site above Lake Garda and because Fracastoro had wanted him to have it since he had a place near by where he was planning on retiring.[6] Flaminio visited the priory, apparently for the first time, at the beginning of April, 1537, and found it falling to pieces.[7] Far from yielding a modest income of forty *scudi* per annum as Flaminio had thought[8] it would take several years of his San Prospero income to restore and furnish San Colombano. Flaminio had hoped to be able to spend the winter of 1537-8 at Bardolino, but now it was evidently impossible. He would have to be patient, as he wrote his cousin, Benedetto Flaminio, a law student at Bologna, and meantime find some rich man to stay with.[9]

However, although he was in Ferrara in June to pay his respects to Vittoria Colonna,[9] it would appear that Flaminio was able to spend at least part of the summer at San Colombano, because there are some poems by and about him and his place on Lake Garda which could only have been written at this time.

The priory of San Colombano was an ancient red stone monastic building on the flank of Monte Baldo overlooking Bardolino and Lake Garda. It was protected on the east, where it was approached by the road, by a strong tower with cusped battlements. At the other end of the building, and at right angles to it, on the edge of the hill overlooking the lake, was a simple romanesque chapel. The priory itself looked southwards down sloping orchards towards the fertile plain by the lake's gently scalloped shores. The green plain was a scene of tranquil beauty with its russet-tiled houses, sentinel cypresses, and poufs of silvery olive. Far across the lake lay Sirmione.

Garda is blessed with a gentle climate, though the northeast wind can whip the waves into foaming fury. Thus the scene which generally met Flaminio's eyes there was one of

---

[6] Biadego, pp. 216 and 224. See also Fracastoro's poem urging Giberti to give Flaminio San Colombano, *H. Fracastorii et ... N. Archii Carmina* (Padua, 1739), I, pp. 127-30.
[7] Letter from Flaminio to Contarini, April 6, 1537, Biadego, p. 228.
[8] Biadego, p. 224.
[9] Biadego, p. 217.

tranquil composure and classic beauty with a hint of the wonderful and of mighty immanences in the vast lake and the tall bright mountains that rose behind it.

In such a setting Flaminio turned again to classical poetry. He remembered his old university friend, Count Nicolò d'Arco, now relatively close at hand in Mantua, and sent him a formal eclogue in the Theocritean-Vergilian tradition. While Alexis played the flute the two youthful shepherds, Thyrsis and Alcon, Flaminio and Arco, sang antiphonally the first poems which they had composed together on the banks of the Reno, i.e., in Bologna. Many of these quatrains have verses that have already appeared in other works by Flaminio.[10]

This eclogue to Arco may have been inspired by a hexameter epistle which Arco must have sent Flaminio about this time,[11] for in it Arco says that he has heard that Flaminio is now living in Verona in the service of the reforming bishop, Giberti. He is glad that his friend has realized one of his aims, to lead a wholesome, quiet, and studious life. But he misses Flaminio's company and conversation, which he can no longer enjoy, although he is not far away in Mantua. How happy were those days in Bologna when they shared their troubles and composed together on the banks of the Reno and when Flaminio helped him with difficult passages in Greek and Latin literature. 'Now I hear that you are working on the Fathers and on Greek, and that you hear Fracastoro explaining the secrets of nature. But do not disdain your old friends—Come! Can you not hear the groans of Lelio and Strozza, as well as my own?'

We do not know whether Flaminio and Arco ever visited one another, but there is an epistle in hendecasyllabes from Flaminio to the courtier poet, Lodovico Strozza (V, 19), inviting him from Mantua to San Colombano and trying to tempt him with the delights of Garda. Flaminio imagines Strozza in tiresome attendance upon the Duke while he reclines by Garda's

---

[10] 'Vos mihi, quae quondam Thyrsis puer, et puer Alcon' is one of the Antonio Mario poems, Gruter, IV, 26–9, and Ubaldini, fol. 21ʳ–22ᵛ, but the biographical facts clearly indicate Flaminio as author. It is written from Garda, but at a time when Flaminio is still with Giberti in Verona, i.e., in 1537.

[11] In the edition of Fracastoro's and Arco's poems (Padua, 1739), II, pp. 213–4.

glassy water under the perfumed myrtle tree. Flaminio offers his friend reading, relaxation, and poetry at Garda with him.

A fuller description of the hospitality that Flaminio can offer appears in another epistle, V, 24, in which Flaminio invites Giberti's secretary, Francesco della Torre, to ride out from Verona the following morning to visit him at San Colombano. Flaminio says that he will have lunch prepared for his friend under the trees by the spring. 'There will be sweet milk, fresh cheese, eggs, ripe melons, plums yellower than new wax, and delicately flavoured tiny fish that shine in my stream. The old farmer will sing jolly songs while we eat, and his two daughters will dance for us. Then you can take your siesta in a vine-covered arbor while the arching laurel whispers softly. When you are rested we will read the pastorals of Vergil and Theocritus, to me the most beautiful and loveliest of poems. When it is cooler we will walk in the valley, then have a light supper. Then you will return to the town.'[12]

Though Flaminio returned for a while to Giberti's household, he was now looking for somewhere else to go.[13] A letter of his to Pietro Pamphilio, seneschal of the Duchess of Urbino,

---

[12] Apart from the poems written from Bardolino the only poems that Flaminio wrote in the Verona period were: 'Cum molles dominae formosus Hylas hyacinthos,' one of the Antonio Mario poems in Gruter, *Delitiae Ital.*, IV., 32; 'O sidus almae Cypridis,' a *lusus pastoralis* addressed to the evening star by whose light he is hastening to an assignation with Hyella, another one of the Antonio Mario poems in Gruter, IV, 31, and Ubaldini, fol. 23$^v$–24$^r$; 'Hanc pateram Chio spumantem, auroque nitentem,' II, 10, on Cardinal Benedetto Accolti's gift of a golden cup; 'Descripsit ille maximus quondam Plato,' I, 41, on Contarini's *Magistrates of Venus;* 'Contarene, tuo docuisti, magne, libello,' II, 24, on Contarini's *Immortality of the Soul;* 'Perdideras Varium; nostro sed tempore laudes,' II, 23, on Benedetto Lampridio's Pindaric odes; 'Docte puer, magni pulcherrima cura GIBERTI,' II, 9, on Giberti's nephew's dedication to poetry; 'Jam luculenta, MARCE, pecunia,' VI, 63, a trite Horatian ode on the contrast between country life and the pursuit of wealth (this is one of the poems which appears in the standard editions of Flaminio's works but which is ascribed to Antonio Mario by Ubaldini, fol. 23$^r$–23$^v$); 'Gratulor, tua vota liberales,' VI, 29, an epistle containing interesting biographical material, addressed to Francisco Robortelli who was going to teach classics in Venice and spend the summers in his native Serravalle. (Robortelli later became a famous scholar.)

[13] Flaminio did not get on too well with Giberti, see Caraffa's letter rebuking Flaminio, Kaminski, *Regnum Dei*, II, pp. 12–14.

dated Verona, August 9, 1537,[14] reveals that Flaminio's desire for a new home has become known. The Archbishop of Salerno, Federico Fregoso, a former member of the court of Urbino and an outstanding scholar of Provençal poetry at whose home Bembo had already written his *Prose*, had invited Flaminio, through Pamphilio, to come to stay with him. Flaminio's reply is interesting for what it reveals of the relationship between patron and protégé. Fregoso's invitation is gratefully declined. Flaminio wants more freedom than he has had so far to go where he wants to go. He cannot again commit himself to any one person. However, he goes on to say that Salerno is so good, and he has so much regard for him, that he would love to be able to stay with him for five or six months at a time. It is a great pleasure to be able to live and die with one with whom one is in complete concord—pleasing and honest conversation is the greatest source of tranquillity of soul, of contentment. When he has not such company he converses with God. To make himself more worthy he is giving up all studies but Christian ones.[15] After the hot season he will re-read the New Testament and St. Augustine—another indication that Flaminio's reading was taking a dangerous turn; for an interest in the New Testament and St. Augustine was soon to be considered virtually heretical.

The translation of the psalms, which Flaminio had been working on in 1533, had been abandoned when Fracastoro told him that the work was putting his life in danger.[16] However, it seemed a pity to Pole that what Flaminio had done should be completely lost. Therefore, at his urging, Flaminio took up the paraphrases of thirty-two of the psalms, which he

[14] Atanagi, *Lettere 13*, pp. 294-5.

[15] Flaminio's growing religious devotion is revealed by a letter that he wrote Contarini on April 6, 1537 (Biadego, p. 228). In this letter Flaminio tells Contarini how, now that he has leisure, he spends an hour and a half every morning reading the offices and that he has gained more from this, with more pleasure, than from all his study and reading because the whole of this holy book is full of the most moving words which illuminate faith, increase hope, fire love, teach humility, patience, and all the other virtues, make us recognize the vanity of worldly things and the beauty and nobility of the divine, give us a thousand ways to praise the Lord God, to thank him, to love him, and venerate him wholeheartedly. . . .

[16] See Flaminio's prefatory letter to Paul III, *Paraphrasis in Duos Et Triginta Psalmos* (Venice, 1538), sig. A ii<sup>r</sup>–A iiii<sup>v</sup>.

had completed, and polished them for publication. In November, 1537, he went to Padua to stay with Cortese to see his paraphrases through the press. On November 12 Cortese wrote to Contarini from Padua[17] that he was expecting Messer Marcantonio in Padua and at the monastery of Praglia in a few days. He was coming to see his paraphrases of thirty-two of the psalms through the press. The paraphrase is diffuse and large. He thinks that it should be very useful. He regrets that ill health prevents Flaminio from doing further work. Already this little has completely robbed him of sleep.

Flaminio's *Paraphrase of Thirty-two of the Psalms* appeared in Venice in January 1538 and, on Giberti's insistence, was, like the Aristotle, dedicated to Paul III. The preface indicates Flaminio's conception of his duty as a translator.[18] He says that he has, in the light of modern scholarship, corrected the translation from the Hebrew, which was not always sufficiently careful, 'and, since the language of the Jews is very concise and elliptical . . . I decided that I should make some additions of my own, in some passages, to make the prose full and complete. These additions are almost always enclosed in parentheses.'[19] Flaminio goes on to discuss other difficulties that face the translator, such as the Hebrew use of tenses; for David often uses the present to refer to past or future events and the past to refer to the future. Then there is the question of political allusions. One has to read Kings to understand the psalms. All these difficulties Flaminio will try to iron out in his paraphrase.

However, there is a further problem in translating the psalms. David cannot be treated like any other ancient author because he was a prophet who prophesied the coming of Jesus. Therefore one cannot rely upon Jewish sources alone for the exegesis of his text. We are Christians, after all, and we must remember David's message to us. The Jews, of course, laugh at this sort of translation. But does it matter? They have the richest spiritual food at hand and they prefer to feed upon scraps. We must, in translating the psalms, consider their relevance to us, as part of God's revelation to man which was completed in the New Testament.

Thus the paraphrase of the first psalm is not properly a para-

[17] Cortese, I, pp. 123–4.  [18] Sig. B i$^r$–B viii$^v$.
[19] This is not true.

phrase at all but a sermon based on the first psalm, explaining its application to Christianity. Similarly the paraphrase of the second psalm would more rightly be labelled a commentary. A loose paraphrase of verses one and two is followed by a reference to the Crucifixion and Resurrection; after verse four a reference to the destruction of the Temple is inserted; while verse six, 'Yet have I set my king upon my holy hill of Zion,' is interpreted as prophetic of the Crucifixion.

Somewhere around this time, perhaps as a reward for his paraphrase of the psalms, Flaminio received another benefice from Giberti, the abbey of Saints Fabiano and Sebastiano in the valley of the Lavino.[20] The abbey, which is now a farmhouse, is a few miles to the right off the road that leads through Bazzano to Bologna, up the Lavino past Rivabella, at the intersection with the road that leads down from Mongiorgio. On the top of the mountain, at Mongiorgio, the Countess Matilda (1046–1115) had built a castle and a chapel. In the valley, at about the same time, Benedictine monks had built themselves a convent, with a strong tower attached to it, and a plain, but spacious, romanesque church with three aisles. There was also a lazaretto and a cemetery. Behind the church, towards the river, there are now fruit trees and beehives. They may well have been there in Flaminio's time. The Lavino is a 'torrente', a stream that flows down from the mountains, full of stones but little water in midsummer, where women wash clothes and men bathe. The horizon all around is bounded by moderately high hills with higher mountains in the background. In the early sixteenth century the Olivetan monks had still been there, but they had left now, and the property served only to provide income for the favourites of the Church. Despite the many pensions with which it was charged, the abbey of Saints Fabiano and Sebastiano brought Flaminio two hundred pieces of gold (scudi) a year.

As the autumn of 1538 approached and his health worsened, Flaminio decided that he could not spend another winter in the north. Now, with his three benefices, he had the means that permitted a modest independence. He decided to leave Verona and the Alps for ever for the radiant warmth of Naples. He

[20] Cuccoli, pp. 46 and 47, footnote.

remembered how he had been welcomed there by Sannazaro in 1514, how Vergil had gone there to write, and die.

His ode on his setting out for Naples (II, 7) reflects the conflicting emotions of a sick and homeless man whose normal yearning for a settled life in the warmth of a family is contrasted with what he knows must be his fate as a lone man of letters. His health demands that he undertake a journey both perilous and exhausting for him. It will take him to a place of beauty which he knows already, where he can join a company of poets whom he admires and with whom he feels a spiritual affinity—the bleak fact is that they are all dead. But the traveller must go his lonely way, perhaps to join the immortals there.

The ode is interesting as an account of sixteenth-century life, for the poet describes the traveller's kit and the dangers of a journey. (Bandits infest the roads, while by sea there is always the possibility of shipwreck.) Flaminio says that if he reaches Naples safely he will hang up his cap and spurs and sword, and the other arms that a traveller is obliged to carry, in the chapel to San Nazaro that the great Sannazaro had built at his villa, Mergellina, and that he will never travel again, not for all the wealth of Persia, not for all the riches of the sea.

The following passage, on the folly of restless voyaging and the blessedness of a settled life on the land, comforted by one's wife, growing old as one's sons grow up around one, is heavily indebted to Horace, but the detailed account of the occupations of the farmer reveals first-hand experience and is realistic. The man is happy who has never left his ancestral home, who lives content with a small piece of land. He tills the soil, prunes the vines, irrigates the fields, bringing water down from the hills, shears the sheep, and washes them in the river. In familiar surroundings, amid familiar people, he enjoys the life of the gods, and after his death his family bring annual offerings to his grave—a reference to pottery bowls here suggests that the life of the farm that Flaminio is describing is that of San Prospero outside Faenza.

What a good life that is for one who has been born to it! But Flaminio, the humanist's son, was destined to other things, a more exciting but less satisfying life. He was to die with a cardinal at his bedside, but no parent or friend, and he was to be buried in the church of strangers, in the church of St.

Thomas of Canterbury, attached to the English College in Rome.

The journey from Verona to Naples was very long. At Ravenna Flaminio already felt like turning back. Then, when he finally reached Naples, he could not find suitable lodgings. Heavy-hearted, he turned back to Sessa where his old friend from Verona, Galeazzo Florimonte, now lived. He accepted an invitation to stay with him for the winter. He would try Naples again in the spring.[21]

To Carlo Gualteruzzi, Cardinal Farnese's secretary who was handling the problems associated with his benefices, Flaminio wrote:

> Could you ever believe it, that I should have returned to Sessa through not having found lodgings for my money in Naples? And yet it's true. . . .
>
> [Florimonte is, in his writings, an Aristotelian] but in fact he is a most refined and pleasant Epicurean, and he who delights in this heresy will always prefer to live five months in Sessa in Messer Galeazzo's delightful place, and then die, than live fifty years in Rome in the palace of the pope. And, to tell you the truth, I suspect that this philosophy would appeal to me, too, more than that one which has been created in the bishop's palace in Verona, and that this hook would hold me here by the gullet, though proposing to me certain other reasons and apparent pretexts, so that the mind need not blush at it. . . .
>
> The bearer of this letter is that young man who accompanied me, and who is going back home. Please, sir, if he needs to, let him rest a couple of days in your house and find him some company for Bologna, or for Pesaro, because he is afraid to travel alone. I am very fond of him, because he is a good young fellow and has served me excellently.
>
> Sessa, November 11, 1538[22]

Sessa is a pleasant little town on the slopes of Mount Massico which has been renowned for its wine from classical times. Tucked between ranges of low volcanic hills that run at right angles to the shore, Sessa looks down over gentle folds planted with olive groves to a fertile plain by the sea. Florimonte's house was a little out of town.[23] It had an attractive terrace with

---

[21] Cuccoli, p. 72.
[22] Atanagi, *Lettere Facete*, I, pp. 304–6. See *supra*, p. 75, note 4.
[23] G. Tommasino, *Tra Umanisti e Filosofi . . . Philalethes* (Maddaloni, 1921), pp. vii–viii and 93.

a view of the sea, a garden, and a fountain, for which Flaminio composed the inscription which can still be read (II, 3). Flaminio was fortunate in having a friend who could offer such pleasant hospitality and the winter in Sessa must have been agreeable.

In the spring of 1539 Flaminio returned to Naples, but again found no suitable place to stay. Therefore, in July, he accepted an invitation from Giovanni Francesco d'Alois, count of Caserta, to visit him there.[24] Flaminio stayed in Caserta until early 1540. He regained his health there and wrote his second book of *lusus pastorales* (VI, 20).

To aid him in writing this second book of *lusus* Flaminio summoned Catullus's muse from Lake Garda (IV, 1): for Catullus was both the love poet, *par excellence*, especially the poet of unhappy love, and the poet of Garda and Verona where Flaminio had been living. There seems to be no other significance in the invocation of Catullus's muse. These poems are not written in his metre or manner and, except for the poems on the death of Hyella's goat which *might* owe something to the famous poem on the death of Lesbia's sparrow, they are not written on similar themes. Rather, in this second book of *lusus pastorales*, Flaminio has written something like a pastoral romance. Admittedly the plot is both simple and uncomplicated, but these are the songs of an *Arcadia* without the prose links. Hyella and Iolas were lovers. Iolas' father arranged for him to marry Nisa. The grief was more than Hyella could bear, and she died, like Juliet, when she was not yet fifteen. Hyella's favourite goat followed her to the grave. All the woodland, its creatures, gods, fountains, and gardens grieved for Hyella. Iolas, distraught at the suffering that he had caused, realizing his love for Hyella now that it was too late, died too.

The story is told through the poet's, later Iolas', dialogue with Hyella, or with the creatures or things that formed part of Hyella's life. Many of the poems are variations on single themes, such as the death of the goat, Hyella in the underworld, etc. They vary in length from six verse epigrams to one hundred verse elegies incorporating elaborate mythological *exempla*. The tone, as befits the distinguished middle-aged philosopher treating the trivia of adolescent love and the adorable little creatures

[24] Cuccoli, p. 72.

that inhabit the pagan countryside, is often mock heroic. Flaminio appears to have written much of his pastoral tragedy with his tongue in his cheek in an excess of good spirits at finding himself in good health in the ever-new wonder of spring (VI, 20 and IV, 25). The metres are iambic couplets, iambic trimeter, and elegiac couplets. At this period Flaminio seems to have been extraordinarily fond of effects of alliteration and assonance.

Flaminio's choice of the goat as the character through which the tragedy should be revealed shows a delicate sense of comedy and lightness of touch. The first poem about the goat, 'Caper, Capella caelitum beatior' (IV, 2), pictures the idyllic pastoral scene before tragedy struck. It is also something of a take-off on Flaminio's own ode on idyllic human life 'Fortunate senex, senex beate' (V, 39), written about an elderly cleric living in scholarly retirement outside Rome (see supra, p. 49). With epic dignity the goat, surrounded by a crowd of nannies, goes to the peaks of the high mountains 'when the sun reveals the heavens in gleaming day and the happy grasses grow white with hoary dew.' At midday the fair shepherdess leads her flock to a cool fountain. Here the favourite goat rests with his head in her lap, while she strokes his beard, makes wreaths for his head, or sings. When night raises up her star-crowned head and the meadows ring with the chirping crickets, Hyella drives him home to his stable and prepares him his supper of salted leaves. What goat has a happier life?

The companion piece, 'Caper, capellis ire dux ad pascua' (IV, 3), reveals everything changed. The goat leaves the stable last and drags his feet. Now nothing is sweet to him, not thyme, nor shade, nor a cool drink. The beautiful Hyella is dead. In the following *lusus* (VI, 4), the countryside grieves, its gods, the satyrs and fawns and goat-footed creatures, Hyella's garden, the fountain, the groves, and the valley where she pastured her she-goats. If Proserpina is wise she will make Hyella the shepherdess of the underworld; for she was the most skilful cheesemaker in the neighbourhood, the best at weaving pretty baskets, and the leader of the choral dances, while the country folk stood agape.

A more ambitious poem in elegiac couplets (IV, 5)—the poems on the goat were in the more informal iambic trimeter and the one on the gods is in hendecasyllables—tells how the fountain is swollen with tears at Hyella's death. She will no more touch his waters with her rosy lips, no more wash her white limbs in his flowing stream, no more be lulled to sleep by his murmuring chatter, while the lascivious breeze plays between her snow-white breasts and sighs through her golden hair, and the perfumed myrtle blossoms sift down upon her—here we have Flaminio, the translator of Petrarch. The poem continues with the paradoxes of the Petrarchan amorous traditition and with its sweet conceits. As in a Renaissance mythological painting the country gods gather around to hear Hyella sing.

Now, to cut the cloying sweetness of a picture that is becoming too pretty, Flaminio introduces a comic touch. Her goats bleat the refrain of Hyella's song while the kids caper about forgetting to suck and the birds wheel around memorizing the melody. Flaminio completes his Petrarchan picture of ideal pastoralism with an Anacreontic touch. At the sight of such beauty Love turns his darts against himself.

As we have noted before in poems in which Flaminio has made an extensive use of pagan mythology, Flaminio's writing is highly pictorial. Here we have a description of a static scene, carefully composed, with a focus of interest and with minor characters grouped about according to their degree of involvement with the central character. The description is all detailed and exact, no item is unessential, the minor characters are all differentiated by the epithet that is the key to their traditional ionography, and the whole forms a carefully studied and composed picture which could serve as a written cartoon for a painting.

The idyllic picture of Hyella as she was—what the fountain *had* the joy to reflect—is now balanced by the story of the suffering caused to the water nymph, Galatea, by the loss of her beloved Acis, a parallel to the state of the fountain now. The tragic triangle of Galatea, Acis, and Polyphemus was a favourite with Renaissance poets, but the epyllion is appropriate as well as decorative here. Its active grief contrasts with the fixed picture of past happiness that is irretrievably lost, while its frenzied sorrow brings us back to the weeping, flooding fountain.

A further brief recollection of past joy, how Hyella would

intertwine the myrtle boughs to cast shadow on the spring, plait the rushes to form a fence round about, and scatter white hyacinths and red poppies on the water, leads the fountain to a further surge of grief. Flaminio's psychology is sound, even in such a highly artificial work of poetic art. Now the fountain breaks his urn and abandons himself to sorrow, flooding the countryside, feeding the flowers and trees of grief, the violets, the hyacinths, and the cypress. And if any fair maiden comes to wash in his stream he warns her not to stain her body with tears.

'Cur subito, fons turbidule, tuus humor abundat' is a piece of beautiful writing which exists solely for the sake of the beauty which it embodies. It pleases the reader because of the extravagance of its emotions, which assume cosmic proportions. We enjoy, in a never-never land of the imagination, an idealization of emotions that we all, at one time or another, experience—an idealization that flatters our egos, while at the same time it makes us smile; for we know that nothing in life is so good or so bad, that nothing we feel is so important. But it is pleasant to toy with the idea, for a while, that both our happiness and our sorrow can be so complete.

The poem is pleasing, not just because it balances perfect happiness and beauty with whole-hearted grief, flattering our emotions, but because it has been composed with a studied artistry which avoids all excess, puts a rein on rhetoric, and varies the expression of grief through pictures of grief in action, so that one does not wallow in ranting emotion. The rhetorically trained reader, who is, of course, the reader for whom Flaminio was writing, enjoys the evidence of careful planning, studied art, intellectual control over emotion, and fluent ease in the expression of it. This is the scholar's and the artist's escapist literature, into a world of ideal youth and beauty, where the only preoccupation is with love, youth's perennial problem.

After a poem about the suffering of her garden, whose beauty came and went with Hyella (IV, 6), there follows a series of pieces about Hyella's tomb (IV, 7–11), which suggest variations on Poussin's 'Death in Arcadia'. Through these poems written about her tomb we discover why and how Hyella died, and we are able to piece together the unhappy story of Nisa and Iolas.

## INDEPENDENCE AND PASTORALS

In the epitaphs there are echoes of Propertius on the death of Corinna. Here for the first time a flower image appears (IV, 10) which was to remain in Flaminio's mind and to form the basis of one of his greatest lyrics, on the relation of the soul to God, 'Ut flos tenellus in sinu' (VIII, 7).

In these poems we also learn that Hyella's faithful goat has died and lies buried beside her. The dead goat inspires one of Flaminio's cleverest epigrams:

> When fair Hyella perished, the country's delight,
>   Her faithful goat died with her mistress.
> No violent plague, no fierce fever destroyed her
>   Suddenly, but love for her lady.
> Go now, Greece, and boast, in love's name,
>   Of your Pylades, and Orestes, and faithful Pirithoos.

> Deliciae ruris cum pulchra periret Hyella,
>   Cum domina periit fida capella sua.
> Non ipsam violenta lues, non aspera febris
>   Sed dominae subita morte peremit amor.
> I nunc, et Pylades, et amoris nomine Orestas
>   Et jacta fidos, Graecia, Pirithoos.
>                                          IV, 12

The reference to the august heroes of antiquity and to proverbial devotion, and the echo of the great epigram of Simonides maintains the witty, mock-heroic tone of the other goat poems.

Another witty epigram (IV, 13) presents us with Hyella and her faithful goat at the gates of Hell. The dog Cerberus loses his ferocity and fawns and licks Hyella's legs and wishes he could go back with her to the upper world to be an ordinary sheep-dog.

In other *lusus* Hyella's pipe is hung up to Pan (IV, 15) and the shepherds dedicate a grove to Hyella who becomes a tutelary deity (IV, 16). Then the centre of interest shifts to Iolas, already near the end of his story. In the first of the Iolas poems, the dying Iolas invokes Hyella in an elaborate elegy on the irrevocability of death which is illustrated, like the elegy on the fountain's grief, by the myths of Proserpina and of Cybele and Attis (IV, 17); Iolas apologizes for taking Nisa to his bed when his soul belonged to Hyella (IV, 18); Iolas regrets that Hyella ever loved him or, alternatively, that they did not run away together (IV, 19); Iolas rails at the sun which brings back day when the sun of his life has set (IV, 21); in a long nostalgic lament Iolas recalls the happy days that are past, how he and Hyella loved and enjoyed themselves together (IV, 22); Iolas hangs up his flute to Pan (IV, 23); and, finally, weeping under the laurel that he had planted for Hyella, Iolas awaits the death that will unite them for ever (IV, 24).

Flaminio's second book of *lusus pastorales* is a pretty contribution to the history of the Renaissance pastoral made by an established poet who is writing for the writing's sake. It is quite unlike the first book of *lusus pastorales* which was the work of a lyric poet recapturing and making permanent the moods of a moment. The first *lusus* were simple and direct and were written on different occasions and about different people. The second collection of *lusus* was consciously artistic and all the poems were closely related in a single pastoral history. They were all apparently written in a relatively short period of time, namely the spring of 1540. They were intentionally literary works, full of reminiscences of ancient and modern classics, pleasing to the ear through the skilful use of figures of sound, and intended for the delight and amusement of other literary men.[25] They were the diversions of a scholar who was more interested in art than in passion.[26] They show the attention to form that is usually considered to have emanated from the Council of Trent.

This same spring Flaminio wrote a pastoral elegy to Florimonte, inviting him to come to Caserta to visit Alois who was ill with a fever (V, 8). The elegy has a refrain like the Theocritean-Vergilian incantation, 'Huc ades, Galatee; quid moraris,' and is permeated with the lively good spirits that seem to have sustained Flaminio through the composition of the Hyella-Iolas story. Flaminio tells Florimonte that he has just finished his little book of pastorals.

Another poetic epistle written about the same time to Carlo Gualteruzzi (V, 22)[27] thanks him for expediting his business, an apparent reference to Flaminio's effort to return the abbey

---

[25] IV, 25.

[26] It is interesting to read Flaminio's apology for the *lusus*, V, 21: poetry is a fit relaxation for philosophers.

[27] See Flaminio's letter to Gualteruzzi in Atanagi, *Lettere 13*, pp. 298-302, dated Caserta, January, 30, 1540.

in the Val di Lavino to the monks to whom he felt it rightfully belonged. Perhaps stimulated by the example of Giberti, who restored the church of San Stefano in Genoa and then returned it to the monks,[28] as well as under the influence of reform thought, Flaminio tried to get the Olivetan monks back to the Val di Lavino. Flaminio, however, was no great radical, nor rashly inclined to give up the revenue he had yearned for for so long. As he makes clear in a letter written to Gualteruzzi from Caserta on January 30, 1540, he wants to see the white monks back in the abbey, but on fair terms. He wants bank securities from the chapter and a free pension. He thinks that the monks will keep their word and give him the pension, even though the abbey is heavily burdened. If they refuse to do so he does not want the process to proceed.[29]

[28] Pighi, pp. 4–5. Giberti also restored the revenues to them.
[29] Atanagi, *Lettere 13*, pp. 298–302.

Chapter 7

# NAPLES AND THE REFORM

THE Reform Commission which Paul III had set up in 1536[1] had produced a series of recommendations which embodied such a shocking indictment of conditions in the Church that the Roman authorities felt it best that it be suppressed. However, inevitably, a copy of the document slipped out and was printed in Cologne in 1538, where it supplied welcome ammunition to the Protestants.[2] The Reform Commission was concerned only with what might be broadly called questions of ecclesiastical administration. The questions of doctrine raised by the Protestants were to be discussed in an oecumenical council first summoned for Mantua in 1537 but not destined to meet, largely because of the political machinations of Francis I and Charles V, until 1545, in Trent.

The Reform Commission found the root of all evil in the Church in the papacy itself. The popes had surrounded themselves with 'yes-men' who told them that anything they did was right. This had led to the sale of benefices, to simony, and hence to all abuses. As the Pardoner said 'Radix malorum est cupiditas'.

The whole Church structure had to be overhauled, beginning with the ordination of priests, who were like the arteries of the

---
[1] See *supra*, p. 85.
[2] For the report of the Reform Commission see Comba, I, pp. 577–86.

Church bringing the life-blood of religion to the people. At the present time ordination was a scandal. Men without experience, of the lowest classes, and with bad moral character were ordained. Hence had arisen a contempt for the priesthood, with the result that veneration for the cult was practically extinct. The Commission suggested that the pope should appoint two or three prelates in Rome, men who were above all learned and pure, to supervise ordination, that the bishops should carry out their instructions in their dioceses, and that no one should be ordained except by his bishop.

Bishops should be good and learned men who would reside in their dioceses. Absenteeism must be abolished. Now most dioceses were run by mercenaries. Bishops should not be away from their churches for more than three Sundays. Plurality, especially in bishoprics, was an abuse.

Benefices, too, should be conferred only upon men of good character and education who would reside in their benefices. Therefore an Italian should not receive a benefice in England or Spain. Benefices should not be charged with pensions, except for charitable purposes. The revenue from a benefice was for the maintenance of the incumbent, for the expenses of the cult and the church, for the repair of religious buildings, and for charity. The exchange of benefices was an abuse, as was their bequest. Priests' children should not have their father's benefices.

Cardinals should not be bishops. Some cardinals should reside in their provinces, but at the present time too many cardinals were absent from the curia without performing any duties anywhere else.

It should not be possible for those in orders to escape punishment for crimes they had committed by bribing higher authorities.

All conventual orders should be abolished by curtailing the admission of novices and by expelling those who had not yet taken vows. The care of nuns by monks was a great scandal and should be ended. The nuns should be put under the supervision of ordinaries. Apostate friars should not be allowed to wear their habits or to retain benefices.

The bishops should investigate the schools in their dioceses to see to it that impiety was not implanted there. Erasmus' colloquies should be banned from the schools because of their impiety. No public discussion of theology should be allowed.

Certain methods of raising money for the Church should be abolished. There should be no dispensation for men in holy orders to marry, etc., etc.

Then the commission turned its attention to Rome itself. Rome should be the 'mater et magistra' of the Christian world, and yet all visitors were scandalized by the priests in St. Peter's, dirty, ignorant men, celebrating mass in filthy vestments. In Rome itself prostitutes walked the streets or rode on mules accompanied, in broad daylight, by nobles, cardinals, and clerks. There were more of them in Rome than in any other city in the world and they lived in the finest houses. Something must also be done about the constant civil disorders in Rome and about controlling its tumultuous families.

The signatories of this report were all Flaminio's friends, Contarini; Caraffa; Sadoleto; Pole; Frederick [Fregoso], Archbishop of Salerno; Jerome [Aleandro], Archbishop of Brindisi; Giberti; Gregory [Cortese], Abbot of St. George, Venice; and Brother Thomas, Master of the Sacred Palace. No wonder Flaminio felt unhappy about his abbey in the Val di Lavino!

Now Reform was discussed everywhere in educated circles in Italy. Juan de Valdes, a Spanish gentleman of 'cap and sword', as Pietro Carnesecchi described him at his trial before the Inquisition,[3] and secretary to the viceroy, had become the leader of a religious circle in Naples.[4] Valdes' group discussed justification by faith alone, but had no separatist tendencies.[5]

---

[3] G. Manzoni, 'Estratto del Processo di Pietro Carnesecchi', *Miscellanea di Storia Italiana*, X (Torino, 1870), 195.

[4] Valdes was secretary to the viceroy of Naples, Don Pedro Alvarez of Toledo, Cuccoli, p. 82.

[5] For Valdes' beliefs see his writings, the record of Carnesecchi's trial, the standard works on the Reform in Italy, works on the individual Reformers, and E. Boehmer, *The Lives of the Twin Brothers Juan and Alfonso de Valdes*, tr. J. T. Betts (London, 1882). The works of Valdes which have survived are: *A Commentary on the First Book of Psalms* (London, 1894); *Le Cento et Dieci Divine Considerazioni* (Basle, 1550 and Milan, 1944)—Nicholas Ferrar made an English translation which was published in 1638, 1646, and 1905; *A Commentary upon Our Lord's Sermon on the Mount* (London, 1882); *Alphabeto Christiano* (London, 1861), ed. by B. Croce (Bari, 1938), also published under

Valdes was not interested in formal relations with the Church, but in the soul's relation with God. His religion was a highly personal one, based on intense emotion. One would enjoy everlasting life and eternal salvation if one believed that Jesus had paid with his blood for all our sins and if one loved him ardently. Valdes drew no inferences from the doctrine of justification by faith. He was not interested in theology. Flaminio became a member of his group when he first stayed in Naples in 1539.

Flaminio, as a poet, sympathized with Valdes' subjective religion and he was, as a man, attracted to the small, thin, ascetic-looking Spaniard with his burning belief, but Flaminio also had a trained mind. He had lived long in ecclesiastical circles, he had worked on philosophy and theology, and he had been reading Lutheran books since 1536. Thus he was aware that the belief in justification by faith alone carried theological implications that could destroy the whole fabric of the Roman Catholic Church as they knew it. Carnesecchi says[6] that in Naples in 1540 Flaminio told him that there was reason to doubt whether confession and penitence were divinely ordained, since there was nothing about them in the New Testament and that St. Augustine, himself, in his commentary on the psalms, had said 'that it can be wondered whether there is a third place in addition to heaven and hell, showing by these words that even he was not sure about it [purgatory]'[7]. Flaminio was clearly plunging farther into heresy than Valdes and following up some of the implications of the new doctrine; yet, as Carnesecchi said, Flaminio himself regularly went to confession, which he found both useful and salutary—in this decade before the Council of Trent when religious issues were suddenly discussed by the educated in Italy after two or three generations of humanism and a much longer period of indifference, orthodoxy was not yet clear-cut and the course that the future would take was open to the wildest inference. Thus it was that most of

[6] Manzoni, 'Processo Carnesecchi', p. 195.  [7] Ibid., p. 194.

the title *Dialogo de Doctrina Cristiana* (Coimbra, 1925); *Lac Spirituale* (Brunswick, 1864) also published under the title of *Instrucción Cristiana para los niños* (Bonn, 1883); and commentaries on St. Matthew, the Epistle to the Romans, and First Corinthians.

the important men and women of the time, even the members of the college of cardinals, were later investigated by the Inquisition. There is a certain parallel today in the treatment of American liberals of the 1930's.

Valdes' circle was an interesting one. Himself an elegant and cultivated nobleman, he invited to his house all those who were remarkable in Naples for their genius, their beauty, their education, and their rank. His house, 'La Chiaia', was a gay and picturesque place which all its visitors later remembered with nostalgia in the grim years that were to follow. But in Naples in 1540 and 1541 life was bright and beautiful.[8] Though Valdes' group was devoted to religion, it loved Christ joyfully. Only in the north do people feel that they have to be miserable about religion.

Valdes' group was graced by many of the outstanding women of the age, women renowned for their beauty and their intelligence as well as for their virtue and piety.[9] There was Vittoria Colonna, Marchioness of Pescara, the widow of Francesco d'Avalos, the victor of Pavia. Vittoria Colonna poured forth her grief for her dead husband in a series of sonnets that her contemporaries found extremely beautiful, roused the fervent admiration of Michelangelo, and was renowned throughout Italy for her chastity. Nevertheless she dressed richly and colourfully and had a gorgeous band of attendants.

Another member of Valdes' circle was that Giulia Gonzaga who had so dramatically escaped from Barbarossa's raid on Sperlonga in 1534. Now, when Flaminio met her in 1539, she was twenty-six-years of age, very beautiful, very devout, and one of the people closest to Valdes. For her he wrote his *Christian Alphabet*, a dialogue between them, and to her he dedicated his translations of the scriptures from Hebrew and Greek into Spanish, and his commentaries on St. Paul's epistles (exclusive of Hebrews), and on the epistles of St. Peter and St. Matthew.[10] Flaminio and Donna Giulia became close

---

[8] See Bonfadio's nostalgic letter to Carnesecchi, J. Bonfadio, *Lettere Famigliari* (Bologna, 1744), pp. 4–6.

[9] For female society in Naples at this time and for the women in Valdes' circle see Amante, pp. 168–88; Cantù, III, p. 234; Cuccoli, pp. 73, 82–3, 90–1; Edmondo Cione, 'Introduction', Valdes, *Considerazioni* (Milan, 1944).

[10] Boehmer, pp. 21–2.

friends, after he left Naples they corresponded frequently, he translated Valdes' *Considerations* and his *Commentary on the Psalms* from Spanish into Italian for her,[11] and she sent him and his friend, Pietro Carnesecchi, a conserve of roses every year for their health.[12] Both she and Vittoria Colonna were posthumously attacked by the Inquisition.[13]

Other ladies in Valdes' circle were Giovanna and Maria d'Aragona, young noblewomen married, respectively, to relatives of Vittoria Colonna and of her husband; Isabella Sanseverino; Isabella Briseña, who became a Protestant and fled to Zürich; Ippolita Gonzaga, Duchess of Mondragone; Lucrezia Scaglione; the poetesses, Maria Cardona, Dionora Sanseverino, and Laura Terracina; and Donna Costanza d'Avalos, Princess of Francavilla, and the aunt of Vittoria Colonna's husband, a woman famous for her defence of Ischia against the French.

The male members of Valdes' circle were Giovanni Mollio; Galeazzo Caracciolo, Marquess of Vico, a correspondent of Flaminio's, who later became a Protestant and went abroad; Flaminio's host, Francesco d'Alois of Caserta; Flaminio's friend, Jacopo Bonfadio, author of the *Annals of Genoa*, who was finally burnt at the stake by the Genoese; Flaminio's friend and correspondent, Mario Galeota, author of an academic treatise on fortifications, who was later arrested by the Inquisition in Calabria;[14] Ferdinando Torres and Onorato Fascitelli, to both of whom Flaminio wrote poetic epistles;[15] the famous preacher, Bernardino Ochino, to whom Valdes now suggested themes for his sermons;[16] the Protestant leader in Lucca and later in England, Peter Martyr Vermigli; and Flaminio's close friend,

[11] Manzoni, 'Processo Carnesecchi', p. 495.
[12] *Ibid.*, pp. 492–3.
[13] C. Corvisieri, 'Compendio dei processi del Santo Offizio di Roma', *Archivio della Società Romana di Storia Patria*, III (Rome, 1880), 261–90.
[14] Amante, p. 288. Flaminio wrote him a poetic epistle, VI, 41, in which Flaminio answers Galeota's urgings that he should publish his *lusus pastorales* —and compete with Sannazaro!
[15] VI, 27, and V, 35, respectively. Flaminio asks Torres to criticize his *lusus pastorales*.
[16] Manzoni, 'Processo Carnesecchi', pp. 195–6. Carnesecchi says that Valdes sent Ochino a note suggesting the theme for his sermon the nights before he had to preach.

Pietro Carnesecchi, protonotary and secretary to Clement VII, later burnt by the Inquisition in Rome.

Flaminio spent the spring of 1539 with this group, but quit Naples with Alois in July, as we have noted in the previous chapter, to spend the second half of the year and the spring of 1540 in Caserta. He did not, however, abandon his concern with religion, which now became the dominant thing in his life. From Caserta he wrote letters on grace and free will to Cardinal Contarini and to Cardinal Seripando, an Augustinian theologian whom he had got to know in Naples.[17] Therefore the conclusion of his dedication of his second book of *lusus pastorales* to Giberti's secretary, Francesco della Torre (IV, 25), is probably quite sincere. Flaminio undoubtedly intended to dedicate himself to religious poetry as well as to religion when he left Caserta. He could not know that it would take Urania nine years to come—if we exclude the poetic translations of the psalms published in 1546.

In the spring of 1540 Flaminio received an invitation from Ferrante Brancaccio, a member of one of Naples' oldest families, to come to stay with him. Flaminio accepted gratefully, leaving Alois and Caserta (V, 16). It was probably also at this time that Flaminio wrote his letter to the Abbot Anisio on the immortality of the soul.[18] This letter is interesting both for Flaminio's opening disclaimer, reminiscent of his correspondence with Bembo and Longueil twenty years before, of his ability to write in Latin, and for its reflection of the religious atmosphere of the Valdes circle. The immortality of the soul is an article of faith. It cannot be proved by philosophy or by the feeble light of nature. Faith is God's gift. Those who have it should live according to Christ's precepts and hope that through his unmeasured goodness our souls, and bodies as well, will be immortal and blessed. If, through pride, we reject the supernatural, we should pray God to enable us to submit our limited intelligence to obedience to the holy faith, as many philosophers have done. When God has given us the gift of obedience, we will not fear death, but ever thirst after it, secure in our trust in the merits of Jesus Christ.

Here we have the essence of the Valdesian teaching. We are

[17] Cuccoli prints these letters in an appendix.
[18] Atanagi, *Lettere 13*, pp. 296–8.

justified by faith alone, but we should live according to Christ's teachings to prove our belief in him. Thus, though the merit is taken from works, works are retained. The Church as a mediator between God and man is ignored. Only the personal relationship counts.

Capponi found in the secret archives of the Vatican a letter from Cardinal Aleandro to the papal secretary, dated Rome, September 6, 1540, in which he discusses who should accompany the nuncio—Contarini was designated at the time—to the meeting at Worms where it was hoped that a reconciliation could be effected between German Catholics and Protestants. Aleandro suggests Cortese or Flaminio. '... Contarini says wonderful things about Flaminio, about his knowledge of theology and other sciences and also about his Greek and Latin ... and Hebrew. This is important in those who are sent because the Lutherans make a greater profession of languages and think more of them than anything else.'[19] On September 13 Alexander Farnese wrote a similar letter to Hieronimo Dandino.[20]

The first letter, however, was effective. Contarini wrote to Flaminio from Rome on September 10, 1540,

> Messer Marcantonio, my friend. His Holiness, wishing to make use of your work, and of the gifts which God has given you, in negotiations of the utmost importance to the honour of God and to the Christian religion, has commissioned me to write to you in his name that, as soon as you have seen this present letter of mine, you should take the road to Rome and come to His Holiness, and you should not fail if you do not wish to stray from the obedience which you owe His Beatitude and be ungrateful to Christ 'by whose blood you were redeemed' and from whom you have had great gifts.... I cannot say more to you, come at once, 'and farewell in the name of the Lord, remembering me'.[21]

Flaminio's reply to this letter is worth quoting in full both for the description of his illness which it contains and for the light that it throws on his character.

[19] Hugo Laemmer, *Monumenta Vaticana* (Freiburg im Breisgau, 1861), p. 301. See also Cortese, *Opere*, I, p. 55.
[20] E. Costa, 'Marc Antonio Flaminio e il cardinale Alessandro Farnese', *GSLI*, X (1887), 384–7.
[21] L. Beccadelli, *Monumenti di varia litteratura* (Bologna, 1799), I, ii, 88–9.

## NAPLES AND THE REFORM

Recently I wrote to Messer Lodovico Beccadello a long letter in which I pointed out clearly that I was not fit for that holy enterprise to which he urged me, and I felt sure that that letter would have moved the compassion of your Most Reverend Holiness in such a way that it would not only have avoided my choice for such a trip, but it would have ruled me out if by chance anyone should have proposed me to His Holiness. But my belief has turned out to be baseless, for Your Most Reverend Holiness has written me a letter which, to honestly tell the truth, has caused me the greatest affliction that I have ever suffered in my life; for I see that His Holiness, to whom I owe greater obedience than to all the world together, commands me to do something which I clearly cannot do without death, and what increases my grief is the fact that I am absolutely sure that my person is not at all fit for so great an enterprise and I marvel that this inadequacy of mine is not very well known to Your Most Reverend Holiness....

If we turn to the matters which are to be discussed with the Lutherans, I maintain with the utmost truth that I am not informed about them, because I have never made the effort to see their writings nor the confutations of them by the Catholics. The little that I have seen of Christian literature has been of simple things, devotional works, and works of spiritual edification, more fit to arouse feelings than to improve the intellect.

If Your Holiness should say to me that I will be able to serve the enterprise with humanistic letters, I have to maintain that I would be mute among those Germans, because I have never had—indeed I have always avoided—the practice of speaking Latin. Nor would you be able to make use of me in the writing of Latin—although it appears a very odd thing to say—but it is nevertheless the absolute truth—that I have never been able to make myself write either prose or verse at another's request. And all that I have written I have written under free impulse—I say free because I have never had it in my power to be able to write every time I wanted to or all that I would have liked. Of this strange nature of mine my patron the Most Reverend Monsignor of Verona can give good witness; for he has never been able to get me to write a single Latin letter, however much I wanted to do it and was embarrassed to deny my benefactor so fair a request—Now I am embarrassed to discuss such things but necessity forces me, so that I can explain myself.

But suppose that I were adequate as to character, spirit, letters, and learning, I would not all the same be able to do my duty, for I am so sick in body.... I could never stand so long a voyage, since my body is most delicate and my kidneys are very weak, without mentioning that piercing cold which would strike me down in ten days, and the stoves which would be deadly to me.

... but it suffices to speak of my new indisposition in particular, which has caused me the most intense suffering these past months and torments me all the time.... I could not accept invitations to Monte Cassino—I could not ride so far—or to Salerno and Badia, which Pietro Carnesecchi wanted to show me ... this extreme heat has so aggravated my disease that if I did not protect myself by resting, and with massage, and daily baths, and with the most careful diet, I would be all covered with ulcers.... Nevertheless, not being content with my own judgment in so important a case ... I spoke to the physician and surgeon who have treated me and who are treating me right now. They both agreed that the journey on horseback would be fatal to me and they were absolutely certain that I would spend the trip in some inn covered with suppurating sores and in desperate plight.

My most honoured Sir, Your Most Reverend Holiness, take it for certain, that if I ever wanted to be well, talented, and lettered, I want it most desperately now, to be able to be of some help in this holy undertaking and to obey His Beatitude, nor do I believe that I can ever feel greater affliction than that which I feel now, knowing that I am impotent. But, since this is God's will, I pray Your Most Reverend Holiness by the love of Jesus Christ and by my long servitude, to have compassion on me and not to wish to precipitate me into certain death, knowing, for the reasons which I have given, that my person cannot be of any use to Religion.... It remains, then, that Your Most Reverend Holiness should add to the many benefits that you have bestowed on me, the most unusual one of making my excuses to His Holiness in such a way that he remains satisfied, because I freely confess that I would never be able to harden my heart to set out on a voyage in certain danger to my life. And it befits Your Holiness' kindness to condescend to this frailty of mine and to procure that evil is not added to evil.... I know that I have written at too great length but I deserve pardon since I am treating, it seems to me, of my life and of my death.

To Your Most Reverend Holiness I humbly entrust my honour and my life and I kiss your hand.[22]

Naples, September 25, 1549

Flaminio was most unfortunate with his health, but even severe illness cannot excuse this sort of disingenuousness.

[22] *Ibid.*, I, ii, 89–92.

Flaminio, as he recognizes himself, protests too much. If he really were so ill and suffering from such a loathsome disease as he describes and this were the fundamental reason for his begging off the expedition to Worms, surely this would be the reason that he would give first. But his lengthy effort to prove that he is *in every respect* unsuitable for the work suggests that he just does not want to do it. It may well be true that Flaminio could not speak Latin, and even that he could not write Latin prose fluently, despite his consummate ease in verse, but his protest that he knew nothing about Lutheran doctrine is difficult to accept, since both we and Contarini know that he had been reading Lutheran works from 1536 onwards. It may be true that the works that he read were chiefly devotional rather than doctrinal—for Flaminio was an emotional rather than a rational person—but the cumulative effect of all these protests is such as to make each one seem inadequate in itself and the reflection of an inadequacy in Flaminio's character. We feel that Flaminio might have learnt to write Latin prose by disciplining or forcing himself, that perhaps vanity set too high a standard, that he had perhaps been spoilt by too much early adulation. The same sort of reaction is elicited by his protest about his complete uselessness in theological discussion. Was it again a fear of not being as brilliant as he was thought to be, or of revealing the fact that he did not have a first-rate analytical and critical mind, or that he lacked strength of character and conviction which drove Flaminio to the purely negative position of refusing to do anything at all? Or, all these things being true, was Flaminio on top of this just too lazy to work hard, too indifferent or too selfish to serve the Church that had done so well by him? Or was Flaminio hiding a secret sympathy with the Lutherans and using every means he could think of to avoid being forced to declare or perjure himself? Perhaps a little bit of all of this lay behind this curious letter which, whatever its degree of dishonesty, does not put Flaminio's moral character in the best light.

Flaminio was highly praised by his contemporaries for the uprightness of his life, for his goodness, and sincerity.[23] We know, too, that he was a warm and lively personality. But

[23] e.g., Carnesecchi, 'Processo', ed. Manzoni, pp. 195–6; Bonfadio, *Lett. Fam.*, p. 19.

there seems to have been a curious negativity about him. He appears to have developed the defence of the weak, a charming but obdurate stubbornness, a refusal to yield and to co-operate, except on his own terms.

While Flaminio lived in Naples he frequented literary circles there, as well as Juan de Valdes' religious group. He was a member of Pontano's Academy[24] and a friend of Bernardo Tasso and of Minturno.[25] It was Bernardo Tasso who established the ode as a literary genre in Italian, and he did so by translating and adapting Flaminio's 'Hymn to Aurora'.[26] Tasso held Flaminio in the highest esteem and invited him to visit him in Sorrento.

Flaminio spent the winter of 1540 and the spring of 1541 in Naples. He left Naples in May a year before the re-establishment of the Inquisition. He went first to Rome in the company of Pietro Carnesecchi; Luigi Priuli, his old friend from the Oratory of Divine Love in Venice; and Donato Rullo,[27] Abbot of Villamarina, a reserved and ambitious churchman, who probably felt sympathy towards Lutheran ideas, but was careful not to commit himself. Rullo later forced himself upon Pole, on the latter's legation to England, and was investigated by the Inquisition.[28] Rullo had cultivated Flaminio with kindness (see V, 14), and Flaminio responded with enthusiastic friendship. Flaminio praised the younger man's helpfulness to him and his friends, and his perpetually open house. He overflowed with gratitude, and rewarded his young admirer with an ode on true happiness, which consists in loving God (VI, 65), and, more tangibly, by using his influence to get him a place in Cardinal Morone's household when they reached Rome.[27]

In Rome Flaminio saw Pole again, back from his legations to Belgium and Spain (1537–9) and from the Diet of Ratisbon (spring, 1541), but, while Rullo stayed with Pole, Flaminio and Carnesecchi put up in the palace of the Cardinal of Mantua, Ercole Gonzaga.[29]

[24] Cuccoli, p. 126.    [25] *Ibid.*, p. 73.
[26] C. Maddison, *Apollo and The Nine* (London, 1960), p. 152. For Flaminio's hymn see *supra*, pp. 57-9.
[27] Manzoni, 'Processo Carnesecchi', pp. 210–11.
[28] Corvisieri, 'Compendio dei processi', pp. 264 and 268 ff.
[29] Cuccoli, p. 115.

After a few days Flaminio left Rome to accompany Carnesecchi to his native Florence. Flaminio intended going on to Verona, but he stopped six months with Carnesecchi in Florence, from May to October. There Flaminio's involvement with Protestantism deepened. Carnesecchi, at his trial, said that Flaminio showed him Calvin's *Institutes* at this time and 'that this imbued his mind with similar opinions'.[30] In Florence Flaminio and Carnesecchi visited Vittoria Colonna at her house there and 'reasoned with her on justification by faith alone, but according to Valdes' opinion, and without making other inferences, and she accepted it in that way'.[31] They also visited Caterina Cibo, Duchess of Camerino, with whom they discussed spiritual matters,[32] and Bernardino Ochino, now in the convent of Montughi three miles outside Florence. They only went to see him once because the road was bad and the weather hot. He said he was collecting his sermons for publication.[33]

As was usual Flaminio had literary friends in Florence as well, Lelio Torelli,[34] secretary to the Duke, Pier Vettori, professor at the university, and Giovanni della Casa,[35] at this time a brilliant sonneteer, destined to influence Milton. Eight years later it was della Casa, now Archbishop of Benevento, who drew up the first Index with one of Flaminio's works on it.

From this summer in Florence we have a letter of Flaminio's to Carlo Gualteruzzi of Bologna[36] regretting that he can offer no constructive criticism of the philosophical treatise by Antonio della Mirandola which Gualteruzzi had sent him. The letter is typical of Flaminio. He has not looked at a page of philosophy or thought about philosophical problems for six years. He started philosophy late and left it early, so he did not learn much, and now he has forgotten what little he knew. Therefore he is incompetent to judge the work, which, however, he read

[30] Manzoni, 'Processo Carnesecchi', p. 195.
[31] *Ibid.*, pp. 201–2.
[32] Cuccoli, pp. 91 and 115.
[33] Manzoni, 'Processo Carnesecchi', pp. 516–8.
[34] Mancurti, MAF, *Carm.* (1743), p. xiii.
[35] W. L. Bullock, 'Lyric Innovations of Giovanni della Casa', *PMLA*, XLI (1926), 82–90.
[36] Atanagi, *Lettere 13*, pp. 302–3.

with interest and pleasure. He asks Gualteruzzi to excuse him with Mirandola, whom he is always willing to serve in accordance with his capacities. He regrets that the first time he is asked the task is beyond him.

Flaminio has not the mentality of the humanist, who would wear himself out in his efforts to promote the advancement of knowledge and scholarship and of his own reputation over that of his rivals. Flaminio could talk brilliantly all night, but he seems to have been incapable of sustained, serious effort. It was probably a matter of temperament, as well as of ill health.

In the summer of 1541 Reginald Pole was made legate to the Patrimony of St. Peter, with his residence in the old gothic papal palace in Viterbo. He took possession in September[37] and forthwith invited Flaminio and Carnesecchi to come to stay with him there, because (as Beccadelli said in his life of Pole), he had seen that his old friend Flaminio had become tainted with heretical ideas and he wanted to guide him back to the true faith.[38]

[37] Atanagi, Cuccoli, p. 115.
[38] Beccadelli, *Monumenti*, I, ii, 326–7.

*Chapter 8*

# VITERBO AND CARDINAL POLE

FLAMINIO'S old friend from Bologna days, Lodovico Beccadelli, had gone with Contarini to Ratisbon. He was now Pole's secretary in Viterbo. In his Italian life of Pole, Beccadelli describes the cardinal as being a man of medium height, fairly thin, with a pink and white complexion, blue eyes, and a typically English, open face.[1] When he was young, he had a blond beard. He was not robust, but he was usually healthy. Pole was a cousin of Henry VIII's, a grandson of that George Plantagenet, Duke of Clarence, who was drowned in a butt of old Malmsey.

Pole was a very abstemious man. He like tasty food, but he limited himself to two modest meals a day, the bigger one in the morning. His table, however, was always well served, because many people of high rank ate with him. His servants were distinguished for their modesty, not their number. He saw to it that they were clean and well-fed and he gave them little to do, looking after himself. However, if they fell ill he visited them and provided them with the best of attention. Pole was moderate in his needs, not attached to wealth, liberal, but not extravagant. He never enriched himself in his posts or through royal

---

[1] L. Beccadelli, *Vita del Polo* (Paris, 1677). The following account of Pole is taken from pp. 92–110.

favour; during the reign of Mary he did not claim the properties of which Henry VIII had deprived him; he never accepted presents or permitted his servants to do so; and he never spent above his income.

His conversation was sweet and agreeable and he could speak to anyone. He even spoke to people of evil life and reputation. He had a gift for expressing himself vividly, and exactly, and he was often witty. He hated flattery, and loved frankness, but he knew how to be honest and frank without hurting those whose opinions he opposed. He was always gentle with heretics; for he was convinced that only by sympathetic understanding could they be brought back into the Church.

Pole submitted himself completely to God and gave thanks for evil as well as good, since both proceeded from God. The serenity and faith with which Pole bore the news of the martyrdoms of his mother, the Duchess of Salisbury, at the age of seventy, and of his elder brother and two cousins, was remarkable.

Pole was born for letters and meditation, not for action. He liked the peace of the convent. He was always working, writing something for the glory of God, or for the benefit of his neighbour. He hated idleness, believing that it was the source of all debauch and crime. When he found the inhabitants of a small town idle, he lent them money to build a factory.

Pole was never precipitate. He waited for the maturity of events and through his patience he achieved success in many difficult situations.

Pole was always associated with the Reform movement within the Church. He was one of its most liberal churchmen. Before the orthodox position was fixed, he, like the majority of the most sensitive and intelligent spirits in Italy in his day, reacted against the primitive and spiritually empty, formalism of popular Catholicism, and embraced the Lutheran doctrine of justification by faith alone. But he always believed that good works were a sign of faith and an inevitable expression of Christian belief. Thus he maintained the necessity for good works, while denying their ultimate merit, as do the Thirty-nine Articles of the Church of England. Putting his doctrine succinctly, Pole told Vittoria Colonna to believe as though her salvation depended upon faith, and to live as though it depended upon good works.² When the Council of Trent adopted its position on justification, Pole submitted to the authority of the Church, though he admitted that he would have worded the article otherwise.³

Pole was a courageous man, but he was not pushing or ambitious. He never jockeyed for the position and power that could so easily have been his. He was a kind and gentle scholarly person with a warm sense of humour, and much Christian charity and compassion. He was a saint in the More tradition, cheerful, just, incorruptible, elevated in spirit, unshaken by disaster, and wholly submitted to the will of God. Vittoria Colonna saw Christ in him.⁴

Pole's friends were the liberal cardinals, Contarini, Bembo, Sadoleto, Morone, and Maffeo; Galeazzo Florimonte, Bishop of Sessa; Giles Fuscherat, Bishop of Modena;⁵ Luigi Priuli;⁶ Lodovico Beccadelli; Marcantonio Flaminio; and Vittoria Colonna. When Pole moved to Viterbo, Vittoria Collona moved there, to the convent of St. Catherine, and stayed there three years to be able to talk to him.

The members of Pole's household in 1541–2 were Flaminio, Carnesecchi, Priuli, Vicenzo Parapaglia, Vittore Soranzo, Bishop of Viterbo, later a victim of Paul IV's Chief Inquisitor, Michele Ghislieri,⁷ and Apollonio Merenda, Pole's chaplain, later condemned by the Inquisition for his views on the sacraments.⁸ Of this whole company only Parapaglia's name does not appear in the records of the Inquisition for this period. This perhaps suggests sinister goings-on in the papal palace at Viterbo. Let us therefore hear how Pole describes life there at this time. In an Italian letter to Contarini, dated Viterbo, December 9, 1541, Pole says that he is very grateful to God and to the pope for the legation to Viterbo. There he has a peace and spiritual satisfaction that he had never hoped for. He has a bit of business to attend to, but that only acts as a sauce to his

² Manzoni, 'Processo Carnesecchi', p. 269.
³ Beccadelli, *Monumenti*, I, ii, 347.
⁴ Corvisieri, 'Compendio', p. 280.
⁵ Beccadelli, *Vita del Polo*, p. 115.
⁶ *Ibid.*, p. 20.
⁷ E. Comba, *Storia della Riforma in Italia*, I (Florence, 1881), pp. 509–11.
⁸ Manzoni, 'Processo Carnesecchi', p. 253; Corvisieri, 'Compendio Processi', p. 268; Comba, I, p. 515.

leisure. He enjoys giving judgment to those who need it. He still spends the morning in private study and does business after dinner, except, of course, in urgent cases, but those are rare. He is occupied for only an hour or two. He spends the rest of the day with that saintly and useful band Signor Carnesecchi and Messer Marcantonio Flaminio. 'I say "useful" because in the evening Messer Marcantonio gives me and the greater part of the household to eat "of that food which does not perish", so that I do not know when I have felt greater consolation or greater edification.' It would be an earthly paradise if Contarini were there. But everything in this world has its defect, so this is as near an earthly paradise as can be expected. He cannot hope for it to last, it is too good. But God's will be done.[9]

The day before Pole wrote this letter, Vittoria Colonna had written to her friend, Giulia Gonzaga, to say that she had only seen Messer Flaminio, 'our best spirit', twice since he came. 'Pole has been too busy to come and I excuse him, but if it were not for Luigi Priuli and Carnesecchi I would be badly off.'[10] However, Vittoria Colonna received more company after they had all become better established in Viterbo, for Carnesecchi said at his trial that 'Pole used to go to convents in Rome and in Viterbo to see Vittoria Colonna and they talked of religion; but there were no witnesses. Marcantonio Flaminio, Priuli and I would accompany the cardinal to the convent, but we did not participate in the conversations, but chatted together in the church or in the neighbourhood. Also Priuli and Flaminio would visit Vittoria Colonna alone and would talk of religion, and also of profane subjects, and everyday affairs. I too went sometimes. We talked only of justification by faith.[11]

Carnesecchi, when questioned, described in detail the evolution of his religious views in Viterbo. After doubts had been put in his mind about the sacrament of confession by Flaminio in Naples in 1540,

> this seed then began to germinate in me more and more with the reading of books by Luther and others of his sect. I began to see

[9] Pole, *Lettere* (Brescia, 1548), III, pp. 41–2.
[10] G. Paladino, *Opuscoli e Lettere di Riformatori Italiani del '500*, I (Bari, 1913), pp. 93–4; Amante, pp. 407–8; Manzoni, 'Processo Carnesecchi', p. 497.
[11] Manzoni, 'Processo Carnesecchi', pp. 268–9.

one of these in Viterbo when I was with the cardinal of England, at least in the company of Flaminio, and this was Bucer on the Gospel of St. Matthew. And I think that I also saw certain speeches of Luther on the gradual psalms although they did not treat of this dogma.[12]

Asked when he began to believe in Valdes' opinions on justification and the certainty of grace, with the inferences that could be drawn from them, 'namely that there is no necessity for the sacrament of penitence, nor for contrition, nor for satisfaction to recuperate the grace lost through mortal sin, nor is there need otherwise to purge the guilt of our sins in purgatory, since Christ has satisfied, as he said, abundantly for all of us by his death,' Carnesecchi replied, 'I think that I began [to believe these things with these inferences] in Viterbo in 1541 when I was with the cardinal of England and with Flaminio....'[13]

In answer to another question Carnesecchi replied that 'I never had a licence to read forbidden books but I read them through my own curiosity, and the first time that I began to read them was in 1541 at Viterbo in the house of Cardinal Pole, and it was the commentary of Bucer on the Epistle to the Romans which belonged to Flaminio.'[14] Asked more generally about the reading of heretical books at Pole's in Viterbo Carnesecchi replied that Flaminio especially read them, more than Priuli, but that this does not mean that they were heretics. They were studying theological questions. This went on in Viterbo until 1547, to his knowledge. After that he went to France.[15] Asked again if they did not, at Viterbo, read many sermons and opinions about and against many articles of the Catholic faith, Carnesecchi replied that when he was there they discussed only justification by faith 'which cannot be said to have been heresy at that time since it had not yet been determined by the Council what one had to believe on that article.'[16]

Again Carnesecchi said, 'In Viterbo Flaminio had with him some writings of Valdes, I believe the book of *Considerations* and the *Commentary on the Psalms*, and he was translating them from Spanish into Italian to please the lady who wanted to have them,

---

[12] Manzoni, 'Processo Carnesecchi', p. 195.
[13] *Ibid.*, p. 197.   [14] *Ibid.*, p. 203.
[15] *Ibid.*, p. 214.   [16] *Ibid.*, pp. 251–2.

Donna Giulia [Gonzaga].'[17] The Inquisition produced an exhibit, a booklet entitled *Meditationi et orationi formate sopra l'epistola di san Paulo ad Romanos*, found among Carnesecchi's papers. It was written by Flaminio, for Donna Giulia. Carnesecchi had had a servant make a copy of it because he considered it pious and Catholic, and so he would continue to consider it until it was condemned.[18]

Questioned about Pole, Carnesecchi said that he checked somewhat the reading of heretical books by his circle by telling them not to be over-curious. This applied particularly to Vittoria Colonna.[19]

Fortunately, at the time of this last trial of Carnesecchi's, all the other people were dead and it was only Carnesecchi himself who was in danger of burning.

Before Cardinal Pole is condemned as a dangerous and deceitful subversive, let us hear the testimony that he gives as to what was going on in his palace at this time. The account is drawn from a letter by Filippo Gherio, the ultimate recipient of Flaminio's abbey in the Val di Lavino and the brother of Flaminio's old friend Cosmo Gherio, the boy Bishop of Fano. Gherio wrote to Beccadelli from Rome on April 29, 1553, about a meeting between Cardinals Caraffa and Pole in Rome at San Paolo fuori le Mura, where Pole answered the charges made against him by the Inquisition. Gherio is excellent at recapturing the atmosphere of suspicion and sinister tension in which Pole lived at the time:[20]

> One day the Cardinal of Naples [Caraffa, restorer and head of the Inquisition] going, or pretending to go, to the seven churches, began with St. Paul's, and reaching it in his litter about eight o'clock, went into the church and stayed there much longer than is customary for his devotions. Cardinal Pole was in the Camera with the Master of the Sacred Palace and, hearing that Napoli had already been nearly an hour in the church, decided that it would be discourteous not to go to see him. Therefore he went down to see Napoli, who was about to leave in his litter. When Napoli heard that Pole had come down, he returned into the church and

[17] Manzoni, 'Processo Carnesecchi', p. 495.
[18] *Ibid.*, pp. 536-7.
[19] *Ibid.*, pp. 503-5.
[20] The letter is printed in Beccadelli, *Monumenti*, I, ii, 347-53.

went with Pole into the Camera where he spent more than two hours, while one of Napoli's men entered two or three times to remind Napoli that it was getting late and time to go. And Napoli always replied, with the utmost urbanity, that he shouldn't envy him that he was able to enjoy a little his friend Cardinal Pole, who was in better form than he had ever found him....

Pole brought the conversation around to his own case, as he knew it. Napoli said that he had never said or written anything about Pole but what was most honourable, and that he hadn't thought of bringing against him anything but his association with Flaminio. To this the cardinal replied, that having himself testified to the world what he felt with his exile, with the risk of his life many times, and with the death of many of his family, leaving everything for the Apostolic Seat, he did not think that he deserved to be suspected for every little thing, and that if they had found him in a room with Luther, they should rather believe that he had wanted to bring him back than that he was letting himself be seduced by him.

Nevertheless, as to Flaminio, these were the facts: He would not deny that he might have been wavering on some points when he came into his house, and that he, to take away his every scruple, had persuaded him to read the Doctors of the Church; for he saw that he was in danger, because of the fine intellect and judgment that he had in literary affairs, in which he was consummate, of making his own judgments in theology, a very risky thing to do. The success he had with Flaminio was shown in his death, which was most saintly and such that everyone should pray God to be able to achieve. Then Cardinal Pole added that if Flaminio never had any sinister opinion, they did evil to find fault with him, but if he did at some time vacillate in some respects, they were wrong to blame him, and they should rather congratulate him since he brought him back by taking him into his company; especially since, if he had become alienated, he could have done the greatest harm because of the fine mind that he had together with the best style that has ever existed in sacred writing. The Cardinal of Naples showed that he was most relieved to hear this about Flaminio, who had been his dearest friend, and he thanked Cardinal Pole for telling him this.

Then Pole took the offensive and went on to discuss the Inquisition, saying that he was not satisfied with the way it was being run. He believed in the use of love, kindness, and understanding in dealing with heretics. When they discussed Donna

Giulia, whom Napoli said he was investigating, Pole replied that he was her friend and that he could win her with courtesy. Pole went on to say that he had heard from the other cardinals what Napoli says about him. Napoli replied that he should not trust the other cardinals. Pole defended himself firmly and triumphed over Napoli. When Napoli said he was sorry that he had not discussed these things with Pole before, so that all rumour might have been scotched, Pole replied squarely that he had given Napoli every opportunity. Caraffa was won over and that very evening reported the conversation that he had had with Pole to the Inquisition, saying that Pole was the best of men and that he hoped that when God desired to replace Pope Julius he would choose Pole.

There is a nice contrast in this letter between the characters of the two men, the one persecuted, but calm, self-possessed, confident in his sense of right, straightforward, and frank, the other, a shifty but highly intelligent paranoid, charming at times, full of excuses and self-justifications, but possessing the power to destroy the other.

There is a letter from Flaminio to Alexander Farnese, dated Viterbo, February 8, 1542, in which he thanks the cardinal for getting the pope's permission to restore the abbey of the Val di Lavino to the Olivetan monks and for his help in the arrangements.[21]

Four days later Flaminio is writing to Teodorina Sauli from Naples. Why Flaminio went to Naples at this time or how long he stayed we do not know. Valdes had died the summer before, providentially—for the Inquisition was established in 1542—and his circle had broken up. Flaminio may have gone south again for his health, but there is no suggestion of illness in his letter. A hendecasyllabic epistle written to Alois (VI, 20), who has invited him back to Caserta, may date from this period. In this epistle Flaminio says he is detained in Naples by business.

Flaminio's letters from Naples are important for what they reveal of his religious thought. Valdes is alive in them and we recognize, too, the voice of Pole. The first letter is addressed to Teodorina Sauli and is dated Naples, February 12, 1542.[22] Flaminio is replying to a request for guidance in the building of

[21] Costa, *GSLI*, X, 384–7.
[22] Paladino, I, pp. 68–71.

a spiritual life. He has found three things useful, mental prayer, Christian adoration, and meditation. Mental prayer he defines as a fervent desire to obtain something from God. Faith, hope, and love are what we should desire. Faith consists in believing in all God's Word, particularly in the gospel of Christ,

> that the only son of God clothed Himself in our flesh and . . . satisfied the justice of His eternal father for our sins.
>
> Christian hope consists in waiting with patience, with eagerness, and with continual joy for God to fulfil in us those promises which He made to all the members of His beloved Son promising to make them like His glorious image. . . .
>
> Love consists in loving God for Himself and in loving everything for God, directing all your thoughts, all yours works, everything you do to the glory of His divine majesty. . . .
>
> Meditation consists in thinking about God. . . . It also consists in thinking about Jesus Christ suffering and mortal, and about Jesus Christ beyond suffering and immortal. In Jesus Christ suffering and mortal, the Christian considers the humility, the gentleness, the love, the obedience to God, the extreme poverty, and the continual ignominy and persecutions to which He was subjected, ending up in His most bitter death upon the cross. . . . In Jesus Christ impassible and immortal and glorified, the Christian considers that He has been exalted by God to the loftiest sublimity because of His obedience, and that He has acquired a name that is above every other name. He considers that He is our high priest, because He constantly intercedes for us; that He is our Lord, because He has redeemed and bought us with His most precious blood; that He is our king, because he governs us with His holy spirit in temporal and in spiritual things; that He is our head, because, as from the human head descends a force which gives life and sensation to the whole body, so from Christ in glory there descends to His majestic limbs a divine force which gives them eternal life and fills them with gifts and sensations that are spiritual and heavenly. He considers that He bears us infinite love, which cares more about us than we do ourselves, which covers with His purity and perfection all our imperfections, which dwells with His spirit in our souls and which, finally, will make us dwell with Him in paradise, glorifying us in the image of His glory.
>
> Who is there who, considering these stupendous things with faith, would not burn with divine love? Who would not fall most ardently in love with God and with Jesus Christ? Who would not judge and consider all the honours, all the riches, and all the

happinesses and pleasures of the world most vile? Who would not consecrate soul and body to God and Christ?

My lady, think always of God and of Christ: live a heavenly life on earth, see God and Christ in everything, do everything for the glory of God and Christ, and love everything for the love of God and Christ.

Flaminio concludes by begging her to ask advice of someone more competent next time and to leave him silent 'praying the Lord God that He give me ears to hear what He says secretly to my heart'.

Fired by an intense enthusiasm and now, as we shall note shortly, in somewhat better health, Flaminio no longer replied negatively to those who came to him for help. Carlo Gualteruzzi, who had been helping him with the legal arrangements about the abbey, wrote to Flaminio to ask him what sort of religious books he should read. Flaminio replied from Naples on February 28[23] recommending the *Imitation of Christ*, but with one reservation. He did not like the use made of fear in that book; for fear of God's punishment can only be a sign of deficient faith. Those who truly believe that Christ has given satisfaction for their sins cannot fear God's judgment. 'Fear of punishment does not befit the Christian, but filial love. However, the Christian should live always in perpetual fear of himself, that his affections and appetites might make him do something unworthy of his profession and of his dignity as a Christian, which would sadden the Holy Spirit which is within him....' Here Flaminio is tackling the difficult doctrinal question of the freedom of the will when God is omnipotent and omniscient. He goes on to say that God considers man not for what he is in himself, but for what he is in Christ, 'and in Christ the Christian is just and holy because the incorporation in Christ makes him share in all the merits of Christ'.

Protestantism now flourished in many places in Italy. The chief centres were Naples, Ferrara, Modena, Lucca, and Venice. In Ferrara the Protestant group was headed by Renée de France, wife of Ercole II, and sister-in-law of Francis I. She even received Calvin there, and Ferrarese Protestantism pro-

[23] *Ibid.*, I, pp. 72–3.

duced an important witness to the faith in Olimpia Morata. In 1544 Renée was denounced to the Inquisition by both her husband and the king of France and was forced to recant. She continued, however, to aid Protestants throughout her life.[24] In Modena the Reform movement was supported by the bishop, Cardinal Morone, who spent two years' imprisonment in the Castel Sant'Angelo as a result (1557–9), by some of the clergy, and by the critic, Lodovico Castelvetro.[25] In Lucca Protestantism flourished under the influence of Peter Martyr Vermigli, the Augustinian preacher. Vermigli had had an enormous following in Naples in 1541 when he denied purgatory in his sermons in St. Peter's on First Corinthians II: 13–15. He was accused by the Theatines and forbidden by the viceroy, Toledo, to preach, but he applied to the pope, and was allowed to continue. Then he moved to Lucca where he indoctrinated his Order until, on a further accusation, he took flight.[26]

On June 15, 1542, Flaminio wrote a letter from Verona saying that he had been in Bologna for several days.[27] Therefore he must have left Naples by the end of May, at the latest. The letter is written to his old friend Count Nicolò d'Arco whom he has not seen since their university days in Bologna but about whom he has been talking with their mutual friend, Lodovico Strozza, and with Arco's son. The letter reveals the old Flaminio, loyal to his friends, but lazy about writing them, suffering from ill health, and now, a new note, having abandoned poetry. However, we notice that he has changed. Now, after twenty-

[24] M. Young, *The Life and Times of Aonio Paleario or a History of the Italian Reformers in the Sixteenth Century* (London, 1860), II, pp. 114–8.

[25] Cuccoli, pp. 80 and 89; Corvisieri, 'Compendio', pp. 268 ff.

[26] Cantù, II, pp. 323–5; Cuccoli, p. 80.

[27] This letter appears in a collection by Bernardino Pino, *Della Nuova Scielta di Lettere di Diversi Nobilissimi Huomini* (Venice, 1582), II, pp. 86–8. No author is given but Cuccoli, p. 118, fn. 1, refers to a letter written from Verona the same day to Arco which appears under Flaminio's name in *Nuovo Libro di Lettere de i più Rari Autori* (Venice, 1545), p. 9, a book which I have not been able to get hold of. However, this is obviously the same letter. Even without Cuccoli's supporting statement one recognizes Flaminio's courtly style, his quirks, and the references to his life. Though Flaminio's works were off the Index by 1582 Pino for some reason or other prints as being by 'incerto autore' a dozen letters by Flaminio, all but one of which had appeared under Flaminio's name in well-known collections.

four years, he has finally found the drive to write this letter. We sense that Flaminio's life has more meaning and direction.

> I should make lengthy excuses to your lordship for never having written him; but it is less trouble and more honest to accuse myself, and at the same time to demand your lordship's pardon for this error of mine, when, to be honest, it arose solely from innate laziness and negligence, which makes my pen seem a pole to me. And if my masters and friends did not know that this was my nature they would have just cause to consider me lacking in affection and courtesy because it is not my custom to write to them unless it is necessary, although I retain my love for them and remember them with all that affection that sincere and virtuous friendship demands....
>
> O my lord, for more than ten years I have been oppressed by such a cruel indisposition that I have never been able in this time to undertake the least mental strain and it is a miracle that I am living with all that. However, the last three years I have been a bit better and I hope, by studying only a little, as I have been doing, to be able to attain to a moderate state of health. Therefore, I beg your lordship to believe this truest of truths, that neither distance of place nor length of time have ever diminished in me that love and respect which I felt for you when I was privileged to enjoy your most affable conversation in Bologna, and of this many gentlemen in many cities in Italy can bear witness....

Flaminio wrote another letter from Verona at this time which is an important document in the history of humanist educational theory.[28] Luigi Calino had asked Flaminio for advice on the education of his son. Flaminio wrote a careful reply which was so highly thought of by Bartolomeo Ricci that he followed its advice in the education of the Este prince in Ferrara.[29] In discussing the current teacher of Calino's son, Flaminio says that he values his own original compositions above Cicero's. Therefore Flaminio is afraid that Calino's son will grow up to be provincial. Teachers should not make their students do exercises based on their own compositions, but use Cicero always. Otherwise there is too great a risk of ineptitudes, vulgarisms, and corrupt Latin. In the imitative arts you must have a good master. If modern painters followed Michelangelo

---

[28] MAF, *Carm.* (1743), pp. 301-6.
[29] *Ibid.*, pp. 306-7.

instead of Moro da Savignano they would be famous and illustrious instead of painters of basins. Few students come out of the communal schools these days with a reputation for good writing and speaking because the teachers are teaching with their original compositions and very few writers are ever first-rate.

In ancient times Latin was common to all and natural. Now it has to be learnt with great effort. Then, teachers were of the first calibre—the old fallacy of the 'good old days'—now, they are very ignorant. Then, the rewards of education were so great that eloquence led men of the lowest rank by a sure and swift road to the highest office of consul. Now, very great effort is required for the most negligible rewards. There are so many obstacles these days to becoming a good writer, especially in Latin, that the appearance of one is miraculous. People are so ignorant today that they cannot distinguish first-rate writers from commonplace. They do not notice barbarous and monkish words. Therefore some people in Rome with a reputation for learning admire the styles of Erasmus, Melanchthon, and certain Italian writers with no understanding of the beauty, propriety, elegance, purity, or copiousness of the Latin language.[30]

The disgrace is that those who have some knowledge of the divine tongue and taste are almost all great men of noble rank, whereas those who are constrained by poverty to teach it are almost all very far from knowing it, and, since they are inept writers and full of improprieties and foolishness, they train their students to be like them.

Students of literature waste time writing verses and prose so plebeian and vile that you would think that they had never studied grammar. They had better spend their time learning something useful instead of becoming the laughing-stock of those who are really learned.

> To learn Latin well one must have the best teachers, who have studied the Latin language and practised writing it for many years, who have a lot of imagination, who know how to vary styles and speech, adapting words, phrases, figures, and rhythms to the subjects. Since such teachers are practically unobtainable

[30] Flaminio has an interesting passage on the stylistic corruption of Muzio.

today, one should get teachers who are modest, and aware of their own limitations, and who, for that reason, follow Cicero, i.e., Cicero should give the scholars their themes and correct them.

This letter makes it clear that in the sixteenth century education was synonymous with Latin style, but it would appear from Ricci's letter about Flaminio's letter that the particular method of teaching Latin that Flaminio advocates, the using of Cicero to set the themes and correct them, a method that he adumbrates more fully in a later letter, was at the time something of a novelty, despite the long history of Ciceronianism. Ricci, writing from Ferrara in 1542,[31] says that the publication of Flaminio's letter to Calino has fallen most opportunely for him. He has been following that method in teaching the prince, but old men have wrinkled their brows and called it monstrous. They will not listen. They turn away and laugh at the new method of learning. But they were impressed by your letter, since you have the reputation of being an expert.

Ricci goes on to ask Flaminio what he is doing in literature. 'Is your Muse forever silent? Have you written yourself out? Or are you suffering so much from your stomach that you are cut off not only from the pleasures of the palate, but also from those of the mind? ... But enjoy life, and let us have the benefit of anything you can write.' He sends his regards to Maffeo, Priuli, and Zanchi.

A letter that Pole wrote to Contarini from Viterbo on July 8, 1542,[32] suggests that Flaminio is now back in Viterbo, for why else would he be asking Contarini to help the nephew of Flaminio's cousin in an important case that he has before the rota of Bologna? This letter is a reflection on the administrative standards of the time among the most upright men.

From Viterbo on August 6, 1542, Flaminio wrote his other important letter on education, to his old friend, Galeazzo Florimonte, Bishop of Sessa,[33] now in charge of the education of the heir of Milan. Flaminio says that he had been undecided what to think when he heard that Contarini had persuaded Florimonte to go to Milan rather than to Loreto. 'It seemed a strange thing to me to see you return to court life in your old

---

[31] See note 29, p. 130.
[32] Pole, *Epistolae* (Brescia, 1548), III, pp. 58-9.
[33] MAF, *Carm.* (1743), pp. 295-301.

age, particularly since I know how much you used to enjoy the philosophic life at Sessa with your old servant.' But Florimonte's letters show that he is very happy and gay in Milan. It gives everyone pleasure to read them.

> I can only conclude that you are either a very ambitious man, and most greedy for favour, and a great hypocrite, since you appeared not to care about such things, or that the Lord Marquis has been so kind to you that you have changed your character and desires. But I am glad to see you in Milan. Such a good companion as you are did not deserve to be buried in the swamps of Loreto. Therefore, I congratulate you on your place and happiness and I pray God that your fortunes may go from good to better.

Florimonte had asked him how he would educate someone in grammar and prepare him for the study of eloquence. Flaminio was glad to reply. He had long been strongly opposed to traditional methods in grammar, which seemed to him long and labyrinthine. This is what he would suggest as a curriculum for the marquis's sons.

First, he would begin with the noun and verb. The inflections should be memorized from Donatus. A lesson, very brief, should be given on active and passive verbs. The student should then learn the comparatives, superlatives, participles, etc., all of this in three months. Then he should begin reading Cicero's letters, the easiest ones as to thought and structure. In the course of the reading the teacher should review the grammar taught, questioning his pupil on the nouns and verbs and their constructions.

Next the teacher should have the student write, using the vocabulary and expressions thus learned, changing the tenses, numbers, etc. Thus he will learn only the vocabulary and idioms of Cicero. Then let him try writing letters in Cicero's style, beginning by the double translation method. Translate eight to ten lines of Cicero into Italian. Then have him retranslate them into Latin. Then compare his composition with the original Latin. Also, the teacher should speak in Italian about the lesson, while the student replies in Latin, using the words of Cicero. Then have him memorize the most important expressions in each letter, and collect them in a little book.

Next study the rhetorical structure of the letter, the order and skill with which the ideas are presented, the technique used in different types of letter: letters of recommendation, narrative letters, polemical letters, etc. Then study the ornaments of Cicero's letters, the figures, *sententiae*. Point out the beauties of style. Distinguish straightforward writing from figurative writing.

Then proceed to Vergil.

It is a good exercise for the student to copy out the letters he studies. That way he learns the style. This is what Demosthenes did with Thucydides.

For a long time the student should not read any authors but Cicero, Caesar, Vergil, and Horace. He should not read Terence, Catullus, or Tibullus because, although they are most elegant, they present too great a danger to Christian belief.

You can learn Latin from poetry, as well as from prose, because the language of the poet, though it may be different from the language of prose, is nevertheless based on the idiom of the language.

Flaminio also discusses the teacher that the marquis has for the children, who is apparently not an Italian, 'And if you would like me to express my opinion on another subject on which it has not been asked, I would never advise anyone to learn Latin from teachers from the other side of the Alps, especially composition, because it seems to me that these subtleties are so much the property of Italy that foreigners who have long since taken our dress, our liberty, and everything else, cannot usurp the glory of true eloquence. This is not to deny that there are men of eloquence and first-rate judgment in other countries. I would cite, particularly, the most Reverend Cardinal Pole. But they are so rare!'

Flaminio concludes, 'You see how I have performed for love of you and how, for longer than I have intended, I have played the humanist, a part that once pleased me so well and which now seems so vain a thing to me. All our company here is well and salutes you. Viterbo, August 6, 1542. Please do not show this letter around because I would not want that teacher to be unhappy on my account, and in fact I was reluctant to discuss him in particular, but wishing to do my duty on the subject of your request, I could not do otherwise.'

## VITERBO AND CARDINAL POLE

It is ironical that it is only when he has ceased being a humanist concerned with the things of this world that Flaminio begins to act like one. Yet his own innate gentleness and kindness, as well as his new-found Christian concern for others, is revealed in his postscript. It is not something that Poggio, Valla, or Poliziano would have thought of.

A letter printed by Pino, without the name of either the author or the recipient,[34] is obviously by Flaminio and is apparently about the death of Contarini. That great and good, man, who had almost brought about a reconciliation between the Catholics and Protestants the year previously at Ratisbon and had then been repudiated by his own side through the shady political manoeuvrings of the anti-imperial party, had retired under a shadow to a monastery in Bologna and had died there on August 24. The letter before us is dated Viterbo, September 12, 1542. The parallels between this letter and Flaminio's letter to Teodorina Sauli of the twelfth of February of the same year are striking and point to a single authorship.[35]

Flaminio begins by saying that it is his duty to write a letter of condolence on the loss of that saintly spirit,

> but truly this cruellest of blows has been felt as much by me, so that I have not been able and am not yet fit to console anyone else; for I myself have the greatest need for consolation, although the loss which we have suffered is so great and of such a sort that human wisdom or worldly eloquence are not sufficient to console us, but

---

[34] Pino, II, pp. 151–6.
[35] Pino, II, pp. 151–6, letter of September 12, 1542, and Paladino, pp. 68–71, letter of February 12, 1542:

| | |
|---|---|
| p. 152: Se siamo morti con lui | p. 69: conoscendosi morto col suo *capo Giesu Cristo* |
| p. 153: Iesu Christo nostro capo | pp. 69, 71: G. C. nostro capo |
| p. 153: i Christiani ... sono membri di Christo | p. 69: i membri del suo diletto Figliuolo |
| p. 152: perche non viviamo una vita ... celeste | p. 69: attende a ... vivere una vita celeste |
| p. 155: amiamo lui sopra ogni cosa, e ogni cosa per lui | p. 69: amar Dio per se stesso e ogni cosa per Dio |
| p. 155: debbiamo humiliarci sotto la potente mano sua | p. 70: si umilia sotto la potente mano di Dio |
| p. 155: benedicendo il suo santissimo nome in ogni tempo | p. 70: benedicendo il suo santo nome in ogni tempo |

we must turn to that one consoler of the afflicted who utters these words of heavenly sweetness, 'Come unto me, all you who labour and are heavy burdened, and I will give you rest.' Believe me, my Lord, if we do not accept this tenderest of invitations, we will never find either consolation, or peace, or quiet in this miserable world, nor will we ever lack reason to weep and sigh. But if we go to our Jesus Christ, if we rest our soul in His arms, the tears and sighs and melancholy will fly far from us, because where Christ is, there is always the greatest tranquillity and peace and perpetual joy in the Holy Spirit. He is the only sugar for our bitternesses, He is the only repose for afflicted minds.

Therefore, my Lord, let us be united with Christ if we wish to possess everlasting joy, let us always remember that in baptism we are dead with Him and revived with Him. If we are dead with Him, why should we allow ourselves to suffer so much for the accidents of the world? If we are revived with Him, why should we not live a life of the utmost tranquillity, a heavenly life, like that one which we will see there after the final resurrection?

Why do we not conform ourselves in every way to the most holy will of God? What is the good of being Christians if we allow ourselves to be conquered by grief and the passions like those who know not God or Christ? Certainly all these defects are born of very little faith, for if we had even moderate faith it would be impossible that another's death, or our own, or the loss of property, or the burden of illness, or any other accident could have the power of upsetting us so much and causing us so much suffering.

Let us recognize in ourselves, then, a deficiency of faith, and let us grieve over this and not over the death of those who are called to God and to an eternal life of beatitude. Let us recognize that this sort of grief does not befit Christians who, if they are true Christians, are members of Christ in death, as in life, and, consequently, are united in Christ with their Christian friends and relatives in death, as in life. And if dead Christians are with Christ in heaven, then living Christians are also with Christ in heaven, as St. Paul says, and as they know through experience who converse with bodies on earth and with the mind in heaven. . . .

But suppose that death could separate us from our friends and relatives, could it separate us from Jesus Christ? . . . And if Jesus Christ is always with us, if He always watches and sleeps with us, why should the death or absence of friends give us such great grief? Is not Jesus Christ enough for us? Is He not worth a thousand friends and a thousand relatives? Is His company not worth more than that of all the angels together? What friend or what relative can give us such faithful counsel in time of doubt, as our Christ? Who can console us in tribulations, restrain us in prosperity, help us in danger, converse with us so sweetly, make us fall in love with God so ardently, as our own Christ? Well then, since we have Christ, why do we grieve so much over the loss of friends and relatives? ...

Therefore, my Lord, let us rouse ourselves now and let us remember that we are Christians, i.e., sons of God and not slaves of the world, spiritual creatures, and not carnal ... therefore, like legitimate sons of God, superior to the vileness of the flesh, let us have a great and generous soul which resists bravely all the assaults of the world, death, the devil, and hell. Let us hold for certain that chance and fortune are empty and profane words, let us believe firmly that our eternal Father, with supreme providence, governs this whole great mechanism of the world, and that He gives to all who are in it, life and death, poverty and wealth, prosperity and adversity. Therefore, if we want to progress from beings sons of God to friends of God, let us humiliate ourselves beneath his mighty hand, receiving everything from His providence, blessing His most holy name at all times, in all places, and for everything ... let us hate ourselves and place all our love in Jesus Christ. Let Him be our lord, our brother, our friend, our master, our delight, our justice, our life, and our only happiness. Let us love Him above all else and everything for Him. ... To Him be glory everlasting. Amen.

With a companion who could think and feel like that, who so radiated spiritual joy, no wonder that Pole felt that he had attained, in the quiet of Viterbo, all that one could ever hope to have of happiness on earth. As Pole foresaw, it could not last for ever, but it did last a few more years.

By the autumn of 1542 the Inquisition was in full swing. Caraffa had been so eager to get it started that, unable to await the granting of funds, he had rented and fitted out a building himself with an audience chamber and cells for the prisoners.[36] The more flagrant sympathizers with Luther were now hunted down. One of the first to go was Bernardino Ochino (1487–1564). This famous Franciscan preacher, considered to be the greatest preacher of his time in Italy, had, throughout the whole of his career, advanced steadily towards a more intense and spiritual relationship with God. After the new and stricter rule

---

[36] Ranke, I, pp. 158–9.

was established in 1528 he became a Capuchin (1534). He was soon the General of his Order (1538–42). He tried to find a way to live in accordance with the will of God. He finally decided that this did not consist in following a rule but in following the Scriptures. He was an ascetic who won a reputation for being a saint. People flocked to hear him preach in Rome, Naples, Venice, Siena, Modena, Lucca, Perugia, Ferrara, Mantua, and Palermo. In 1536, in Naples, he met Valdes and was won over to his belief in justification by faith alone. When he was preaching in Naples in 1540 Carnesecchi said that Valdes would send him a note the night before he had to preach suggesting the subject of his sermon.[37]

In 1542 Ochino was preaching the Lenten sermons in St. Mark's in Venice when he was ordered to appear before the Inquisition in Rome. After some delay he started for Rome, but after conversations with the dying Contarini in Bologna and with Peter Martyr Vermigli in Florence he decided to flee. On August 22, 1542, Ochino wrote Vittoria Colonna a letter saying that he was fleeing Italy and that his doctrine remained what she had approved so many times.[38]

Ochino went first to Ferrara, where the Duchess Renée helped him to safety in Geneva.[39] He was well received by Calvin, and decided to marry and break definitely with Rome. In 1547 he was invited to England by Cranmer and made canon of Canterbury. He stayed until the accession of Mary (1553). Then he went to Strasbourg, Geneva, Basle, Zürich, and Locarno. But the Swiss Protestants found that his views had developed dangerously. He was accused of believing in polygamy and also of denying the Trinity. He was banished from Switzerland in mid-winter.[40] At the age of seventy-six he went with his four children to Poland, where he preached polygamy. But he was attacked by the papal nuncio, and expelled from Poland. He took refuge in Moravia, where the plague was raging. He lost two daughters and a son. Then he himself died, in 1564.

Peter Martyr Vermigli (1500–1562) followed Ochino into

[37] Manzoni, 'Processo Carnesecchi', pp. 195–6.
[38] J. Bonnet, *Aonio Paleario* (Paris, 1863), pp. 121–2.
[39] Alete Dal Canto, *Pietro Carnesecchi* (Rome, 1911), p. 51.
[40] Cantù, II, p. 209.

exile in 1542. Like Ochino he fled to Switzerland via Ferrara, married, and was invited to England by Cranmer in 1547. He was made professor of theology at Oxford, but his views were too extreme for English opinion, and he had to be protected by the authorities. He was brought to London for his own safety, and made a canon. He helped Cranmer in drawing up the second English prayer book. On the accession of Mary he, too, went to Strasbourg, and then to Zürich, where he died in 1562.[41]

Ochino and Vermigli were people whom Flaminio had known in Valdes' circle in Naples.[42] Another case of persecution came to Flaminio's ears in the autumn of 1542. Aonio Paleario, a teacher in Siena from 1530, was charged with heresy before the signory of Siena and the Holy Office in Rome. Bembo and Sadoleto, both later on the Inquisition lists,[42] justified Paleario before the Inquisitor in Rome, and Sadoleto, on his way to a mission in Bologna, stopped in Siena in September, 1542, and defended Paleario there. Paleario also defended himself in an impassioned speech. The governor of Siena, Cardinal Francesco Sfondrati, later investigated by the Inquisition himself,[43] pronounced Paleario innocent, but Sadoleto advised him now to abandon theology and concentrate on Aristotle, where there was less danger.

Paleario's later history is illustrative of the fate of many intellectuals who were investigated but let off in the 1540's. In 1546 Paleario became professor of eloquence at the University of Lucca on the recommendations of Pier Vettori, Bembo, and Sadoleto. In 1555 he succeeded Maioraggio as professor of literature in Milan. In 1567 he was imprisoned by the Inquisition in the Tordinona, a prison on the banks of the Tiber at the Ponte Sant'Angelo. Here he spent three miserable years in a damp cell with the river running by his window. Then, on July 3, 1570, he was hanged, then burnt on the Ponte Sant'Angelo.[44] He was then in his seventieth year.

1542, the year in which the persecutions began, was also the

---

[41] Cantù, II, pp. 323-9.
[42] Manzoni, 'Processo Carnesecchi', pp. 548-9. Vermigli was in Naples in 1540, Ochino in 1541.
[43] Corvisieri, 'Compendio', pp. 268 ff.
[44] Bonnet, *op. cit.*, pp. 305-21.

year in which Paul III first attempted to assemble a council in Trent. He chose three cardinals as presidents and legates, Flaminio's old law professor, Parisio; Morone, Bishop of Modena, who had been to Ratisbon, where so much progress had been made with the Protestants; and Pole, who was popular beyond the Alps, learned, and wise. Pole set out with Flaminio and Priuli. They met Paleario in Florence on the way.[45] Apparently Carnesecchi stayed behind in Viterbo and later left to establish himself in Venice.[46] Flaminio said good-bye to him in a hendecasyllabic epistle, regretting the loss of so good a companion.[47]

The legates arrived in Trent on November 22, but there was war in Germany and not enough bishops were able to attend, so, after waiting a few months, the legates returned to Rome, and nothing was accomplished.

While he was in Trent Flaminio wrote an important letter to Carnesecchi on the sacrament of Holy Communion. Carnesecchi had asked Flaminio what one should say to Lutherans or Zwinglians about the sacrament of the altar. Flaminio replied,[48] citing a list of authorities, notably his old mentor in theology at Verona, Alberto Pighi, that the Catholic Church has always believed in the real presence. In case Carnesecchi does not have these books at hand, since the belief of the primitive Church is of such importance, Flaminio quotes at length from Irenaeus, who knew Polycarp, the disciple of St. John the Evangelist. The statements of Irenaeus prove that the early Church believed that the Eucharist was really the body and blood of Christ, that it used to offer the body and blood of Christ to God in the form of bread and wine, and that this was instituted by Christ and the Apostles. Moreover, these are the beliefs of the Greek, Armenian, and Indian churches, for centuries separated from the Latin Church. Even Bucer, who had at first denied the real presence, recognized his error and admitted it at the Diet of Ratisbon. But some of his followers

---

[45] A. Paleario, *Opera* (Iena, 1728), p. 471.
[46] Manzoni, 'Processo Carnesecchi', p. 197.
[47] 'O dulce hospitium, o lares beati,' in *Carm.* 5 (1549), pp. 178–9, and (1552), pp. 200–201, suppressed by Mancurti along with all the other poems to Carnesecchi.
[48] Atanagi, *Lettere 13*, pp. 304–12, and Paladino, I, pp. 74–9.

are stubborn and refuse to learn from him from whom they first learnt. Flaminio prays that the Protestants may be cured of their arrogant obstinacy, and that they may receive the gifts of love, gentleness of spirit, and humility so that they will cease making rash judgments on the doctrines and usages of the Church and of the faithful, and will begin to believe that those whom they accuse of idolatry are religious, pious, and dear to God, and that those who follow *their* proud presumptions are God's enemies. . . . But they, too, must not harden themselves so that the Protestants leave the Church. They must not hate, or lose their judgment, or charity. . . . They must not persuade themselves that they are rich and blessed when they are poor, miserable, and pitiable.—Pole had gone to Trent saying that an idea should not be condemned solely because Luther had had it.[49]

Carnesecchi's reply to Flaminio's letter[50] is lengthy, wordy, woolly, and obscure, perhaps deliberately so. He attacks Flaminio's authorities, and apparently disagrees with him about transubstantiation and the sacrifice of the mass. Carnesecchi's thought was now more broadly, and more fundamentally, unorthodox than Flaminio's.

By the middle of February, 1543, Flaminio and Pole were back in Viterbo. From here, on the fourteenth, Flaminio wrote to his Neapolitan friend, Galeazzo Caracciolo, Marquis of Vico, that he and the legate and the others were overjoyed at the news of his holy vocation. He thinks that God has shown him exceptional favour since Caracciolo is one of the nobility who, according to Scripture, are not usually chosen. With his typical concern for good works, despite his belief in justification by faith, Flaminio urges Caracciolo to 'pray to God night and day that He increase our faith and that He make it produce in our souls those most sweet and blessed fruits which it is wont to produce in the good soil of all those who are predestined to eternal life, so that our faith may be fertile in good works and we may be sure that it is not feigned, but real. . . . ' Blessed is he who can renounce all worldly things and become a fool in this

[49] Cuccoli, p. 99.

[50] J. Camerario, *Epistolae aliquot Marci Antonii Flaminii de Veritate Doctrinae Eruditae et Sanctitate Religionis . . . ex Italico* (Nuremberg, 1571), sig. G 5ʳ–H 5ʳ.

world for Christ's sake ... and, full of holy joy, can sing with the prophet, 'The Lord is my shepherd, I shall not want. He maketh me to lie down in green pastures, he leadeth me beside the still waters.'

Flaminio's ardour for a revival of true religion, as he felt it, was not affected by the vigorous activity of Caraffa's Inquisition or by the first ominous flights. In Venice in 1543, the most popular devotional work in sixteenth-century Italy was published. Its full title was *Trattato Utilissimo del Beneficio di Gesù Cristo Crocifisso verso I Cristiani, A Most Useful Tract on The Benefits Bestowed Upon Christians by Jesus Christ Crucified*. The publisher said that he was publishing this book without the name of the author so that the subject matter rather than the authority of the author would move the reader. The *Beneficio di Cristo* enjoyed an immense popular success. The first edition was immediately snatched up. A second edition was published the same year at Modena on the order of Cardinal Morone. It was estimated that forty thousand copies were sold, an enormous number for that time.[51] It was the most popular devotional work among the college of cardinals, it was Edward VI of England's favourite reading.[52] Who wrote it?

This question was put to Carnesecchi at his examination before the Inquisition on August 21, 1566. This is his answer:

> The first author of this book was a black monk of St. Benedict, called Don Benedetto da Mantova, who said that he composed it while he was in the monastery of his Order near Mount Etna. This Don Benedetto, being a friend of Marcantonio Flaminio, gave him the book to polish and adorn it with his fine style, so that it should be more readable and pleasing, and so Flaminio, without touching the content, revised it according to his judgment, and I had it from him before anyone, and, as I approved it and considered it good, so he have gave some copies of it to some friends.[53]

Carnesecchi's evidence was corroborated by Cardinal Morone

[51] Cuccoli, pp. 96–7, and Bonnet, *Paleario*, p. 136, who quotes Vergerio as his source.

[52] Bonnet, *Paleario*, p. 136. Edward VI also had a copy of Flaminio's poetic paraphrases of the psalms and of his *De rebus divinis*, *Literary Remains of King Edward VI*, ed. J. G. Nichols for the Roxburghe Club (London, 1857), I, cccxxix.

[53] Manzoni, 'Processo Carnesecchi', p. 202.

in his examination, and by Caracciolo,[54] and one of the charges against Flaminio in the 'Compendium of the Trials of the Holy Office in Rome' is that he revised, corrected, and published the *Beneficio di Cristo*.[55]

*The Beneficio di Cristo* was attacked in 1544, condemned by the Inquisition, and put on della Casa's first Index (1549). The Inquisition collected all copies everywhere and burnt them in huge fires in Rome.[56] It was thought that the book had completely disappeared when, in 1855, a copy was found in St. John's College Library, Cambridge. Let us see what it says:[57]

After original sin, the world became the devil's domain. Therefore, we are always willing to obey the devil's will. But sometimes the grace of God prevents us. Sin entered the world through one man. Redemption entered the world through one man. Just as Adam's sin makes us all sinners, through no fault of our own, so Jesus' sacrifice makes us just, and children of grace, without our doing any good works. Good works cannot be good unless we are already made good and just through faith, as St. Augustine says.

There is no sin that God cannot forgive, because he has punished all our sins in Jesus. Therefore, we are all pardoned. It is gross ingratitude for us to try to justify ourselves with our works, when Christ has wiped out all our sins with his most precious blood, as though the merits and blood of Christ were not enough!

When we have faith in Jesus we become part of his body and are no longer sons of Adam, but sons of God. We must believe the gospel, that Christ died to save sinners and that God punished our sins in Christ. Then our sins are remitted, and we become sons of grace and enter the kingdom of God. Faith is the work and gift of God, as St. Paul says.

Once we are possessed of true faith, we are possessed by an urge to do good works, just as it is impossible to set fire to a bunch of faggots without their giving out light. The man who does evil, but says he believes, and that he will therefore enter

---

[54] Cuccoli, p. 97.
[55] Corvisieri, 'Compendio', pp. 274-5.
[56] Ranke, I, p. 162.
[57] I am translating from Paladino's reprint in *Opuscoli e Lettere di Riformatori Italiani del '500*, I.

the kingdom of heaven, is mistaken. He has not true faith. True faith inspires good works. As fire burns wood without aid of the light, so faith burns sin without aid of works, but as fire is inevitably accompanied by light, so faith is inevitably accompanied by works. If we believe that our salvation depends upon Christ *alone*, we are glorifying him. If we believe that we can earn our own salvation by works, we are discounting Christ and are guilty of pride.

When the sinner doubts, and feels he is damned, he goes to the sacrament and regains the certainty of salvation. He says to himself,

> Has He not spilt His blood to wash away all my iniquities? Then, my soul, why are you sad? Trust in the Lord, who loves you so much that He willed that His only son should die to free you from eternal death, who took upon Himself our poverty, to give us His riches, who took upon Himself our infirmity, to make us strong with His strength, who became mortal, to make us immortal, who descended to the earth, that we might mount into heaven, who became a son of man with us, to make us sons of God with Him.
>
> Therefore, who will he be who will accuse us? God is the one who justifies us. Who will he be who will condemn us? Christ died for us, then He rose again, and He sits on God's right hand and intercedes for us. Then, my soul, abandon your sighs and complaints. My soul, bless the Lord. All that is within me bless His holy name. My soul, bless the Lord, and never forget all His gifts. He is the propitiation for all your iniquities, He heals all your infirmities, He rescues your life from death, He crowns you with mercy and compassion. The Lord is compassionate and clement, slow to anger and great in mercy.
>
> At mass the Christian should always keep his mind's eye fixed on the passion of this our most kind Lord, contemplating, on the one hand, Jesus on the cross burdened with all our sins, on the other, God who chastises Him, beating His most beloved son in our stead. O happy is he who closes his eyes to all other sights and neither wants to see nor hear anything else but Jesus Christ crucified, in whom all the grace and all the treasures of wisdom and knowledge repose! Happy, I say, is he whose mind feeds always on such divine food and who with such sweet and salutary liquor makes his soul intoxicated with the love of God!
>
> '... the Lord participates with His body in the sacrament in such a way that He becomes the same thing as we and we as

He.' Therefore we Christians become one body, and we are incorporated in Christ. Therefore we are all brothers. Therefore if we do wrong to anyone, we are wronging Christ, if we are in discord with anyone, we are in discord with Christ, if we love Christ, we must also love Him in our brothers.... The sacrament obliges us to love our brothers, and to aid and help them in their necessity. Any man who goes to communion at enmity with his brother is at enmity with Christ, and eats and drinks, his own damnation.

Another comforting thought for the Christian is the knowledge of his predestination and election to eternal life. All those who believe in the gospel are elected to eternal life.

> This holy predestination keeps the true Christian in continual spiritual joy. The desire to do good works grows in him. It fires him with the love of God. He becomes an enemy of the world, and of sin ... those who worship God truly in spirit and truth receive all prosperity and adversity from the hand of God, their Father, ever praising Him and thanking Him in all His works, as their devoted, just, and holy Father. They, enamoured of their God, and armed with the knowledge of their predestination, do not fear death, nor sin, nor the devil, nor hell. They do not know what the wrath of God is because they see in God nothing but love and fatherly affection towards them.

But predestination must not lead to fatalism. Though God has determined everything, we still make efforts to procure ourselves food and drink and all we need for our physical survival. So we must do good works to ensure our spiritual survival. God has made us concerned with things pertaining to the perfection of the body, and also with things pertaining to the perfection of the soul.

In this brief outline of the argument of the *Beneficio di Cristo* I have concentrated on the main points of doctrine that were under discussion at the time and that seemed of fundamental importance, namely justification by faith, works, the sacrament, and predestination, and I have tried to indicate the flavour of the work by liberal quotation. It has not been possible to show how carefully and clearly the argument is constructed. It is worked out with meticulous logic and the major points are strongly supported by quotations from St. Paul and the Gospels. Possible objections are honestly and squarely met. There is no denial of their existence. The tone is passionate and mystical but the argument is more strictly reasoned than is usual in a devotional work of this sort.

The *Beneficio di Cristo* was attacked the following year, on behalf of the Inquisition, by Brother Ambrogio Catharino (Lancelloto Politi) of Siena.[58] Flaminio was preparing a reply to this attack when the book was condemned. In the record of the trial of Pietro Carnesecchi, the following statement is inserted, written in Carnesecchi's own hand:

> To this third error are added two others which I think, since they are both of the same nature, can be reduced to a single charge, namely, that I have kept alive among my writings a fragment of a little work of Flaminio's written by him in defence of the book, *Del Beneficio di Cristo*, against brother Ambrosio Catherino, and not afterwards published in any other way, I think because the said book was condemned and prohibited before his defence was finished. This error of mine really was caused rather by the love that I bore the author, than by the belief that I gave the work, not having barely read it once in the preliminary stage in which it was composed, nor being adequate to judge between two so great men, although it was my duty, in case of doubt, to condemn Flaminio since he had written in defence of a book that was condemned by the church.[59]

The preservation of Flaminio's Apology for the *Beneficio di Cristo* was one of the capital charges against Carnesecchi on which he was found guilty.[60]

In April, 1543, Paul III set out for Busseto, in the Parma area, for conversations with Charles V. He took Flaminio with

[58] *Compendio d'Errori, et Inganni Luterani, contenuti in un Libretto, senza nome de l'Autore, intitolato, Trattato utilissimo del benefitio di Christo crucifisso* (Rome, 1544). Politi's refutation is not readable like the *Beneficio di Cristo*. Politi has not made a major overall criticism which he supports with all his powers as the author of the *Beneficio* maintains a single thesis, but rather he seeks to refute the *Beneficio* sentence by sentence. Thus his criticisms often appear niggling and trivial, although some of them are sound logically, while others are mere logic chopping, to the point where a criticism of one passage will contradict a criticism of another. Politi is particularly hard on Flaminio's similes. He obviously does not see life in a poetic light and he forgets that Jesus spoke in metaphors and that often poetic similes can stir the soul where plodding logic cannot.
[59] Manzoni, 'Processo Carnesecchi', p. 192.
[60] See the judgment in Manzoni, 'Processo Carnesecchi', p. 561.

him. They stopped for three days in Ferrara, April 21–24, where they were entertained at the court.[61] They spent May in Busseto. In June Flaminio returned to Ferrara[62] on the way to Venice—to see the *Beneficio di Cristo* through the press?

We hear nothing more of Flaminio for this year except through a letter from Alexander Farnese to the Governor of Bologna, dated November 2, 1543, in which the cardinal asks the governor to order the dataries to stop bothering Flaminio about the abbey in the Val di Lavino.[63] Pehaps while he was in the north Flaminio visited Giberti in Verona, for Giberti's grave illness was talked of all over Italy.[64] Perhaps, too, it was this summer that he went to Serravalle on business in the dog days and wrote to Priuli of his longing for the conversation of Pole and his circle (V, 13).[65]

It would also appear to have been about this time that Flaminio wrote a very interesting poetic epistle to Alexander Farnese (I, 9) inviting him to visit him in the country, at what must have been the abbey in the Val di Lavino. Farnese has had enough of extreme cold, heat, and danger on his many legations for the pope, trying to negotiate the peace of Europe. Now, in the heat of August, he should take a rest at Flaminio's place in the country. There follows a description of what Flaminio can offer him, a catalogue of the pleasures of humanists and high churchmen.

[61] Cuccoli, p. 118.
[62] See the poem written to B. Riccio about his *Apparatus* (VI, 23), dated Ferrara, June 5, in Riccio's *Epistolarum Familiarum Libri IIII* (Ferrara, 1562), fol. 43r–v.
[63] Costa, *GSLI*, X, 384–7.
[64] See Giberti's life by Pietro Francesco Zino in Giberti, *Opera* (Hostiliae, 1740), p. xliv.
[65] This letter must have been written in the August of 1543 or 1544 because it obviously belongs to the period when Flaminio and Priuli were members of Pole's household, i.e., 1541–6. Flaminio did not join Pole's household until October, 1541, therefore it could not have been 1541. In July and August, 1546, Pole was ill in Priuli's villa in Treviso. Since Treviso is a mere nineteen miles from Serravalle and thus within daily visiting range, and since there is also no reference to Pole's illness, the poem could not refer to 1546. We know that Flaminio was in Viterbo in July, August, and September of 1542, and that he was in Trent with his friends in the summer of 1545. Therefore the only possible years when this letter could have been written are 1543 or 1544 and we know that Flaminio was in the north of Italy in 1543.

If we compare this poem with those written from Bardolino or San Prospero we will notice that Flaminio's standard of living has risen. He can now receive on a considerable scale, and offer gentlemanly forms of entertainment. The picture of life on his estate, in fact, calls to mind Jonson's description of Penshurst, although actually what Flaminio possessed was very humble in comparison with the wealth and splendour of the Sidneys.

Flaminio tells Farnese that, at his place in the country, he can read Horace, Homer, and Vergil, that he can visit the caves and cool springs, and that the laughing and joking will make him forget his troubles. He can watch Pholoe dance and hear Meliboeus sing, he can lime birds, fish, hunt deer, rabbits, and wild goats, and go hawking. Flaminio suggests that he bring with him Maffeo, Mirandola, and Amaseo and a few other cultivated men, but not too many, 'you cannot savour the blessings of the countryside if you do not leave the superfluous pomp of the city behind in the city'.

Another poem also written in this period, but later on in the season, invites Farnese to San Prospero for the vintage (I, 16). The switch from the epistolary hendecasyllables to the more formal sapphic stanzas makes for a more serious work of art. The sapphic stanza inherited from Horace a tendency towards completeness, towards polished perfection. Each stanza must express a single idea in pictorial imagery, delicately, sensitively, briefly, and yet contain a link to couple the miniatures together in a chain of argument. Flaminio chose the sapphic ode to send Farnese a more formal invitation to visit him and, in doing so, generalized and idealized experience to a far greater extent than in the literary epistle.

> Now Phoebus brings the day to a close after a shorter
> Turn and calms the mad Lion's rage,
> While a softer season brings
>   Autumn bedeckt
>
> With a crown of ripe grapes. He advances joyfully
> Through the lovely countryside, and at the sight
> Of him the apples blush
>   With gladness.

## VITERBO AND CARDINAL POLE

Then golden-haired Semele's son, rejoicing
At his comely companion's return, goes forth
A long way to meet him, and they both
   Join hands and dance.

The Bacchic band leaps about them, the jolly
Pans, and Dryads with streaming hair.
The sweet flute sings, mingled
   With the shepherds' pipes.

Venus herself descends into the fruitful
Fields, and handsome Mirth and Pleasure—
Yet you can harden yourself to remain
   In the tiresome town!

You perpetually hover over the whole world, Farnese,
With your flying thoughts, long anticipating
What the fierce Turk and the German
   Is planning and Britain

In her distant part.[66] But free yourself
For a few days from the care of empire,
The countryside will restore you more active
   To your great task.

>Jam diem gyro breviore claudens
>Phoebus insani rabiem Leonis
>Sedat, Autumnumque refert decorum
>   Mollior aestas,

>Ille maturis redimitus uvis
>Laetus incedit per amoena rura:
>Ejus aspectu exhilarata ducunt
>   Poma colorem.

>At puer flavae Semeles sodalem
>Candidum gaudens rediisse, prodit
>Obviam longe: socias choreas
>   Jungit uterque.

[66] This Horatian commonplace was exactly true of Alexander Farnese.

> Saltat hos circum thiasus, jocosi
> Panes, et passo Dryades capillo,
> Fistulis mixtum resonat suavis
>     Tibia carmen.
>
> Ipsa pomosos Cytherea in agros
> Migrat, et pulcher Jocus, et Voluptas:
> Tu tamen durus potes in molesta
>     Urbe morari,
>
> Semper et magnum celeri per orbem
> Mente, FARNESI, volitas, quid acer
> Turca, quid Rhenus paret, ac remota in
>     Parte Britannus,
>
> Providens longe. Sed omitte curam
> Imperî paucis vacuus diebus:
> Te magis tantos vegetum ad labores
>     Rura remittent.                    I, 16

Flaminio was later to say that he wrote no poetry during this period—which was, of course, not strictly true—but this ode shows that when he did write he had lost none of his refinement, delicacy, or taste. Here there is the right amount of pomp for the ode, coupled with the right amount of gentleness and warmth for an invitation to a high-ranking friend. There is no empty rhetoric. The personified figures are exact abstractions of reality. The sketch of Farnese's preoccupations, apparently conventional could not be closer to the truth. Flaminio is a complete master of the classical tradition and an artist with an unfailing sense of taste and proportion.

Then winter came. In a brief ode (I, 12), in the elegiac tone that suited his genius so well, Flaminio says farewell to the countryside, as silence settles over the fields after the autumn's festivities:

> Now the soft season has passed with the coming
> Of winter, and the leaves fall
> From the tall trees, and the warm west wind
> Shrinks and withdraws before raging
> Boreas' mighty wrath, and the song-birds,
> The joy of the field, follow.
> And so I, too, will leave the sweet countryside,

## VITERBO AND CARDINAL POLE

Until beautiful spring with her shining
Hair restores Zephyr's warm breeze. Farewell,
My garden, my delight. Farewell,
Bright springs. Take care of yourself, my little villa,
Dearer to me than the proud palaces
Of princes, I am going, but I leave my heart
And my soul here with you.

>Jam bruma veniente praeterivit
>Aestas mollior, et cadunt ab altis
>Frondes arboribus: tepor Favonî
>Immanes Boreae furentis iras
>Formidans abit: illum agri voluptas
>Canorae volucres sequuntur. Ergo
>Et nos dulcia rura deseramus,
>Dum Ver purpurea coma decorum
>Reducat Zephyri tepentis auram.
>Horti deliciae meae valete,
>Fontes luciduli valete, salve
>Mihi villula carior superbis
>Regum liminibus, recedo, sensum
>Sed meum hic animumque derelinquo.
>
>I, 12

This winter Flaminio wrote Giberti's epitaph (I, 25)[67]. He also wrote a letter from Rome on February 14, 1544, urging his cousin Cesare Flaminio, to give up duelling.[68] It is written in the same spirit as the letter to Teodorina Sauli and the *Beneficio di Cristo*.

It was perhaps about this trip to Rome that Flaminio wrote two whimsical poems to Pole in which he pretended to be a little dog and begged for a lift in his master's coach to Rome (I, 35 and 36). These poems show a gentle sense of humour.

There were other occasional poems written at the time, including a series of epigrams from Viterbo[69] and three letters of recommendation (V, 3, 5, 10). These letters of recommendation are truly remarkable. Any man who has to write them could well envy Flaminio the ease with which he is able to set

---

[67] Giberti died on December 30, 1543.
[68] Paladino, I, pp. 86–9.
[69] II, 17; II, 16, and two in *Doct.*, fol. 28ʳ; I, 32; V, 31; I, 33; I, 39, 40; V, 45; V, 30; VI, 33; VI, 34.

forth a man's main qualities and qualifications in a way that is likely to please the recipient of the letter and get the candidate employment. And he did this in verse, too, effortless, natural verse. Moreover, it would appear that Flaminio's judgment was sound. One man whom Flaminio recommended and whose subsequent career is well known is Gulielmo Sirleto. When Flaminio met him he was a poor teacher, teaching poor boys free (V, 10). Flaminio recommended him to Cardinal Seripando, whom he had known in Naples in 1540, and Sirleto rose in the Church to become one of its leading scholars, the librarian of the Vatican library, and a cardinal himself. His cousin, Benedetto Flaminio, whom Flaminio recommends to Lelio Torelli, secretary of Duke Cosmo of Florence, had quite a respectable legal career (V, 3).

In Venice, in 1545, Flaminio's *Explanation* of the whole psalter appeared, dedicated to Alexander Farnese. Here each psalm is preceded by a brief outline and followed by general remarks, or notes on obscure passages, obscure expressions, historical allusions, and customs. This is not properly a commentary on the psalms, but an annotated edition of them. In his dedication to Alexander Farnese Flaminio explains the genesis of the work:

> I could wish that my state of health had permitted me to complete that paraphrase of the divine songs of David which I had begun in earlier years and which I had dedicated to your grandfather, Pope Paul III ... [since] Bernardino Maffeo ... has told me many times that it would give you great pleasure. And what could I wish more than to please so illustrious and eminent a man in such a pious thing, especially since your liberality is so great that you never cease honouring me with new benefices? But, since such is the state of my health that I have not the strength to offer what I ought, I am sending you what I can, this brief explanation in which I have treated all the psalms....[70]

It is interesting to compare Flaminio's commentary on the psalms with Valdes', which, however, was a commentary only on the first book of the psalms, according to the Hebrew division. There is a marked difference between the two works.

[70] *In Librum Psalmorum brevis explanatio ad Alexandrum Farnesium Cardinalem amplissimum* (Paris, 1546), fol. 2r-v.

Valdes and Flaminio do not comment on the same passages and, although their overall interpretation of a particular psalm may be the same, they often put their emphases in different places. Flaminio's commentary is not derivative. It is also much less controversial than Valdes'. In fact it is difficult to understand why it, along with the prose paraphrases of the psalms, and Flaminio's later religious lyrics, was put on the Index. On the other hand it is easy to understand why the Church, once it had adopted its official position on justification by faith, should have banned some of Flaminio's Italian letters.

*Chapter 9*

# TRENT

IT was not until 1545 that Paul III was able to reconvene the Council of Trent. The cardinal-legates were now del Monte (later Julius III), Cervini (later Marcellus II), and Pole. Flaminio probably went to Trent with Pole and Priuli on May 4. On the way there Pole and his companions were magnificently received in Mantua at the court of Ercole Gonzaga.

It took the Council a long time to assemble and settle down to work. It was not possible to begin business until December 3, 1545. So the Italian cardinals, with their suites, spent the long summer at Trent enjoying villa life and the humanist distractions that were natural to them. There is a very important description of these in Vida's *De Republica*,[1] written in its final form in 1555, but begun much earlier and approved of by Pole, to whom it was dedicated, before his departure for England in 1553.[2] Since one of the other personages in the dialogue was del Monte, who was pope when the work was being prepared for publication, and since Cervini, who was destined to be del Monte's successor, was alive, it seems very unlikely that Vida is guilty of gross misrepresentation here.

In his dedication, Vida tells Pole that he has written the *Republic* to fill the gap left in philosophic literature by the loss

---

[1] Published by G. Toffanin in *L'Umanesimo al Concilio di Trento* (Bologna, 1955), pp. 75 ff.
[2] *Ibid.*, pp. 77–8.

of Cicero's *Republic*. Hence he decided to publish for Pole the record of a conversation that he, Vida, had with Flaminio one day in Trent many years ago when Flaminio attacked all forms of society and he was obliged to refute his arguments. Vida recalls the occasion of the discussion. It was the summer of 1545 and the bishops were assembled at Trent, but the Germans refused to begin discussions, and there was a tiresome delay. One day Priuli and Flaminio walked out to see Vida in his suburban gardens at the Golden Cross, where Cristoforo Madruzzo, Bishop of Trent, had let him have a house for the summer. 'I was having my morning walk, and so I received them in a shady arbour, because it was the hottest day of the year.' Pole came a little later, then the other two legates, del Monte and Cervini. Gradually the conversation moved around to a discussion of the State. Vida had launched into a long encomium of the advantages of organized society when del Monte interrupted him:

'Let's have some discussion. . . . You should first explain the nature of society. And I think that Flaminio here will not agree with you in your praise of human society, which is the origin of the State, as the fountain of all goods, since we frequently read in the most famous poets of the great sweetness and felicity of life at the beginning of human history when states did not yet exist and cities were not yet founded and men wandered alone, free of all social ties, and led their lives as free men in the fields, far from all fear of the law and of punishment, when, in sum, to quote a noble poet, the earth produced its fruits spontaneously and the hard oaks oozed dripping honey.'

When del Monte had said this, all looked at Flaminio, waiting with closest attention to see what kind of case he would build up against the whole concept of the State and society itself, if not in complete seriousness, at least for argument's sake.

'I would not like to take on a role', said Flaminio, 'which is so totally antipathetic to me. . . . Also I enjoyed hearing what Vida was saying. . . . '

But the others urged Flaminio to take up the argument. Finally he gave way and suggested that he and Vida try to find the truth by discussion, as they did in the Old Academy.

Flaminio began by saying that he did not think that Vida could really believe without qualification all that he had said. He must have made his statement to sound out the opinions of others and to get their views, 'For who is so blind and so bereft of common sense that he cannot see that innumerable, almost infinite, evils burst on the human race with the foundation of states and that an enormous upheaval followed that compact of men in society, which you praise to the skies, and that he who first brought men, who were scattered in the woods and on the mountains, together into society was the author of many great evils? . . .

'Theseus brought the pastoral people of Attica together and built Athens. The people exiled him in perpetuity for his pains. Their lives before had been tranquil and secure, now they were disturbed and confused. More and worse crimes are committed in cities, in proportion to their population, than in the countryside and villages and tiny towns. In the country, where there are less crowds, everyone will admit that men are less clever and less malicious . . . they cultivate equity and justice in a sincerity of life, instructed in no artifice of dissimulation, simple, innocent, faithful, open, true, and, to cover everything by a single word, antique. The more people there are together the more corruption and contagion there is.

' . . . society has disturbed everything. It was invented to satisfy man's desires, that cities should be stuffed full of enticements to all desires, both of the mind and of the body, and that all the gatherings of men should abound in extravagant living and wantonness. No philosopher can deny that humanity has deteriorated and been deformed from the time that cities were first founded until now, when it is rushing headlong into night and disintegration. Only the name of justice and of the other virtues remains as subjects for discussion by philosophers. There are more men killed by other men than by disease or disaster.

'Before the foundation of cities, there was a single universal state with God as its governor. Men worshipped Him, following nature and silent reason; they voluntarily submitted themselves to Him; and there were as many republics as there were houses or families. The elder ruled the younger, the wives obeyed their husbands, children their parents [it is obvious that Flaminio was a bachelor], . . . whose wills they considered sacred, and at home they never lacked examples from which to learn. There were not so many arts, so many facilities developed for human pleasure, so many enticements to worldliness and voluptuousness, with which men's spirits are softened and made effeminate. They didn't feast, they didn't drink, they didn't smell of pomades and perfumes [he also knows nothing about anthropology]. Any shelter sufficed for protection against the wind and rain. Now, we build magnificent villas at great expense. They have marble floors, and coffered ceilings, and gleam with gold and silver and ivory. And we acquire paintings, statues, reliefs, works of gold and silver, bronzes, various kinds of jewels, fine clothing, necklaces, horses, properties, beds, and tables heaped high with the rarest of foods. We are clean and elegant and brilliant, we have the best chefs and pastrycooks, we seek out the rarest fish and birds—there is no limit to our desires or to our expenditure.

'This would be bearable if there were equality. But as it is, some people have so much money that they satisfy all their desires and spend their time building up the sea and levelling mountains, while others work, enslaved by another man's money, and, ruined by the daily growth of interest, fight against hunger.

'In the days when there were no states, there was no passion for power, which observes no law, human or divine. . . . Thus it is that people fear their kings and governors more than the enemy, trembling before their cruelty, their avarice, their lust, and their pride. . . .

'Man is born free, and the love of liberty is innate. Servitude is worse than death. Those who herded us together into cities and put us under the rule of law subjected us to everlasting servitude. Now we are subject to laws, and to magistrates who interpret them, and how many magistrates are just and moderate?

'What, I ask you, can you think of that is more contrary to nature than not to live according to one's own will and judgment —especially for a man who has been brought up innocently, and in whose heart is liberty—but to be compelled always by the order and command of another, to be forced to shape himself according to another's whim, and to do nothing except in the way the other person wants him to?

'Laws teach us not justice, but how to litigate. Man has the potentiality of being spontaneously good. He doesn't need a lot of threatening laws.

'No state can be properly governed, since everything is in a state of flux, and human affairs are subject to fortune. Do you think that in any society, whether great or small, the community interest is really observed? Is it possible to give to each one according to his worth? . . . What is the source of all forms of taxation, if not society? . . . Those who run states run them to their own advantage.

'O who will take me away from the crowd and from that confused life full of fears and traps forged from all the refuse of crime and restore me, straightaway, to that blessed solitude, to that happy separateness in which each man lived in his own house in complete security, far from all fears! O who at long last will take me away from... the constantly shifting and conflicting multitude, which suffers all the time from so much hatred, discord, dissension, contempt, strife, rivalry, competition, hostility, and civil war and place me... in that placid and tranquil life in which fortune can do little, the life that Justice brought down from heaven....

'Even were I to be crucified for it, I will openly say what I think, and I would like my voice to be heard by all nations: Hear me, nature, hear me, humanity. It being admitted now that with the building of cities man's ills have multiplied... and since our race continually grows worse so that heaven's vengeance threatens, since we are reduced to such a pass as not to be able to support either our vices or our remedies, I think that we should leave the cities and every social grouping and return to the solitudes of the fields and leave this cruel beast, the State, turning our backs on kingdoms, empires, honours, dignities, ambitions, wealth, and the empty glories which torment us so here. Let us wrench ourselves from this mad and perverse society that justice may descend a second time on earth. What, I ask you, is sweeter and more pleasing than living according to nature?'

Here we have the words of Rousseau two hundred years earlier. Toffanin, in his edition of Vida's *Republic* in *L'Umanesimo al Concilio di Trento*, says that these views were very dangerous ones and that Vida attributed them to Flaminio because he was dead.[3] It seems to me that both these statements are unlikely. If these views were dangerous why is del Monte, pope at the time that Vida was writing, represented as encouraging Flaminio to take up this line of argument, and why are he and Cervini, soon to be pope, represented as being indulgent to Flaminio's views after he has spoken? Also, if these views were dangerous, is it likely that Pole, himself in trouble with the Inquisition, as we have seen above, p. 124, would have allowed Vida to ascribe them to his dead friend Flaminio who was close to being condemned posthumously by the Inquisition? But, if Vida had no particular reason to ascribe these views to Flaminio except, of course, for the sake of argument, to give

[3] Published by G. Toffanin in *L'Umanesimo al Concilio di Trento* (Bologna, 1955), pp. 23 ff.

himself the opportunity to build up his picture of the ideal State in book two of the *Republic*, is there any reason to believe that these might actually be views that Flaminio held, that they were not, at any rate, too gross a travesty of Flaminio's thought? The answer is yes. We have already come across this primitivist and anarchist strain in Flaminio's poetry (*supra*, p. 89) and we will see it again in his translation of the psalms made a few months later (see *infra*, p. 165). Thus it does appear that these views were ones that Flaminio, at times at least, probably held. One other fact should be noted, that Flaminio's speech is a long and somewhat repetitive diatribe that reads like the unedited record of an actual argument, like the words of an enthusiast carried away. Vida's *Republic*, then, may well represent a real discussion that actually took place in the summer of 1545 during the long wait for the Council of Trent to assemble.

Towards the end of 1545 the pope offered Flaminio the secretaryship of the Council of Trent. Flaminio wrote Alexander Farnese an elegy in which he begged the cardinal to explain to his grandfather that he could not accept because of failing health. Farnese replied that the pope understood and that he would like Priuli in his place.[4]

In Trent at this time Flaminio wrote a poetic paraphrase of thirty of the thirty-two psalms which he had previously paraphrased in prose (1538). He wrote them in twenty nights while he was a guest of Farnese's. Then his health broke down. As Flaminio told Farnese, he could write only at night. Therefore, he had to go without sleep or without poetry. The long psalms kept him up until daybreak, and so put his life in danger.[5]

Already, in his preface to the prose paraphrases of the psalms, Flaminio had complained about the fact that, in their rejection of medievalism, humanist teachers also virtually rejected

[4] Costa, *GSLI*, X, 384–7.
[5] Cuccoli, pp. 235, 237 and MAF, *Carm.* (1743), pp. 244–5. Flaminio describes his nocturnal composition in two other poems. One of these was published by Torrentino just before the verse version of the psalms in *Carm.* 5 (1548), p. 270, and (1552), p. 8, but was not republished by Mancurti in the standard edition of Flaminio's works. The other poem, V, 44, is addressed to Fabrizio Brancuti, who wrote down the poems as Flaminio composed them during the night. He is mentioned in 'Processo Carnesecchi', p. 254, as having been in Pole's household and having fled to France to the Lutherans.

Christianity.⁶ This sane and balanced view of humanism Flaminio had learnt from his father who, as early as 1515, in writing to Leandro Alberti about the Dominican saints' lives which he was writing or editing, had deplored the fact that much of the Christian witness was being lost because moderns refused to read monkish Latin and cared only for style, and nothing for content. It would be well if children learnt something of holy living and dying and were not nurtured solely on the worldliness, frivolity, and superstition of the pagans.⁷ It was to make the psalms available to formative youth that the younger Flaminio began to translate them into the kind of Latin verse that was popular in the middle of the sixteenth century. Echoing Horace's boast of his poetic achievement (III, 30), Flaminio says that he is the first to translate David's poetry into Latin verse. Here one does not read of Jupiter's insane passions, or of the drunken orgies of Bacchus, or of the Pythian games, or of pagan rites. Instead, here is the praise of God Almighty, He who steers the planets in their courses, who stills the great ocean, who rewards the just and punishes the wicked, and nourishes all living things. It is Flaminio's aim to make this sacred poetry accessible to the young. He also wanted to please Cardinal Farnese. When we realize that this distinguished prelate was still only twenty-six years of age, we appreciate why Flaminio refers to his youth. Flaminio asks Farnese to read these poems when he is tired of listening to the noble legates of kings discussing matters of supreme importance and takes refuge in his lovely gardens with his learned friends, Mirandola and Maffeo.⁸

Flaminio's 'To the Reader'⁹ also affords an interesting reflection on the changed spirit of the times. It illustrates the mood of the Council of Trent. Flaminio addresses himself to the 'Christian reader', he tells how he was able to write these poems through God's favour, and he prays, and asks for his readers' prayers, to be able to finish the psalter, not for his own glory, but for God's. There is a tone of official Catholicism about this. There is no trace of the emotion of personal and subjective religious thought. Despite the fact that it was

⁶ *Paraphrasis in Duos et Triginta Psalmos* (Padua, 1538), sig. A iiiᵛ–A iiiiʳ.
⁷ GAF, *Ep. Fam.*, pp. 275-7, and L. Alberti, *De Viris*, fol. 105ʳ.
⁸ MAF, *Carm.* (1743), pp. 244-5.
⁹ MAF, *Carm.* (1743), pp. 243-4.

favoured by the Protestants, Flaminio's verse translation of the psalms was never, for its own content, put on the Index, as were the prose paraphrases and the explanation.[10]

Indeed, in his address to the reader Flaminio explains his method of translation in what reads like a statement of mannerist principles, and mannerism was a style fostered by the Church. He has not translated David word for word, but he has not added much either—his religious duty would forbid that. Moreover he feels certain that he has added nothing contrary

---

[10] Cuccoli, p. 92. There are, however, some passages even in the verse translation to which a rigorous churchman, looking for the least suggestion of unorthodoxy, could take exception. For example, in translating psalm 30, verse 7, which in the contemporary Vulgate version reads, 'Domine in voluntate tua praestiteras monti meo fortitudinem,' 'Lord, by your will you had given strength to my mountain,' Flaminio writes,

> Certainly you had secured my kingdom
> And my fortunes so that they appeared
> Like a mountain to all. But this had befallen
> Me through no virtue of mine,
> But through your great liberality.
>    Tu scilicet regnum meum,
>    Measque fortunas ita stabiliveras,
>      Ut montis instar omnibus
>    Habere visa sint. At hoc nulla mihi
>      Virtute contigerat mea,
>    Sed liberalitate maxima tua.

This interpretation of 'in voluntate tua' as meaning 'through your grace and through no merit of mine' is also found in Flaminio's *Explanation*, pp. 116ᵛ–117ʳ. It is interesting to note that this interpretation of 'in voluntate tua' is not found in Valdes' *Commentary on the Psalms*. Indeed a comparison of Flaminio's three works on the psalms with Valdes' commentary shows that Flaminio did not derive his ideas from that source.

Despite this passage and some few others of the same tenor, Flaminio's verse translation of the psalms is a much less controversial work than either the prose paraphrases or the *Explanation*. For example, in commenting on 'propter nomen suum', 'for his name's sake', in verse 3 of the 23rd psalm, he writes in the *Explanation*, p. 95ᵛ, 'nullis meritis meis, sed propter infinitam bonitatem suam', 'through no merits of mine, but through his infinite goodness', and this same interpretation is found in the prose paraphrase, p. 97ʳ, which, incidentally, he wrote and published before he met Valdes. However, in the verse version of this psalm he writes merely, 'benignitate maxima', 'through his very great kindness', and there is no qualifying 'through no virtue of mine' as in the verse version of the 30th psalm quoted above.

to the poet's thought, nothing which does not clarify some obscurity or add some grace to the beauty of the poem, the sort of grace that a wreath of roses and violets, artfully made, adds to the beauty of a golden-haired girl.

It often happens that certain things are in the air, that several people will become interested in the same problems at the same time, and that the same style will develop more or less simultaneously in different centres without there being any influence of the one upon the other. Wallace and Darwin thought of natural selection at about the same time. Flaminio, the French poet, Salmon Macrin, the Scots poet, George Buchanan, and the chancellor of the University of Paris, Jean Gagny, all thought of translating the psalms into Latin verse more or less simultaneously. Gagny was filled with consternation at the appearance of Flaminio's psalms in 1546 when he was about to publish his own (1547). He was worried that his versions would now appear unpleasing and insipid trifles.[11]

Flaminio's verse translation of the psalms was published in Venice in 1546 and was republished in Paris in the same year by Henry Stephanus in a volume of poetic translations of the psalms by several hands. The other principal translators were Buchanan and Macrin.

Stephanus' preface reveals that he, too, felt that humanism had become something of a scandal for men who were supposedly Christian. Christians born were always willing to write poetry about the pagan gods, but they neglected their own God because, as they say, sacred literature does not admit ornament! That is a shocking reason, even if it were true, but he will prove that it is not by the translations of the psalms which he is publishing.

Stephanus' preface also reveals the beginning of a prejudice that was to last well up to the time of the Romantics. Tragedy and epic are more serious forms of literature than the lyric. Therefore a man of intellectual substance will exercise himself in these forms. The lyric is trivial, and the product of an irresponsible and undisciplined talent. Thus Stephanus affirms that Buchanan is the greatest translator of the psalms because he has already trained himself by the translation of the Greek tra-

---

[11] Quoted by Mancurti, MAF, *Carm.* (1743), pp. 318–9.

gedies. Flaminio could have been sublime, had he not ruined himself by a long addiction to love poetry.

Stephanus also sheds a new light on the composition of Flaminio's verse versions of the psalms. Although Flaminio gives the impression that all thirty of them were written at the same time in Trent, it would appear from Stephanus that some of them, at least, were written much earlier, perhaps when Flaminio was at Trent for the first time in 1542. It would be quite like Flaminio to begin a project and then let it drop for four years. Also this would then parallel what we know that Flaminio did in writing his poetic epistles (see *infra*, p. 176). When urged by Vicenzo Geri to bring the numbers up to fifty, Flaminio says that he stayed up one night and wrote four epistles, the last to Fracastoro who had once cured him of a serious disease. However, it appears from its tone and content that the epistle to Fracastoro was written twenty years before, in 1528, when Flaminio was actually suffering from the disease to which he refers. This letter to Fracastoro, 'FRACASTORI venerande, cui medendi' (V, 49) was probably a poem which had been lying among Flaminio's papers and which he decided to use only in a moment of desperation to fill up a self-imposed quota. It had probably been suppressed because Flaminio had written a similar poem to Fracastoro, 'FRACASTORI venerande, anima mihi carior,' at the same time and had allowed it to circulate, with the result that it appeared in *Doctissimorum* (fol. 29v–30v). Knowing that this poem was about, Flaminio was naturally reluctant to publish a similar and, as he undoubtedly felt, inferior, because less philosophic, one on the same subject. However, he was forced to do so by Geri's pressure. In the composition of the psalms, Flaminio was engaged in a similar, nocturnal, verse marathon, and it would be quite understandable if he utilized any material that he had at hand to help himself get through it, but still felt, and claimed, that the verse translation of the psalms was made in 1546 at Trent.

This seems to be the best way to reconcile Flaminio's statements with Stephanus'. It does not seem likely that Flaminio had already written all the psalms in 1542 and that he merely polished these versions in 1546. If that were the case, it seems virtually certain, from what we have seen of Flaminio so far, that he would have told Cardinal Farnese in his letter that he was offering him now what he *could* since ill health prevented him from offering him what he *would*.

We must quote exactly what Stephanus says about Flaminio, not just because of the light it sheds on the date of the composition of the psalms, but because it illustrates the revulsion against humanism, the new seriousness, and the growing belief that poetry should concern itself with religion and morality in the narrower sense. Stephanus says to Buchanan:

> I will tell you the answer that I gave to an Italian four years ago [i.e., in 1542] in Rome. For when discussion arose about Flaminio's verses, I praised the labour and care that he had expended in translating the psalms. 'But', he said . . . , 'what a disaster, for since he has become addicted to those religious works that you mention, his poetry has fallen off a lot from its wonted elegance and wit. . . .' Then I said, 'If you say that there is no place in the translation of sacred poetry for a certain kind of effeminate, or rather meretricious, ornament, I agree; for nothing is more alien to it. But if you are talking about virile imagery, full of majesty, then I think that you have, as they say, missed the boat entirely, for it demands just this ornament. And so, on the contrary, I say that it is too bad that Flaminio had already so broken and enfeebled his Muse with a too effeminate pandering to love poetry that, when he ought to have risen up higher, that is, in serious argument, the way to sublime poetry was not open to him. This is what I said then about Flaminio, my dear Buchanan. I now add this: if he had previously exercised himself much and long in writing tragedies or translating them from the Greek (labour that has long since brought you a great name), perhaps you would not be as lucky as you are now in triumphing so easily and effortlessly [over him].

Whether Buchanan is a better translator of the psalms than Flaminio is a matter of taste. Certainly Buchanan's translations are more even than Flaminio's. They are always brief, sober, clear, straightforward, reliable, serious, and reflective, rather than emotional, and Buchanan always possesses a certain monumental dignity, undoubtedly because, as Stephanus says, he had had a lot of practice in translating Greek tragedy. Flaminio's translations are, on the other hand, uneven. They vary considerably in quality, but they are, on the whole, mannered, fluent, pellucid, and pretty. They illustrate again Flaminio's extraordinary facility in writing verse—everything is always smooth and easy. Moreover, Flaminio incorporates quite a lot of explanatory material without being verbose—indeed he sometimes succeeds in translating a psalm in less words than Buchanan.[12] However, the power and passion of David are almost always lost, and Flaminio's versions are usually musical, but superficial. Flaminio's hasty composition is reflected in his occasional lapses into trite and tired Latin expressions, e.g., in psalm 1 Flaminio refers to the foliage of a tree as 'suus honor'; in psalm 12 he describes the decline of morality in hackneyed classical phraseology:

> Now kindly Truth has been driven away by lying
>     Falsehood, and has left the cities,
> Together with Faith, and holy Modesty, and her sister,
>     Lovable Sincerity,[13]

> Mendacio jam pulsa turpi veritas
>     Recessit alma ab urbibus,
> Fidesque sanctusque pudor, et soror illius
>     Sinceritas amabilis,

—this is the equivalent of the Authorized Version's, 'They speak vanity everyone with his neighbour: *with* flattering lips *and* with a double heart do they speak'; in psalm 100 he echoes Catullus:

> Ergo Deum canamus, O
> Viri et pudicae feminae
> Viri et pudicae feminae ...

and in psalm 13 he echoes Catullus again, 'Adeste castae virgines, pueri integri,' and he uses the familiar Horatian filler, 'Ab Indo ad ultima Britanni litora'.

Flaminio's prettiness may be illustrated by his version of the 23rd psalm, where the sheep that God pastures flow with milk and bring forth the most beautiful offspring. However, even in this psalm we see that Flaminio had the capacity to write moving religious poetry. In translating the well-known verse about the valley of the shadow of death Flaminio writes:

[12] e.g., psalm 1: Vulgate, 90 words; MAF, 126; Buchanan, 141. Psalm 114: Vulgate, 87 words; MAF, 87; Buchanan, 126.
[13] We recognize here the views of the Flaminio of Vida's *Republic*.

> If I go alone, unarmed,
> Through lonely places, haunted
> By death in many disguises,
> I shall walk on, unafraid,
> Safe with God as my guardian.

> Si sola solus per loca
> Inermis eam, ubi plurima
> Imago mortis territat,
> Interritus perrexero,
> Custode securus Deo.

On the other hand Flaminio sometimes makes a successful adaptation of the Hebrew poem to Latin verse, Horatian tradition, and contemporary taste. This is the case in his versions of psalms 13, 15, 114, 121, 122, 127, 128, 134, and 137. In his version of psalm 122, 'I was glad when they said unto me, Let us go into the house of the Lord,' Flaminio has succeeded in recapturing the joy of David on going up to Jerusalem; in psalm 127, 'Except the Lord build the house,' his complete reliance upon God; in psalm 128, 'Blessed *is* everyone that feareth the Lord,' Flaminio has expressed Jewish aspirations and ideals in Roman terms, with the moral odes of Horace's third book in mind:

> Blessed is he who has given himself in holy
> Servitude to God,
> Who is always ready to carry out what He commands
> In His most holy words.
> He does not cultivate his father's fields in vain,
> But his land gives back
> The seeds that it has received in its fertile bosom with
>     great
> Increase to the farmer.
> His chaste wife manages his home well[14] and adorns it
> With the best of children,
> Like a fertile vine which the diligent pruner
> Dresses carefully.
> New sons grow like green shoots
> On a fair olive,
> And the chattering crowd surround the table,

---

[14] This concern with domestic economy is typically Roman. David does not worry about it.

Filling the parents with joy.
This is the life of the good, with such
Rewards the kindness
Of their Father on high rewards them. If you worship
    Him,
You will joyfully enjoy
The good things of the sacred city, you will live
Long enough to see your children's
Children prosper, and blessed Happiness will reign
In your father's fields.

    Beatus ille qui piam sese Deo
        In servitutem dedit,
    Semper paratus exsequi sanctissimis
        Quod ille verbis imperat.
    Non is paterna rura inaniter colit;
        Sed quae feraci semina
    Sinu recepit fundus, illa maximo
        Reddit colenti foenore.
    Uxor pudica bene regit domum, et optimis
        Exornat ipsam liberis,
    Foecunda vitis instar, apta diligens
        Quam curat arte vinitor.
    Proles novella crescit, ut virentibus
        Oliva pulchra ramulis;
    Et mensa turba garrula circumdata
        Cumulat parentes gaudio.
    Haec est piorum vita; eosque talibus
        Remuneratur praemiis
    Summi benignitas patris; quem si coles,
        Urbis sacratae commodis
    Laetus frueris; usquedum vivas, tuae
        Prolis beatae liberos
    Florere cernes; patriis Felicitas
        Regnabit alma finibus.

Flaminio's version of the 137th psalm, 'By the rivers of Babylon, there we sat down . . . and wept,' comes as something of a shock. Here we have Flaminio really adapting his material to contemporary taste. He has made the lament of the Jews over their captivity into a pastoral, with the devastator of Jerusalem as the interlocutor. The poem lacks the emotional intensity of David, but it is quite successful in its own way.

Flaminio translated most of the psalms into iambic couplets. There is one in the pythiambic couplet, four in iambic trimeter, and six in iambic dimeter.

Flaminio occasionally left Trent in 1545–6 to visit friends in the neighbourhood. We have a poetic epistle to Jacopo Peregrino of Verona (V, 15) saying that he is leaving Trent the next day to go to see him.

There is also a letter written from Verona on May 12, 1546, to Luigi Priuli, at Trent.[15] Flaminio says that he has heard from Rome that he is going to be made a bishop. He begs Priuli to intercede with Signor Maffeo so that this does not happen. He does not want to be a bishop. He does not dedicate his works to get rewards, but in appreciation of past rewards. He could not, if he were made the richest man in the court, write to order in either prose or verse. He could not do it under the threat of punishment either. Only very occasionally has he been able to write at another's request. He wants to be free from all other gifts. The only thing he would like is his abbey freed of pensions. Every hour he feels his powers diminish. He cannot write. He would like to spend the little of life that remains to him with as little exertion as possible and content himself with the sufferings that God will send for his own good, without finding any for himself. Writing is a great travail. He is old. He wants no more studies. He wants to rest with the knowledge that Christ was crucified and that is all.

Flaminio's attitude towards offers of employment in the Church is curious. In an age when all artists worked for commission it is odd that Flaminio feels so strongly that he can do nothing without inspiration. Many commentators have suggested that this talk of inspiration is just a blind for Flaminio's Lutheran prejudices, that he did not want to accept church employment in the 1540's because he did not want to have to participate in the condemnation of doctrines in which he believed. It does not seem likely that this is true. Flaminio could not have known in advance what would be condemned and what not. There had been good hope of reconciliation with the Lutherans. Contarini had been very near to success in Ratisbon in 1541. In Trent in 1546 the miracle might have happened.

---

[15] Atanagi, *Lettere 13*, pp. 315–18.

Moreover, Flaminio had no particular reason to feel that his views were so very dangerous when he knew that many of the highest churchmen shared them. It seems more likely that Flaminio was unwilling to accept a steady job because he had become used to the client's position, and had never had the incentive to earn his own living, because he had, from the beginning, been able to keep himself without it, because he had been spoilt by early adulation, and because he did not have the health and the physical strength to give him the sustained drive to take on a long-term task. Flaminio seems to have had none of the ambition typical of the humanist. The only thing that he wanted was a comfortable income, and the freedom to do what he pleased. He liked to be able to live in the country, to study and write when he felt like it, and to enjoy lively and educated company.

On May 20, 1546, Cardinal Bembo wrote to Fracastoro from Rome. He sent his greetings to the three legates, to Priuli, and to 'the learned and pious and saintly poet, Messer Marcantonio Flaminio'.[16]

On June 28, 1546, Pole left Trent for ill health and never returned. He spent July and August in Priuli's house near Treviso.[17] At the beginning of September he went to Padua, where he stayed in Bembo's house. On October 27 he got a dispensation from the legation to Trent, and was called to Rome. He reached Rome just before the end of 1546. In the autumn of 1546, on the suspicion of the plague, as he affirmed, or for political motives, as the emperor suspected, the pope transferred the Council from the no-man's-land of Trent to his own city of Bologna.

Trent had brought Flaminio together again with his benefactor, Cardinal Alexander Farnese. A sheaf of occasional poems followed. In May, 1545, Farnese had been sent on a mission to Charles V in Germany. Flaminio described his passage over the Alps with allusions to Mercury and to the young Ascanius (II, 8). In 1546 Farnese found fifty-six fragments of the *fasti consulares et triumphales*, lists of the consuls and of the

[16] Bembo, Italian letter to G. Fracastoro in *Opera Fracastorii* (Bologna, 1739), I, p. 91.
[17] Flaminio's 'votum' to the breeze to cool Pole, ill in the heat of summer (I, 37), was probably written at this time.

triumphs of ancient Rome, in his excavations in the Forum. This find was of very great historical value and was celebrated by Flaminio in the epigram, 'Haec Saxa publicis notata litteris' (VI, 4). In July, 1546, Farnese led the papal forces over the Alps to the aid of Charles V. His illness in Germany, real or simulated, provoked two anxious epistles (V, 38 and 28) and an ode to celebrate his recovery (I, 45). Later an espistle to Maffeo and Mirandola told of the joy in Rome at the news that Farnese was returning safely (V, 9). Finally Flaminio collected poems by several hands praising Farnese and presented them to him with a dedicatory epistle (V, 1).

*Chapter 10*

# ROME TWENTY YEARS AFTER

FLAMINIO, too, went to Rome in the autumn of 1546. He stopped first of all with Mario Bandino,[1] then with Pole in his house near the Vatican. Flaminio seems to have been in good health in the beginning and to have enjoyed Rome tremendously. He wrote an enthusiastic letter in verse to Francesco Torelli of Forlì asking him how he could stay away from Rome, the most noble city that the sun has looked or ever will look upon (VI, 32).

However, Flaminio soon had a hard blow to bear. On February 25, 1547, he wrote a letter to Caterina Cibo, Duchess of Camerino, whom he had known in Florence in 1541, consoling her on the death of her daughter. This letter is full of piety and intense spirituality and is written in a rush of feeling that one finds nowhere else in Flaminio. There are no sentences. When we come to the end we understand. As a postscript Flaminio has added, 'On this same day, at eighteen hours, the Signora Marchesa [of Pescara, i.e., Vittoria Colonna] left the world with such a joyful spirit, and with such faith, that we must not honour her death with other tears than those born of sweetness, and of pure and holy joy.'[2]

[1] Flaminio, V, 18, told Mario Bandino that he would stay with him for ten days on condition that he was not pressed to stay longer.
[2] Feliciangeli, *Caterina Cibo* (Camerino, 1891), pp. 231-4. For the account of her death see Amante, pp. 350-1.

Despite this loss, however, Flaminio found Rome good at this time. He again frequented the old literary circles meeting in gardens. Now it seems to have been Biagio Pallai who dominated the scene. He had splendid gardens climbing up a hill behind the Vatican. In the bottom of a valley, a sunny fountain was surrounded by marble seats placed among shady laurels. From here a broad alley, roofed by thick vines, led through fruit trees of all sorts to a slope covered with a grove of perfumed lemon trees. On top of the hill were two marble pools and above them a terrace where Pallai gave his dinner parties. In the centre was a fountain in the shape of a theatre with columns supporting shady vines. On either side were fountains falling from the rock, which was made to look like the stalactites of Tivoli. These fountains irrigated the lemon trees. Beside these fountains were little houses which served as kitchens. A hill rose on the left, covered with a grove of laurels whose berries attracted large numbers of birds. Near the house chickens, ducks, and peacocks wandered about.[3]

Under the stimulus of Pallai and his circle Flaminio found the inclination to write humanist poetry again. He had always shone in lively, witty company. Pallai had written a series of clever poems praising a feed called 'turunda', which he used to catch thrushes. These poems had circulated in cultivated circles in Rome and were much admired. Flaminio entered into the spirit of the thing and himself wrote a collection of poems on 'turunda'.[4] These poems were built around a witty conceit. Flaminio pictures 'turunda' as a country wench whom Pallai has discovered and dressed up and introduced to Roman society. Like Lorelei Lee, Turunda tells how she got on, and the protégée's tone is often amusing. Turunda's meteoric success lands her on Olympus, where we have a kind of apotheosis.

Flaminio's epigram on Cardinal Rodolfo Pio's fountain in the Quirinal gardens (II, 13) was probably written at this time, as were some dozen and a half occasional poems, most of them interesting for the information that they give about Flaminio's life in this period. It is spring, and Flaminio is think-

[3] Gnoli, 'Orti', p. 28.
[4] For the inspiration of Pallai's 'turunda' poems in getting him to write again see V, 42 and 36. Flaminio's 'turunda' poems are I, 55–64.

ing of leaving Rome for San Prospero.[5] He sends his Muse as messenger to his neighbour there, Ercole Severoli of Faenza. Will he leave Rome, too (VI, 18)?

It is summer, and Flaminio is waiting for Matteo Dandolo to come to Rome from Venice. What is keeping him? The blandishments of his wife? But it is not as though he were going to Germany. Rome is only three days' ride from Venice (VI, 13).[6] Dandolo apparently came to Rome, because an epistle, which must have been written in the summer of 1547 shortly after the poem to Dandolo, complains that Donato Rullo did not come with Dandolo, as had been expected (VI, 14). Rullo was presumably at this time with Morone in Bologna.

Flaminio had been very enthusiastic about life in Rome, but, as the summer wore on, he became restless. He wrote a beautiful ode to his farm (I, 15), full of an almost hopeless yearning, that suggests Ronsard's 'A la Fontaine Bellerie'. How he would like to return to its peace and coolness, to its chattering springs and rustling branches! How he would like to milk a goat with his own hand and quench his thirst with her milk! He prays to the Muses to rescue him from the noisy and tumultuous city.[7]

---

[5] The property that Flaminio refers to must be San Prospero since his neighbour is Ercole Severoli, who comes from Faenza. The poem refers to leaving Rome; therefore, it must have been written at a time when Flaminio possessed San Prospero (i.e., after 1536) and when he was resident in Rome. The only possible springs are those of 1547, 1548, and 1549. We know that Flaminio was ill in the springs of 1548 and 1549. Therefore the date must be 1547. But he did not get away that spring as he had hoped.

[6] This poem must have been written in the summer of 1547 because Flaminio was in Civitella in the summers of 1548 and 1549. Another poem to Dandolo (V, 12), which may have been written earlier this year, tells how Flaminio enjoyed the winters that he spent as his guest, chatting by the fireside, and how much he misses him now. He asks for letters. The time referred to in the poem must be the 1530's, when Flaminio was living in Verona, close to Venice. It appears that the poem itself was written about 1547 because Flaminio refers in it to his move to Rome.

[7] This poem could only have been written in 1547 because it was published in 1548 and refers to a summer when Flaminio was in Rome. Also the vocabulary would suggest the date 1547. The adjective 'discolor' to describe the grass occurs only here and in one of the Turunda poems (I, 56) which must have been written about this time since it was published in *Carm. 5* in 1548, while the adjective 'tumultuosa' is used of Rome only in poems of this period. The description of the farm fits San Prospero. Cf. the other San Prospero poems, I, 22, 17; III, 1, 2; VI, 2, 3, 5, 6, 7; I, 46–54.

A little later he wrote a hendecasyllabic epistle to his old friend, Lodovico Beccadelli, with whom he had spent so many happy summers at Pradalbino in the old days, asking him why they were both staying in Rome instead of going to Pradalbino and the Val di Lavino (VI, 17). He also wrote an envious epistle to Onorato Fascitelli, who was in the country, telling him that he was stuck in Rome, and asking him to send what he had written (V, 33).

The summer passed. With autumn Flaminio's eagerness to leave Rome increased. He wrote an epistle in pythiambic couplets to Antonio Mirandula suggesting that they both set out for the benefice that Mirandula had just received from Farnese at Dovadola on the road that leads over the Apennines from Florence to Forlì (I, 21). Another epistle (V, 35) would suggest that Flaminio did, in fact, make this trip. It is written from San Prospero, which is only twenty-two miles from Dovadola. It is an invitation to Nicolo Ormaneto to come to visit him in the country.

This same year, when Flaminio appears to have enjoyed continuous good health and unwonted vigour and good spirits, he wrote a lively and humorous epistle to his old friend Galeazzo Florimonte of Sessa, now with Morone and Cervini in Bologna (I, 26).[8] Florimonte was a funny fellow and inspired funny poems. Flaminio wrote him an eclogue (V, 8), an epistle (I, 26), and an epigram (VI, 60), all three of them comic, the eclogue, the most serious of the three, through the use of the mock-heroic, the other two through cheerful insults to Florimonte's poetry. Flaminio wrote many other poetic epistles to friends at this time.[9]

The only prose letter of the period which has survived is one which Flaminio wrote on December 31, 1547, 'to a certain lady of princely family'.[10] It shows that Flaminio's religious

[8] This poem must have been written in 1547 because Cervini moved to Bologna only at the end of 1546 when the Council, of which he was then president, was transferred there. Morone had been in Bologna as legate from 1545. The poem could not be later than the beginning of 1548 because it was published in the spring of 1548. Since Flaminio was ill early in 1548 and the poem is very cheerful and makes no mention of illness it was probably written in 1547.

[9] See, e.g., V, 40; VI, 31; VI, 22; V, 17; VI, 21; V, 2; V, 23; VI, 15.

[10] Atanagi, *Lettere 13*, pp. 318–23.

views have not changed. It also reveals that, despite the fact that he lived in the age of viragoes and associated with them, his views of women's capacities were very conservative. Flaminio had apparently rebuked the lady for her harsh criticism of a preacher, and she had taken his criticism in good part. Flaminio is relieved, and thanks God for her humility. He feels a great repugnance to the office of monitor, and had only admonished her for this because it is the duty that man owes to man to try to help his fellow to perfection. We are all weak and imperfect. It is a sign of God's grace to be able to accept correction that is offered in affection. Man himself is completely depraved, every good thing that appears in him is the work of Christ. Through the means of faith he regenerates his elect. Man is more perfect and noble the more he realizes that he is nothing in himself but everything in Christ. ...

> But sometimes the flesh, in the guise of zeal, leads us to errors. The special error of the day is to declaim everywhere on theological subjects and to be bitter critics of preachers. This is reprehensible in men, but intolerable in women who should not teach, themselves, but learn in silence. The Church of Christ is like the court of a great prince. Each one has his place and duty. The whole is disorganized and no longer functions smoothly if one tries to perform another's duty. Each man serves God best by staying modestly within the bounds set for him, by keeping his condition. A woman's duty is to be chaste, sober, and obedient to her husband, to educate her sons in the fear of God, to govern diligently her house and family, to be modest in speech, in dress, and in all her conversation, doing all her work for the glory of God and for the benefit of her neighbour. Her whole life should be a sacrifice to God. This is the best sermon of all. Men are converted by example.
>
> To do this one needs the help of the Holy Spirit. Therefore we must always pray for it, to be able to say with the Apostle, 'I no longer live, but it is Christ who lives in me. To whom be glory everlasting.' Amen.

Flaminio was never again to know such a good year as 1547. In the spring of 1548 he fell ill.[11] An elegy to the Christ child

[11] A letter to Ulisse Bassiano, dated May 27, 1548 (Atanagi, *Lettere 13*, pp. 339–40), tells us that Flaminio is beginning to get better. An earlier epistle in hendecasyllables (V, 7) written to Bassiano tells him that he is ill with a fever and asks him to visit him. This epistle was published by the middle of 1548 in *Carm. 5* (Venice).

(VIII, 22), added to the *Carmina Sacra* by the publisher Torrentino in the 1552 edition of *Carm.* 5, was probably written at this time. It tells of Flaminio's fever and chills and prays for health, or strength to bear his suffering cheerfully. A hendecasyllabic epistle addressed to Pietro Carnesecchi, one of the poems to Carnesecchi that Mancurti suppressed in his effort to free Flaminio from the taint of heresy,[12] tells how Flaminio was cured by a Greek doctor called Emanuele Chio. Flaminio tells Carnesecchi that now his fever, with its thirst, is abating and that he is beginning to be able to sleep. Now he feels like eating again, and wine tastes less bitter. He takes no more poisonous drugs, but is being treated with massage and a light diet. He thinks it doubtful that a better or more experienced doctor exists. Certainly there is none kinder or less mercenary, who treats his patients with the affectionate devotion of a parent, or a child, or as though they were his brothers. Chio is a doctor in the Hippocratic tradition.

By May Flaminio was well enough to write poetry. A letter which he must, on internal evidence, have written from Rome about that time tells us about his manner of composition:

To M. Ulisse Bassiano:

I do not know whether you will laugh at my madness or rather pity me. Messer Vicenzo Geri writes my verses! This good young fellow came into my room yesterday, looking very serious, and he asked me how many epistles I thought I'd written. I told him forty-two. 'You're wrong,' he said, 'there are forty-six, and I am telling you this so that you'll be encouraged to persist until fifty.' I laughed and said that if he had stayed up as many nights as I had he wouldn't treat me so badly, persuading me to continue going without sleep. And he said, 'Oh Messer Marcantonio, stay up again tonight and somehow or other get to fifty.' And so I stayed up last night, I never closed my eyes, 'I let poetic passion rage,' and I began with him to give him good for evil [V, 46]. Then, I remembered that Marcantonio Faita, the cardinal's [Pole's] assistant, would be upset if I didn't honour him equally with his comrade, particularly since he'd written much to me. Therefore I wrote him his little letter [V, 47]. Then I remembered Triphon

---

[12] Published in *Carm.* 5 (1548, 1549, 1552), in the last edition on pp. 214–15. Since this poem was published in 1548 it must refer to the 1548 and not to the 1549 illness.

Bentio so celebrated by Molza, an old friend and a faithful defender of my verse. I wrote him his [V, 48], joking with him, because he's the sort of person who can take it. I came to the fiftieth—to whom should I write it? To Fracastoro, who cured me once of a very serious, almost hopeless attack of fever [V, 49].[13] And so I had no sleep all night. How vain we are, I most of all! However, I am happy to have lost this night to show, as best I can, my affection to these other four friends. But the greatest man in the world couldn't persuade me another time to break my firm resolution not to stay up any more to write verses. Now you must see them and go over them with your accustomed diligence. I will send them this afternoon . . . and you will note on a piece of paper everything that you don't like.[14]

Then Flaminio goes on to discuss 'stupet in aliquo',[15] a phrase that Ulisse Bassiano had apparently queried. This is a Vergilian expression used of Pallas, who 'stupet in Turno'. It is stronger than 'admirari'. He uses it of Signor Stefano [Sauli] who looks at the ornaments and beauties of Cicero and 'stupet'. He asks Ulisse Bassiano to kiss the Reverend Signor Stefano's hand for him. He would have come to lunch with Signor Stefano this morning, but he wants to have a bit more sleep today than usual and he does not want to talk much.

As I have remarked earlier (*supra*, p. 163), it appears that the poem to Francastoro (V, 49, of the standard edition) was an old piece that was thrown in to make up the number. It seems that the epistle to Marcantonio Faita (V, 47) must also have been made up from material that Flaminio had at hand, for the subject of the epistle is the death of Vittorio Colonna, which took place in February, 1547. Since the letter begs Faita to console Flaminio for Vittoria's 'bitter' death it seems unlikely that this poem was suddenly struck off in the middle of a

[13] The four poems to which Flaminio refers here are numbers 46-9 of book 5 of the Cominian edition. They were numbers 48-51 of the fifth book as it was originally published in *Carm. 5* in Venice in 1548 and in Florence in 1549 and 1552, but Mancurti dropped two epistles to Carnesecchi from the final (1743) edition of Flaminio's poems. Thus Vicenzo Geri was either wrong in his count or Flaminio or his publisher added one epistle to the earlier part of the book before it was printed.

[14] Atanagi, *Lettere 13*, pp. 337-9.

[15] Used in the epistle written to Cristoforo Longolio from Genoa in 1521 (V, 28).

busy night some fifteen months later. On the other hand the poem, like all of Flaminio's obituaries, including the other one on Vittoria Colonna (V, 4), is heavily indebted to the classics and seems artificial and lacking in feeling.

That leaves us with the epistles to Vicenzo Geri and Tryphon Bentio (V, 46 and 48), which probably were written that night. They consist of twenty-seven and twenty-six lines respectively, of very competent occasional verse. Neither of these epistles is exceptional for its cleverness or invention, but both are easy and pleasant to read. Flaminio is the sort of man who would have made an excellent after-dinner speaker. He always had something appropriate and often amusing to say, and the words came easily. Indeed Flaminio was much sought after as a conversationalist.

A second letter written to Ulisse Bassiano on May 27, 1548, is headed 'Civitella,' apparently Civitella San Paolo, which is about twenty-five miles up the Tiber from Rome in the hills on the right bank.[16] This second letter to Bassiano[17] replies to some criticisms that Bassiano has made of Flaminio's poems. It is a warm, friendly, tolerant, and intelligent letter:

To M. Ulisse Bassiano. Civitella, May 27, 1548.

Wonderful Messer Ulisse, my dearest and honoured friend: Although I have received the licence to use 'merere' in the meaning which I explained to you in my previous letter and although I feel certain that it can be used in that way, nevertheless, I have decided to use another expression in its place, which is in no way controversial, because it seems to me that it isn't good to use very rare expressions that can give rise to discussion. And for the same reason I have also changed that 'in quam nupta fuit', because that expression appeared strange not only to you, but also to Messer Basilio, and it would appear that way to almost everyone. When I got your letter I had already satisfied your desire as to Faerno, satisfied I say in that I made honourable mention of him in my

---

[16] L. Alberti, *Descriptio Italiae*, fol. 75ʳ and Cuccoli, p. 125, fn. 1. Pio Paschini, *Un Amico del Cardinale Polo: Alvise Priuli* (Rome, n.d.), p. 99, cites a letter that Pole wrote on June 6, 1549, from Civitella San Paolo to the papal nuncio in France in which he enclosed greetings from Flaminio and Priuli. It is on the basis of this letter that I have identified Flaminio's Civitella with Civitella San Paolo.

[17] Atanagi, *Lettere 13*, pp. 339–40.

verses,[18] ... I am sending you them along with some others which I have written in part to satisfy certain other dear friends of mine. But you should not believe now that I want to go on for ever, that to satisfy all my friends 'I would write long Iliads'. I have reached the fiftieth and I don't want to go beyond. I am telling you this so that you won't get the urge to suggest any other new subject to me. I have done my part in accordance with my frail powers. Now you do yours, since your age is far more fit for it than mine. Would you read diligently these verses of mine, and would you let me know what corrections you think should be made? I am beginning, through the grace of God, to get better, and to feel the benefit of this air. Recommend me to your most kind host and to the Reverend Father Don Honorato. Don't say anything to Faerno about the hendecasyllable. Farewell in God.

In these last two years of his life (1548–9) Flaminio seems to have been preparing himself consciously for immortality. He tried to get his poetry into final form by submitting it to the criticism, not only of his young friends Ulisse Bassiano and Basilio Zanchi, but also to the criticism of Lelio and Ippolito Capilupo,[19] called the modern Quintilians. Even some of the earliest pieces were discussed and revised. He also seems to have tried to leave poetic memorials to all of his friends. He mentions one hundred and twenty-seven of them in his verse, and most of these people were recipients of whole poems. Moreover, during this period Flaminio tried to explain his poetry and to make clear what his aims and principles had been.

Flaminio's critical letters show him to have been a creative classicist. He believed in following the ancients, because only in their works could one find the pure and uncorrupted Latin tradition. But he believed that Latin was a living language, and therefore capable of continuous development. How could anyone feel otherwise in the midst of that tremendously rich flowering of Latin literature that took place in the Renaissance in Italy?

Flaminio wrote a very interesting letter against the Ciceronians, that is those who believed that a modern writer could

[18] VI, 33. In this epistle Flaminio thanks Cardinals Cervini and Sfondrati for giving his friend Faerno a benefice which will enable him to live comfortably.

[19] See the epistle addressed to the two brothers asking for their criticism of his poems, V, 51.

use only the words that the ancients had used, in extreme cases only the inflected forms that were actually found in ancient texts. The letter was written to Basilio Zanchi and was undated.[20] Flaminio supports the right of the modern to innovate, with enthusiastic firmness, in clear and logical argument. Zanchi had apparently advised Flaminio to change the epithet, 'floricomum', 'with flowers in her hair', which Flaminio had used of spring in one of his earliest odes, the second ode to Guido Postumo published in 1515, an ode which was not destined to be republished until the eighteenth century.[21] Flaminio disagreed with Zanchi' objection to 'floricomum' and gave his reasons: Zanchi's criticisms imply either that new words cannot be created—but this is contrary to the judgment and practice of the great ancients, Aristotle, Cicero, and Horace, who all approve of neologism, and even teach how one should go about it—or that neologism, while permitted to the ancients, is not permitted to us—but Horace said, 'Licuit, semperque licebit/Signatum praesente nota procudere nomen.'

Some people argue that neologism was permitted when the Latin language was not lost, but that it is not permitted now. But Latin is not lost today. If so, how is it that we write it? How is it lost when its beauties are preserved in so much prose and verse? How is it lost when these beauties are not only understood today, but used? How is it lost when today one writes better than since the age of Caesar and Augustus? He will go farther and maintain that today many understand and use more the propriety and beauty of the Latin language than the majority of Roman gentlemen did at the time of Caesar and Augustus. Why? The reason is obvious: today we learn from Cicero and Caesar and the other masters of the Latin language whereas they learnt from their servants and from the people—we have Cicero's authority for this.

The Latin language is preserved today, known, and used by many who have formed themselves on the best stylists. Therefore, why should we not have the same right to innovate as the ancients? Why should it be counted to our discredit what was always praised in the ancients?

[20] Atanagi, *Lettere 13*, pp. 324-30.
[21] It was among the poems from various sources that Mancurti added to the end of Flaminio's second book, II, 33.

Of those who admit neologism, some argue that it is permissible only when the word is necessary, i.e., when it is needed to express new philosophical or theological concepts, but not when it is decorative. But the ancients invented purely decorative words—Flaminio gives a long list of compound descriptive adjectives analogous to his 'floricomus'.

The best way to form new words is from two roots. These compound words make one's writing very pretty and flowery and have much significance, since two concepts are embodied in one word. Forbidding poets the right to form new words for ornament would do them great injury.

But everyone should not be creating new words. It requires excellent judgment. The rest of the piece must be such as to give authority to the new word placed in it like a star. Moreover, one should be sparing with neologisms and should see to it that they harmonize in structure with the neologisms of the best writers. He cites for praise Navagero's 'silvipotens' on analogy with the ancient 'ignipotens', 'armipotens'.

As for 'floricomus': Vergil observed that a predecessor had formed 'lauricomus', and on analogy created 'auricomus', and someone else, 'silvicomus'. Why is 'floricomus' less laudable? Is it not a lovely image for spring? Is it not a sonorous word? He finds it very pretty and he cannot imagine that it does not strike Zanchi the same way.

Now Flaminio handles the possible objection that if a neologism were so beautiful the ancients would have created it. This is not true, because each poet has his particular originality.

He has dilated on the subject to such an extent because he considers it of the highest importance to poets. He also wanted Zanchi to understand that it was through no lack of respect for his judgment that he decided to retain 'floricomus'—that is why he wrote, so that Zanchi could meditate his arguments—but through a firm conviction that one is allowed to disagree on literary matters and remain friends.

We see here that Flaminio, despite his rather romantic habits of composition by night and only, with the exception of the four hendecasyllabic epistles which he wrote at Vicenzo Geri's urging, when the mood is upon him, carefully thought out what he was doing and was very definitely a conscious artist weighing the effect of words. He thought logically, clearly, and independently. He was able to take criticism, and to defer to his friends when he felt that they were right, but he remained politely firm when he felt that his own judgment and instinct were sound. He was never violent or strident in argument, but he brought up possible objections and met them and, with gentle humour, mocked his opponents out of existence.

1548 was a big year for Flaminio. In that year his nephew, Cesare Flaminio, published two books of his uncle's poems, and the verse translation of the psalms in Lyons, the chancellor of the University of Paris, Jean Gagny, published fifty-nine of the lyrics in Paris[22] in his anthology of humanist poetry, *Doctissimorum nostra aetate Italorum Epigrammata* (Flaminio, Molza, Navagero, Cotta, Lampridio, Sadoleto, etc.); and Flaminio was given pride of place in the edition of *Carmina Quinque Illustrium Poetarum* (Bembo, Navagero, Castiglione, Cotta, and Flaminio) published in Venice. Moreover his *Explanation* of the psalms, accompanied by the prose translations, was republished in Lyons in 1548.

The Lyons edition of Flaminio's poems, published by Gryphius, was prefaced by a letter by Cesare Flaminio, dated October 13, 1547. In this letter Cesare said that he was publishing two books of lyrics, which his uncle had corrected and arranged and sent to Francesco della Torre, who had died last year, together with his verse translations of thirty of the psalms. Cesare says that Flaminio had refused to give permission for the publication of these youthful exercises of his, which were unbecoming a man of almost fifty.

The largest group of new poems in the Lyons edition was the book of *lusus pastorales*, about the unhappy love of Hyella for Iolas, which was written in Caserta in the spring of 1540, hardly when Flaminio was a youth, though before his religious conversion. There were, in all, twenty-nine new poems in the Lyons edition, twenty-three pastorals and six other poems.

Gagny's Paris edition contained another twenty-three new poems. However, all but one of these were epigrams of little importance and of very early date. Some thirteen were written before 1530, two or three before 1520. The only new poem in the Paris edition which was not an epigram was the hexameter

[22] Actually sixty lyrics, but numbers 17 and 60 are identical epigrams to Molza.

epistle written to Fracastoro in 1528 asking him to cure him, 'FRACASTORI venerande, anima mihi carior ipsa', which has already been discussed (*supra*, pp. 88-9 and 163). However, the Paris edition republished two of the 1529 amorous epigrams written at Serravalle in 1526: on whether or not he should snatch a kiss from Nigella and on Nigella's sitting on his knee, poems that were published in all the sixteenth-century editions of Flaminio but that were omitted by Mancurti from his definitive edition of Flaminio's poems along with everything else that might detract from the saintly character of Flaminio that he was seeking to establish. In addition, the Paris edition republished all but one of the *lusus pastorales* about the Hyella-Iolas love story and all but five of the other poems published in Lyons. Since Gagny did not republish the verse versions of the psalms, the result of this selection was that Gagny represented Flaminio as being a pastoral love poet above all else.

However, the most important selection of Flaminio's poems that appeared in 1548 was the one in *Carmina Quinque Illustrium Poetarum*, where Flaminio was given by far the largest representation. Whereas only two books of his poems had been published in Lyons and Paris, four books and the verse translations of the psalms were published in this Venetian anthology. That is, the Venetian edition published a whole new book of twenty-four early pastorals and a whole new book of fifty-three poetic epistles, as well as sundry new miscellaneous poems. Now virtually all the poetry that has so far been discussed in the biography was published.

In the winter of 1548-9 Flaminio fell ill again. He apparently suffered from malaria, which attacked him in the bad weather. From his account of things, it would appear that the parasite had now infested his spleen. We find the first reference to this illness in a letter that Flaminio wrote to Galeazzo Florimonte, now Bishop of Aquino, from Rome, on February 22, 1549.[23] However, a poem that could not have been written later than mid-April, 1549, states that he is now in the fifth month of his illness (VIII, 13). In that case Flaminio must have fallen ill in December, as he was to the following winter.

[23] Atanagi, *Lettere 13*, pp. 330-7.

The letter to Florimonte is extremely important for its statement of Flaminio's poetic principles. Apparently Florimonte had attacked Flaminio's poetry, undoubtedly partly in fun, and Flaminio replies here good-humouredly in his own defence. He will not attack Florimonte in a 'scazon', as he wants him to. He is not so enamoured of his own compositions as to attack those who do not like them. He does not like some of the poems of the most famous writers, Horace, Catullus, Propertius. Therefore why should he think it strange if someone does not like his? He did not know whether to answer Florimonte's objections. He would gladly have kept silence, but he was afraid that Florimonte might consider this pride, and a scorn for his opinion, since men who were, objectively speaking, more qualified judges than Florimonte praised his verses.

Well then, Florimonte's criticisms of Flaminio's poetry were threefold, that the material was trite, that there was little invention, and that the style lacked poetic spirit. Flaminio accepts all these criticisms as genuine, but maintains that they are unimportant. If he is trite, then so is Homer, Sophocles, Euripides. What about Horace's first ode, or the one on the death of Quintilius? As to the second point, is poetry really better for being adorned with rare conceits, subtle, recherché, and far removed from the common intelligence? Then you would prefer Ovid, Statius, Martial, and Claudian to Homer, Hesiod, Theocritus, Vergil, Catullus, and Tibullus. If you compare the dialogue of Homer with that of Ovid, you find that Homer's characters almost never use conceits outside those of common parlance. Therefore, every mediocre poet says he could do as well. On the other hand, Ovid's characters exhibit such ingenious, subtle, and out-of-the-way cleverness, that even a great talent has to confess that he would have the greatest difficulty in equalling him. Homer and the other first-rate poets did not write simply through want of genius and invention, but through sound judgment, for a poem delights more the closer it is based on expressions of common usage. Only inferior poets write in an exotic style.

As to the third point, that his style lacks poetic spirit, he tells Florimonte that when he has more taste and more knowledge of the beauties of the Latin language and of poetry, and when he examines carefully the means and ways he uses to present his conceits, he is firmly convinced that he will not find his epistle so devoid of poetic spirit as he finds it now. The excellence of a poet consists in his expressing common ideas in uncommon, but not bizarre, forms and manners. He who can do this rouses the admiration of him who has a taste for poetry. He cites examples of what he means from Vergil's *Georgics*.

He did not write in his own hand because he took a drug the day before and he could not have written so legibly.

Flaminio tells of the onset of his disease in an epistle to Giulio Sauli (VI, 53). When Flaminio was consoling Sauli's mother while the young man lay dangerously ill with a fever, suddenly he felt a pain in his left side, and a parching fever swept through his body, like the fierce flame that lays hold of an ancient wood and swallows everything up.

Although he was very ill this spring, Flaminio wrote as never before. Everyone flocked to see the great poet, who apparently lay dying, and Flaminio rewarded with hendecasyllabic epistles those who came to visit him and who hastened to do him favours before it should be too late. He wrote twenty epistles about his illness to various people, as well as four epistles to his three doctors and a general letter to all his friends (VI, 35–59), and the joking hendecasyllabic that we now expect to Galeazzo Florimonte about the epitaph that Florimonte supposedly had ready (VI, 60). All this is competent, fluent, occasional verse of the highest quality and reveals Flaminio's extraordinary ability to treat the same theme over and over again with a variety that seems in no way sought after. He also wrote an elegy to the sleep that he wooed, warm, witty, and humorous (VI, 62), and a whole book of religious poetry (VIII) the like of which is found only in the early centuries of Christianity.

In a brief epistle to Alberto Lino (VI, 35), Flaminio tells of writing one of his religious lyrics while he was suffering from the pain in his side. He says that he was not trying to gain the applause of learned men, but he was worshipping God, who thought that a man spoke elegantly when he spoke devoutly. If Lino preferred the opinion of proud critics, who would consider his verses inelegant, then he need not read them. In the poetic dedication of the *Carmina Sacra* to Marguerite de Valois (VIII, 1), Flaminio tells her that he wrote these poems while he was suffering from a long-lasting fever. In his dedicatory epistle in prose, he is more specific. He says that he wrote these poems when he was ill for months with a quartan fever, and he promises her more of the like, if he recovers.

The *Carmina Sacra* were found among Flaminio's papers after his death and sent by Priuli to Carnesecchi, then at the French court in the service of Catherine de'Medici. Carnesecchi presented the poems in manuscript to Mme Marguerite, Henry II's sister, to whom they were addressed. He then persuaded Robert Stephanus to publish them. At his trial Carnesecchi told how he went to Stephanus' shop,

> both to make his acquaintance, since he was a famous man and excellent in his profession, and partly also to sound him out as to whether he wished to print certain hymns of Flaminio, *De rebus divinis*, composed by him shortly before his death, and when he was ill, and addressed to Mme Marguerite, sister of the king and now Duchess of Savoy, with a dedicatory epistle to her. I barely obtained his assent, since he appeared, I don't know why, to have a small opinion of them. But I think this was because it was a small work and one that would earn very little, and that he was busy with other things that were more important. However, despite all this he published them.[24]

The *Carmina Sacra* are written in the iambic dimeter, the metre of St. Ambrose and of the medieval Church. And, with the music of the early Church Flaminio has re-created its atmosphere. Gone are all traces of humanism and the frippery of classical poetry. Flaminio is classical only as St. Ambrose was. His *Sacred Poems* opens with morning prayer,

> Now Lucifer, herald of kindly
> Day, drives the shadows of night
> From earth and sky, and doing so
> Bids us abandon our beds
> And pour forth prayer from the depths
> Of our hearts to the heights of heaven. . . .

> Jam noctis umbras Lucifer
> Almae diei nuntius
> Terra poloque dimovet,
> Simulque nos cubilibus

[24] Manzoni, 'Processo Carnesecchi', p. 360.

> Monet relictis, pectore
> Preces ab imo fundere
> Ad templa summa caelitum. . . .
>                                    VIII, 2

The noonday prayer (VIII, 3) asks God to warm cold hearts, as the sun warms the earth, that all worldy things may seem sordid to them and that, volatilized by the heat of their love, they may fly across the expanse of heaven to join themselves in an insoluble bond with their Father on high. In the evening prayer (VIII, 4) the bedridden poet, watching the rhythm of light and dark, prays, as he sees the evening star rise and night descend, that night may not descend also upon his soul. May the eternal light never recede from the hearts of the devout.

Then we come to prayers that arise more specifically from his disease. Flaminio asks Jesus to hear him (VIII, 5). As the earth gapes open for rain in the heat of the sun, so his soul, afflicted, weak, and thirsty, pants for manna from heaven, God's sweetest refreshment. 'O my Saviour, cool my spirit. Change the fears, the pains, the tears to eternal joy, that your praise may take the place of these sobbing laments and that my voice may ring out day and night in songs of thanksgiving. And I pray, do not judge my acts, my words, my thoughts,[25] but wash away all my sins with your blood.[26] May the pain of your wounds cure me; may the bitterness of your death fill my heart with sweetness, that I may have the strength, willingly, to bear my cross.'

The image of the thirsty soul is developed further in one of Flaminio's greatest lyrics (VIII, 7):

> As the tender flower in the bosom
> Of a kindly earth unfolds
> Its shining blossom in beauty,
> If it is nourished by dew and rain,
> So my tender soul
> Flourishes when it is fed
> On the sweet dew of the kindly Spirit.
> If it lacks it, it wilts straightaway,
> Like a flower that has sprung up
> In arid soil, if it is not
> Nourished by dew and rain.

[25] See Flaminio's comment on psalm 6.
[26] A possible allusion to the doctrine of justification by faith alone. The *Carmina Sacra*, too, were for a time on the Index.

Ut flos tenellus in sinu
Telluris almae lucidam
Formosus explicat comam,
Si ros et imber educat
Illum; tenella mens mea
Sic floret, almi Spiritus
Dum rore dulci pascitur.
Hoc illa si caret, statim
Languescit; ut flos arida
Tellure natus, eum nisi
Et ros, et imber educat.

Here the imagery and the language are extraordinarily simple, yet extremely beautiful, and the comparison of the soul to the weak and ephemeral flower, with its allusion to the psalmist, is perfectly fitted to express the adoration of the Christian who feels that his soul is nothing in itself, but everything in Christ. The Italianate diminutive 'tenellus' adds to the delicacy and dependence of the flower-soul and to the warmth of the expression of devotion. The poem, although it consists solely in the application of the flower simile, is full of imagery that suggests the mother-child relationship. 'Tenellus' refers to something that is young and soft and delicate; 'sinu' is the word for 'bosom'; 'almus' means 'nourishing', 'feeding'; 'educare' is the verb regularly used of bringing up children; 'pascere' means 'to feed'; 'natus' means born. The poem gains greatly from the emotions elicited by such overtones. We feel the dependence of the soul on God as that of the child on his mother. It looks to God for its drink as the baby looks to the breast of its mother and, of course, as the flower looks to the sky.

The simple imagery of this lyric, the comparison of the soul to the simple, everyday flower, the simple vocabulary, and the repetition of the same few simple words all reinforce the impression of the child-like simplicity of the soul. In this brief devotional lyric Flaminio has captured the spirit of the teaching of Jesus. We remember the parable of the lilies of the field and Jesus' warning, 'Except ye become as little children....'

Other lyrics are more theological or philosophical: Blessed is he who picks up his cross daily and strides at Jesus' side (VIII, 6); How vain are the things of the world, beauty, wealth, intelligence, only Jesus offers happiness (VIII, 8); May I always remember that Jesus left heaven for earth, that I may leave earth for heaven (VIII, 9); Leave all to follow Jesus, and Jesus will never leave you (VIII, 10); He sighs with love for Jesus, all day, all night, at home, outside (VIII, 11); He hymns Jesus, the creator and the redeemer (VIII, 12).

In the thirteenth lyric Flaminio describes his illness. Now the fifth moon is waxing to the full since his emaciated body has been consumed with fever. He trembles with chills, then burns with fierce fever like a dry torch that has been set on fire. He has lost so much weight that he is barely a shadow of himself. His spirit is bowed beneath the burden of misfortune, like a flower in a rainstorm. He prays Jesus to lift him up. He does not now pray that the disease leave his body, but only that Jesus give him strength and endurance . . . and that his mind remain vigorous and strong, through His Spirit, so that it may always sing His praises joyfully. Jesus is kind and good and has suffered horribly himself. Therefore He is prompt to succour those who are in pain. He bids his soul lay down its bitterness and fears and complaints with faith and call upon the sweetest name of its king. He is a tower of strength to those who call upon him.

In the following piece (VIII, 14) Flaminio grieves that he is old, that his hair is thin and greying, that his life is slipping by like the water of a river, and that pale death plucks at his ear, warning him, yet he, wretched creature, still pursues dreams and vain shadows. He is about to appear before the tribunal of the supreme judge, yet his mind is still fixed on worldly things. He prays Jesus to hold out His hand to him, to save him while he is still alive.

The last eight lyrics become more intensely emotional and concentrate, in baroque fashion, on Jesus' sufferings and the poet's love. In number 15, Flaminio prays to Jesus to feed him on the holy blood of His wounds, which gives him strength and fills him with sweet joy. 'This is the goblet of heavenly love . . . my mind, drunk with drinking it, forgets itself and all worldly things and thinks only of God and of your love. . . . Love, you lead the son of God on high down from the seats of heaven and you clothe Him in mortal body, which you then place on the bitter cross. Lovable, sweetest love, stir up such great flames of love in my heart that they burn these heavy bonds of body, that I may fly on your wings, in blessedness, to the best of Jesuses.'

In the sixteenth lyric Flaminio prays God that he may not think, do, or say anything that is displeasing to Him, that he may be friendly and kindly to good and evil alike, following the example of the best of fathers who lights all with the life-giving light of His sun, and gives to all food and drink. The seventeenth lyric is very interesting because it tells of his conversion or possibly reconversion from something bordering on Lutheran heresy to orthodox Catholicism. The poet asks Jesus how he can thank Him for saving him. 'Once I wandered from the flock like a miserable sheep and got lost among frightening ravines, and was about to be devoured by rapacious wild beasts. Thus I, most wretched of all, was rushing blindly into all manner of evil, when the bright light of your blessed spirit shone, and revealed to me the way that leads to the eternal kingdom of the blessed in heaven. This light of yours drove fires of the sweetest love into my heart. From that time, holy one, my whole being has burnt for you. Wounded with passion I seek you. My heart yearns to see your bright countenance, to enjoy your embraces. It now thinks of nothing but of you alone. The passionate lover does not feel such intense desire for his beautiful mistress, the two parents do not love their infant son so strongly. My heart is soft, and melting in the heat of love like wax in the burning sun. O flame that restores my heart, burning out all the dross, kindle me ever more each day. Come, burn me, consume me, until the whole of me becomes your torch.'

The typical baroque preoccupation with wounds, blood, and sweetness appear again in the eighteenth lyric. 'Oh blessed Jesus, if they who cherish trivial things knew how sweet it is to enjoy your holy love, how they would loathe their madness! The bitter wounds of your body flow with such sweetness that whoever sucks them would scorn wealth, honours, everything that he loved, and would joy in the glory of God, alone, forgetful of self. But people are blind and prefer stinking, pestilential pits to these springs. Many thanks to you, mightiest Jesus, who wash and nourish me with your purest blood.'

In the nineteenth lyric Flaminio dedicates his heart and mind to Jesus. Without the constant guidance of the Holy Spirit he is like a two-year-old child who creates all manner of dangers for himself if he is not constantly looked after by his nurse. 'Sweet, kindly Spirit, please possess me wholly, and your flame will fire my heart with love.... The sun, the moon, the light of the stars, the everlasting flow of rivers, the beautiful forest, the field loaded with crops, all that I see, may it make me perceive and touch with my hand the extraordinary kindness of the holy, blessed Divinity. Hence may I learn to be kind, and to help everybody, to harm nobody. Pure, whole, and beloved of God, may I spend what life remains to me; then may I fly beyond the highest stars of heaven to eternal bliss.'

The eroticism of medieval and of baroque religious poetry appears again in 'Amore totus langueo' where the poet calls on Jesus to show him His face, to give His lover a lover's kiss, for 'You are my soul's spouse,/She weeps for you, she calls/Upon you continuously.' Then, in the final lyric of the book, Flaminio commends his spirit to God:

>Blessed king of heaven
>Who so love mortal man
>That, for his salvation,
>You wash away his sins
>With your kind son's holy blood,
>Receive your servant's spirit,
>As he prays. He gladly
>Quits his feeble body,
>Relying on your unique benignity
>He seeks the stars of heaven
>On high that he may, O best
>Of Fathers, enjoy your presence
>And everlasting happiness.

>Rector beate caelitum,
>Qui sic amas mortalium
>Salutem, ut almi filii
>Cruore sancto laveris
>Peccata eorum; suscipe
>Servi precantis spiritum,
>Qui fretus unica tua
>Benignitate languidos
>Artus libenter deserit,
>Ut alti caeli sidera
>Petens fruatur, optime
>Pater, tua praesentia,
>Et sempiterno gaudio.
>          VIII, 21

Flaminio felt that he was dying. He wrote his old friend, Luigi Priuli, a final epistle (VI, 36):

> Ah, dear Priuli, why do you wear
> Me out with your tears? This grief of yours
> Makes my death bitter, though God with his benign
> Spirit grants that it can be sweet.
> We lived together, joined in a narrow bond
> Of love such as the sun that shines from the ultimate
> Indies to most distant Britain has scarcely
> Seen. The same studies, the same
> Desires made us one. There was nothing that the one
> Liked that the other did not like also.
> We lived in the same house, we ate at the same table.
> The joys, the sorrows, the prosperity, the adversity
> Of the one equally affected the other,
> So that one did not grieve less or rejoice
> More than his friend. This is what was.
> Now I am called to the blessed home of heaven
> Where, my various duties done,
> Eternal joy awaits me. Therefore,
> If you have your friend's interest at heart, put an end
> To your lamentations and complaints and follow
> With joyful applause my departure to the halls
> Of heaven. And try to live a devout life.
> We will soon be together again.

> Ah cur me lacrimis tuis, PRIULE
> Care, conficis? hoc tuo dolore
> Mors mihi fit amara, quam benigno
> Deus numine donat esse dulcem.
> Una viximus arcto amore juncti,
> Qualem Sol radians ab ultimo Indo
> Vix cernebat ad ultimum Britannum.
> Nos unum studium, una nos voluntas
> Fecit unanimes. Nihil placebat
> Uni, quin idem amaret alter. Una
> Nos domus tenuit, alebat una
> Mensa. Laetitiae, dolor, secunda,
> Adversa unius alterum movebant;
> Ut numquam minus hic doleret illo,
> Gauderetve. Sed haec prius fuere:
> Nunc caeli vocor ad domos beatas,
> Ubi me vario labore functum

### ROME TWENTY YEARS AFTER

> Manent gaudia sempiterna. Quare,
> Si cordi tuus est tibi sodalis,
> Pone flebilibus modum querelis,
> Et plausu aethereas euntem ad arces
> Laeto prosequere, et piam labora
> Vitam vivere, mox simul futurus.

But Flaminio did not die this time. In a letter written to Caterina Cibo on May 4, 1549,[27] Flaminio tells what happened. He says that he is still very weak, but he knows that she would like to hear about the favours that he received from God in his illness. God favoured him in mind and body. Though he spent twenty days and nights without sleep—he only had six hours sleep in all that time—his head was always clear and his senses sounder than when in health; yet normally after the loss of one night's sleep he is completely dazed and depressed.

> And what is more marvellous, when the fever and the pain brought me to a state of extreme weakness and lack of breath, I unexpectedly felt my limbs fill with strength, with such a sweetness that it seemed as though I were in the most delicate bath in the world, and I felt completely comforted. I had there the best doctors in Rome ... and they all confessed that they had never had a case in which the work of God was seen so clearly; for against all the laws of medicine he kept me alive. ...
> God showed me interior favours as well. He changed my nature and temperament suddenly, because my whole body is full of choler and fiery humours which rise up in me on the least pretext, and, in this illness, so they tell me, I never showed the least trace of anger or impatience, although the torments of the disease were enough to make the most patient and gentle man irritable and choleric, and I am absolutely certain that this was the work of God, because I didn't make any effort to bring this about, and I never thought about wanting to be patient and gentle, but God made me like that without any effort on my part.

Flaminio goes on to say that he had no fear of death. He remembered the sweetest words of the Holy Spirit, that for the elect Christ has destroyed sin, the devil, and hell (Romans VIII: 38) ... and God made him feel in his heart that he had been promised eternal salvation through Christ's passion and

---

[27] Feliciangeli, pp. 235–40.

he was as certain as though he had seen it with his bodily eyes and he said ardently with St. Paul, 'I am certain' (Romans VI: 6; I Corinthians XV: 26).

Then, as the illness progressed, although my senses were always clear and sound, nevertheless in a certain way I lost the function of reason, in that I no longer perceived anything else in the world, but I rested solely on God and Christ. I couldn't turn my thoughts to anything else, always my mind's eye saw God, who caressed me as a fond mother her ailing baby. I always saw Christ who led my soul to Paradise, and this interior vision filled me with such jubilation that I began already to taste the joy of eternal life.

I was so fixed upon this sweetest sight that I could no longer talk about anything and then I learnt why Christ calls his elect sheep and children, and at the same time I learnt why Christ also says that whoever believes in Him will never see death, because, in truth, when the doctors thought that I was already close to the last hour, then I felt so much sweetness in my spirit that I would have been in Paradise before I would have perceived the separation of the soul from the body and hence I would not have seen death. In short the joy of dying was so multiplied in the flesh and in the spirit, that, when I realized that I was beginning to get better, I was assailed by a great temptation which lasted more than three hours, for it seemed to me too hard a thing that, being arrived at the gate of Paradise, I was forced to return into this valley of misery and sin. But then, by God's grace, I realized the way self-love was deceiving me and I said to myself, 'O ungrateful and thankless creature, is this the gratitude that you show towards the goodness of God who has shown you so many favours? When He led you to heaven, you followed Him there with the greatest of joy, when He leads you back to earth, do you follow Him with such ill will? Is this the obedience that you offer God? And so you love yourself more than the will of God?

And so now I am content to live and die when and how it pleases God. We should submit in everything to God's will, joyfully accepting from His hand health and infirmity, life and death, and every other thing.

He begs Caterina Cibo not to let this letter out of her hands.

In a poem to Girolamo della Torre (VI, 39) Flaminio tells how he was cured. He was near death with his fever and the intense pain in his side and preparations were already being made for his funeral when Cardinal Caraffa came to see him. Caraffa prayed, and the fever and the pain left him. He regained strength and his affectionate friends changed their heavy laments and tears to song and rejoicing. Flaminio bids his friend thank God for the restitution of his life and give all the credit to Cardinal Caraffa. Later Flaminio sends his Muse as messenger to Francesco Bolognetti (VI, 55) to tell him that he has recovered and he writes a joking epistle to Florimonte (VI, 60) telling him how glad he is that he escaped his epitaph.

By the end of the month Flaminio's letters on his poetry begin again. On May 30 he wrote to Ulisse Bassiano from Civitella[28] discussing notes that Bassiano had made on his poetry, citing his authorities, and giving reasons for his usage. One of the poems that he discusses is an epistle that he wrote to Pietro Carnesecchi expressing his joy at the news that Marguerite de Valois, the king's sister, sings his poetry.[29] It was because of her appreciation of his poetry, as well as because of her well-known interest in religion, that Flaminio dedicated the *Carmina Sacra* to her.[30]

Another poem that Flaminio comments on is one that he had written to Mariano Vettori (VI, 57), who had invited him to come and convalesce with him. In the epistle Flaminio had asked Vettori if he honestly thought that that was in his best interests, and he went on to say that there in Rome he had goats, chickens, the best wines, shady gardens, good doctors, and people who were fond of him. Bassiano had objected to the goats, chickens, and best wines, saying that this suggested gluttony, or at least high living. Flaminio denied this. It is clear from the poem that he is still ill, and this is an invalid's diet. Hens and goats are used by Horace as a sign of frugality, and he does not think that any gourmet, wanting to describe delicate and desirable dishes, would particularly write of hens and goats.

Flaminio expresses gratitude for other criticism, which he accepts fully. Then he goes on to discuss the versification of the psalms, which Bassiano had urged him to continue. He tells

---

[28] Atanagi, *Lettere 13*, pp. 341–5.
[29] Published by Stephanus at the end of *De Rebus Divinis*, p. 34, and in the 1552 edition of *Carm. 5*, pp. 320–1, but suppressed by Mancurti along with all other poems to Carnesecchi.
[30] See the dedicatory epistle to *De Rebus Divinis* (Paris, 1550).

Bassiano that he had better pray God to give him the power and the understanding that so great an undertaking requires. He will make no resistance to the inspiration, if he feels his heart moved. But under the present circumstances many months go by when he has no inclination to write poetry, he does not know how to finish as he has begun, and the continual hard work, with staying up at night, consumes his wits and his life. He prays that it may be the will of God that he never again have the impulse to write in either verse or prose because of his age and ill health. 'Now these enterprises which have thus been set on foot fall to you young men.'[31]

On June 27 Flaminio wrote again to Bassiano from Civitella[32] After I had written to you I received your letter. Although it doesn't need an answer, I want to write ten lines nevertheless for my own satisfaction. I know that there are critics so proud that they take offence if their criticisms are not accepted as oracular, but I consider this a most odious tyranny. As I want my friends, when they have given me their opinions, to allow me to do what I want with my compositions, so I earnestly desire that they should do what they want with theirs. However, I don't know an answer to your answers. It is enough that I have told you once what I think. But I cannot now restrain myself, for the love I bear you, from explaining my meaning in general terms.

I say, then, that epigrams, odes, and similar poems are, in my judgment, like little gems, which have no value unless they are very fine and very pure. Moreover, many things are permitted in prose and in long poems which are not permitted in this sort of small poem which the very least shadow of imperfection can injure greatly with those who have good judgment, the only ones we should count in this case. But don't think now that I place myself in their number. Therefore I say to you from the bottom of my heart, and I pray you, and I entreat you from the great affection which I bear for you, that you should not ever follow my opinion, except when your conscience tells you clearly that it is good. And all the more should you mistrust me because, for many years now, all my studies have been directed towards sacred writings, towards St. Bernard and other writers of that sort, who are most elegant in their thoughts, but are barbarians in words.

---

[31] Somewhere around this time Flaminio wrote in a similar vein to Cardinal Bernardino Maffeo (VI, 11), who was urging him to write.
[32] Atanagi, *Lettere 13*, pp. 345–6.

And, as they used to say at home, 'He who works in the mill gets covered with flour.'

Again, on July 4, 1549, Flaminio wrote to Bassiano[33] about a hendecasyllable he wrote against one Pietro Myrteo (VI, 24) who went about Italy pretending that he was related to Flaminio and hence receiving favours, free lodging, and money from Flaminio's friends. Flaminio did not want to be too severe on him. It did not befit a gentleman and a Christian—in fact Flaminio said in the poem that he would be willing to admit Myrteo as a relative, even as his son, as soon as he began leading a decent life.

In May, 1549, an unpleasant event had occurred, which augured ill for the future. Della Casa drew up a list of books that were condemned as heretical.[34] On that list was the *Beneficio di Cristo*. Apparently della Casa had no idea who had written it,[35] but Pietro Paolo Vergerio, the Bishop of Capodistria, who had been attacked from 1544 onwards by della Casa, the nuncio to Venice, and who was about to defect to the Lutherans,[36] did. He wrote sorrowfully, commenting on the Index, that many think that the *Beneficio di Cristo* is full of unction, piety, and simplicity, and better than any other work to instruct even the uneducated in religion, especially about justification. 'Two people wrote this book, one began it, another finished and polished it. Both these men are in Italy and well known. They are petted by the chief dignitaries of the court of Rome. Will they proclaim themselves and defend their work and the heavenly father? Or do they want to hide and to enjoy in peace the advantages and pleasures attached to their ton-

---

[33] Atanagi, *Lettere 13*, pp. 347–8.

[34] G. della Casa, *Il Catalogo de Libri, Li Quali* nuovamente nel mese di Maggio nell'anno presente MDXLVIIII sono stati condannati, et scomunicati per heretici.

[35] See della Casa's letter to Carlo Gualteruzzi, dated Venice, July 7, 1548, in which he says that Donato Rullo has just given him a copy of *Carm. 5*. He praises Flaminio's poems for their antique spirit, with an enthusiasm that precludes any knowledge of the extent of Flaminio's involvement with the heresy which he was persecuting.

[36] On July 3, 1549, Vergerio was stripped of his dignities by the pope and censured. He was later excommunicated and banished. Like other Italian Protestants he fled to Switzerland, Germany, and Poland, see Cantù, II, pp. 378–443.

sures?[37] We do not know how Flaminio reacted to this attack. There are no references to the *Beneficio di Cristo* in his surviving letters.

From Civitella Flaminio wrote to Bassiano again on July 14[38] about a letter that Bassiano had written him about his decision to study law so that he would be able to earn his own living as a professional man instead of having to depend upon patronage. Here is Flaminio's reaction:

> Since you are in a position in which you cannot live at leisure in your own house, and since you have not such a great disregard of either the world or your own person that you want to live from hand to mouth with no concern for comforts or discomforts, you are practically forced to choose between one of two courses, either the life of a courtier or that of a professional man who earns his living. And although I did not follow the second course, more because of my health than for any other reason, nevertheless I would advise everyone ... to prefer it to the first one, which, apart from being very uncertain and deceiving, has many bad points. But one thing makes me doubtful about your plan, namely that the study of law is very laborious and that your constitution is very delicate and therefore not really fit for so much hard work.... [Moreover] our lord God has given you so great enthusiasm for Christian devotion, that one would expect that this practice of law would rather be conducive to the salvation of your soul than the contrary, while leading the life of a courtier you would expose yourself to many perils, the more you were a favourite of the great, not to say more—you know too well, anyway....
>
> I like 'Tua benignius dextera', and so it shall be revised. And I like much more the greetings which you sent me in the names of the Very Reverend Seripando and of the Reverend Master of the Holy Palace, not so much for the respect shown to me as to you....

Sometime in this period Flaminio wrote Ulisse Bassiano about the Lord's Prayer, in answer to his request.[39] Flaminio says that there are two manner of men who profess the Chris-

---

[37] Cantù, III, p. 283. The reference to the tonsure, which Flaminio certainly never had, makes one wonder if Vergerio really did know who had written the book. But the attack on its anonymous authors would sting all the same.

[38] Atanagi, *Lettere 13*, pp. 349–51.

[39] Atanagi, *Lettere 13*, pp. 351–5.

tian religion. First of all, there are those who confess God in words, but deny him in deeds. The Lord's Prayer is not for them, because they have not the Christian spirit and are not Christ's but the devil's, until they change their thoughts and life. They cannot pray with faith or recognize God for father, or desire that his name be made holy, or that his kingdom come, or that his will be done. They can say this prayer with their lips, but not with their hearts. This kind of praying is vain and feigning.

Then there are those who confess God with words and deeds. These are the truly pious and good Christians. They put all their efforts into the observation of God's commandments, repenting of their sins, and trusting in God's mercy, through Jesus Christ Our Lord. To them the Lord's Prayer belongs. They pray with faith, they recognize God for father, they desire His glory, that His will be done on earth as it is in heaven. . . .

The sinner cannot obtain pardon if he does not repent. We have this on Scriptural authority. On the other hand, God is merciful and only expects human perfection and holiness from us, not divine. To obtain God's pardon we must repent and we must forgive our debtors as God forgives us.

During this summer Flaminio wrote a few occasional poems. The last of the hendecasyllabic epistles of the sixth book number 61, is addressed to Basilio Zanchi. Flaminio tells his friend that he is now sending him his second book [of epistles][40] for criticism. He asks for his candid judgment. He asks him to read and reread his poems and to note anything that he considers inelegant or unlatin. He says he will even throw them all into the fire if that is where he thinks they belong.

Another epistle to his old friend Federico Fantuzzi of Bologna (VI, 54) tells him that he has been ill but that he is better now and is preparing to go to the Val di Lavino. We hope that Flaminio did get away and that he was able to spend his last autumn in his beloved countryside.

By the end of November Flaminio was back in Rome, and ill. On the thirtieth he wrote a letter of consolation to Lelio

---

[40] Flaminio could only be referring to the second book of epistles, i.e., VI of the Cominian edition, here because that and the *Carmina Sacra* are now his only unpublished works, and there was no second book of *Carmina Sacra*.

Torelli, principal secretary of the Duke of Florence:[41] God gives us suffering to chasten us. Christians gladly accept and bear their crosses. He is sure that Torelli has this feeling and that this letter is therefore unnecessary. However, he goes on to say,

> The Christian is different from others because those who have not the spirit of Christ flee the cross as something horrible and unbearable, whereas the true Christian carries it willingly with Christ, to reign with Christ, with the full knowledge that the tribulations, the life, the death, the world, the present, and the future serve their felicity who are the servants of God. With these and other similar arguments men of piety make themselves superior to all human accidents and, being united with Christ crucified, feel so much sweetness beneath the bitterness of the cross that all the pleasures in the world could not equal it. . . .

In 1549 the Florentine publisher, Torrentino, had published a second edition of *Carmina Quinque Illustrium Poetarum* with a few more poems added to Flaminio's first book. This constituted the most complete edition of Flaminio's poems published while he was still alive. In that book of 316 pages Flaminio's poems occupied 217 pages, i.e., he was by far the most important author as to representation. He was also by far the most important author as to variety of contribution and consistent high standards. From beginning to end Flaminio's pen never faltered. There were no lapses in taste, phrasing, or harmony, while at times Flaminio rose effortlessly to the greatest heights attained by the Latin lyric. There was never a sense of strain or showiness about Flaminio's writing. He was a natural classic, achieving his successes with quiet confidence.

Flaminio was already ill when he wrote the letter to Lelio Torelli and he would have liked to have been able to leave Rome, but Paul III had died and Pole wanted him to stay in Rome with him for the conclave. Pole was nearly elected pope in the conclave on the morning of Thursday, December 6, seven days after its opening. He was supported by Cardinal Farnese and the emperor's cardinals and was for that reason opposed by the French cardinals, who bought votes. Nevertheless Pole had twenty-six votes. With twenty-eight votes, twenty-seven plus his own, Pole would have been pope, but he

---

[41] Atanagi, *Lettere 13*, pp. 355-7.

refused to canvass, he would not seek election. The conclave dragged on for two months. Pole finally urged the cardinals to make a choice. The long delay was harming the Church. On February 7 the conclave agreed on a compromise candidate, Cardinal del Monte, who took the name of Julius III.[42]

Meantime Flaminio lay gravely ill. On December 14, 1549, he wrote his last letter from Rome to Ulisse Bassiano:

> Magnificent Messer Ulisse, my respected friend, Do not be surprised if I do not write to you as is my custom because I am so ill with the quartan fever and with my stomach and with my head that it seems to me that it will require a big effort to stay alive. Do not be surprised that I have written the ode that pleases you so much, because a just disdain excited my spirit seeing that almost everyone who visits me comforts me, ... as though I were miserable. However, I wanted to demonstrate that he who fears God is far from being miserable but has a share in felicity when, according to the judgment of the world, he appears to be most wretched.
>
> I was extremely pleased to hear these past days from Messer Iacomo da Parma that you are now living in the company of the illustrious Count Torelli. I kiss his hand.
>
> As for the papacy, take it for certain, that I shall see my cardinal come out as willingly as cardinal as as pope. Indeed I assure you that he will come out more willingly cardinal than pope, although no one could believe it, not knowing him intimately as I do. Since you like your law studies so much, look after yourself, so that no illness forces you to abandon them.
>
> I recommend myself to you with all my heart.

On February 22, 1550, Girolamo Ponte wrote a letter to Giulio Zarrabini of Imola, a relative of Flaminio's. He told him how 'to Flaminio's quartan fever, on the eleventh of this month a flux was added. Two days later there was continuous fever and a pain in the side. Flaminio died on Monday at two at night.'[43] The Monday was February 17. Flaminio died in Pole's house with Cardinal Caraffa at his bedside. Beccadelli describes his last moments:

> Cardinal Caraffa happened to be in the street when Iacopo Ercolani was bringing the viaticum to the dying Flaminio. He

[42] Beccadelli, *Vita del Polo*, pp. 38–45, and Ciccarelli, fol. 244$^v$–246$^r$.
[43] Quoted by Cuccoli, p. 125, fn. 6.

accompanied the priest on foot. Then, when he came to Flaminio's room, the cardinal suggested that the priest should make Flaminio recite the symbol of the faith and Flaminio, in a clear voice, professed his belief in everything, including the Holy Catholic Church. Then Cardinal Caraffa suggested again to the priest that he should ask him if he believed in the article about transubstantiation, which could be called the touchstone to distinguish a Lutheran from a true Catholic, and Flaminio, as far as he was able, raised his voice, and accepted this dogma of the Catholic faith. Then Caraffa came up by the bed of the sick man and helped him until the last gasps of his life, showing to all Rome with what religious sentiments Flaminio had finished his mortal career.[44]

Poor Flaminio, he seems to have been so miscast for this melodramatic scene, with the Chief Inquisitor hiding behind the priest, catechizing him in the shadowy, candlelit room. And what horrors of final persecution are suggested by the story that Caraffa said later, when he became pope, that he would like to dig Flaminio's body up and burn it![45] However, Flaminio was prepared to die and was probably by then soaring through the stars, exalted in his anticipation of his union with love. He probably did not care whether he died with the fierce Dominican or with the gentle Pole at his side. He was at last going to join his Jesus, and that was all that mattered.

Flaminio left most of his property to Pole. He asked him to give the benefice in the Val di Lavino to Beccadelli and he left two houses in Serravalle to a nephew and niece, his sister's children,[46] the *Carmina Sacra*, as we have seen, were sent by Priuli to Carnesecchi to present to Mme Marguerite. On Pole's order Flaminio was buried the following day in the English church in Rome, in St. Thomas of Canterbury's attached to the English College, in the Via Monserrato.

---

[44] Beccadelli, *Monumenti*, I, ii, 328, fn. 29, and A. Caracciolo, *Vita Pauli IV* (Cologne, 1612), pp. 52–5. This account is taken by those who are anxious to prove that Flaminio was an orthodox Catholic as an indication that he had recanted, but the creed is accepted by all the major Protestant Churches and Flaminio was always orthodox about transubstantiation—see his letter to Carnesecchi from Trent, January 1, 1543. It was on the doctrine of justification by faith that Flaminio should have been tested.

[45] Schelhorn quoted by Cuccoli, p. 94.

[46] Cuccoli, p. 126, and p. 126, fn. 2.

Flaminio's death, though it must have been expected, shocked the literary and ecclesiastical world. Pier Vettori wrote to Bartolomeo Ricci, 'With him died nobility, probity, and all good qualities. I am amazed that the animals don't moan. . . . Now Flaminio is in heaven with David. . . . What we are grieving over is our own deprivation, not his, not seeing his most likeable face again, which was so dear to us, not enjoying his sweet company, not listening to his wisdom.'[47]

Ricci wrote to Giovanni Battista Pigna of his grief at Flaminio's death. He will grieve to the end of his life, though no amount of tears can bring him back. He loved him for forty years. It was a friendship between two people who were like each other, and who had the same friends, Giulio Camillo, Priuli, . . . What a loss to scholarship! He was Ricci's great support. It was he who urged him to publish the *Apparatus Latinae Locutionis*. . . . He has now gone to the heaven to which he always aspired with his holy life.

Aonio Paleario wrote to Cardinal Bernardino Maffeo from Lucca on March 7[48] that he was very much upset to hear of the death of Marcantonio Flaminio, one of the best of men and one who was very friendly to him. He had not yet recovered from the shock of the deaths of Sadoleto and Bembo (both in 1547):

> Flaminio had spoken of me to people from Lucca just before he fell ill and, when he was already suffering most acutely from the quartan fever, he still asked Lilio, of whom he knew I was very fond, where I was,[49] what I was doing, how many more children I had had, and how he could help me. He would have done everything for me if he had lived.
>
> Since I received Lilio's letter I cannot get Flaminio out of my mind. It is a bitter thought that that genius worthy of immortality is suddenly extinct. I cannot stop thinking of his pleasantness, his greatness, his industry, his vigilance, his piety. There is nothing I would rather do than think and talk of Flaminio.
>
> I haven't heard how Pole is taking it. He is strong and grave, a man of the greatest wisdom, but what bitterer blow could strike a man?

---

[47] Camerario, sig. D$^v$–D2$^v$.
[48] Paleario, *Opera*, pp. 600–2.
[49] Paleario had left Siena and had become professor of eloquence at Lucca on the recommendations of Vettori, Bembo, and Sadoleto in 1546; see Bonnet, *Paleario*, p. 189.

On April 21 Maffeo answered Paleario from Rome:[50]
Flaminio's death has inflicted an irreparable loss on literature... on religion... and on all good men.... But since his death was such a pious Christian one that we cannot doubt that he has attained everlasting felicity, we should rather rejoice for him, than be upset over our own loss, especially since he has left many monuments of his genius.

Do you think that a man like Pole needs our consolation? He has shown he can endure great suffering with fortitude. I sent him your letter anyway. He was very moved by your devotion to him and praised your style.

—It is extraordinary to the modern reader how the humanist can think of style whatever the circumstances!

On March 20, 1550, Pier Vettori wrote to Pole from Florence[51] that he did not seek to console him... for Pole is a source of strength himself, but he did want to say a little about the serious blow literature had suffered:

Although I am an inferior man of letters I was foremost in loving him for the sharpness of his intellect, the sanctity of his life, his exceptional erudition, and the elegance of his manners.... We have lost the flower of poets and the glory and splendour of this century. He was equal to the ancients in the variety and elegance of his poems.[52] He was excellent at clarifying obscurities in ancient writers.... Perhaps no future age will see his like.

Pole answered this letter on March 29:[53]

...for it seems to me that I have not known anyone endowed with greater piety towards God, or more removed from all greed for those things which men commonly admire, or more diligent in all the duties of Christian charity. And so, at the extinction of such a man, whom I loved uniquely and by whom I felt myself most greatly loved (if that is, he is extinct who has changed death for immortality), I cannot deny that I too was deeply shaken.... But if you felt such deep grief on his death because of your admiration for his probity and his learning, what do you

[50] Paleario, *Opera*, p. 603.
[51] Brutus, *Epistolae Clarorum Virorum* (Lyons, 1561), pp. 239-43.
[52] Corrado, too, felt that Flaminio was the equal of the ancients, Sebastiano Corrado, *Epistolae ad Atticum* (Venice, 1544), commentary, fol. 41ʳ–42ʳ.
[53] Brutus, *Ep. Clar. Vir.*, pp. 243-7.

think I feel who constantly enjoyed all these good things and who moreover, constantly received the greatest delight from his most agreeable conversation, and the greatest profit from his most loving advice in all my undertakings of every sort? But we must submit to God's will.

There is one consolation, no one could have an easier access to eternal life and blessedness than Flaminio, who has always lived with the greatest integrity and chastity, and who has departed this life in piety and holiness.

Flaminio, like Valdes, was fortunate in the date of his death. Soon there was no place in Rome for the humanist, for the man of tolerance, sympathy, and understanding, for the man who wanted to examine every idea and to form his own opinion on it. Pole, who almost became pope in 1550, was being persecuted by 1553. In 1555 Caraffa became pope and adopted the name of Paul IV. By 1557 Pole was recalled from the legation to England and Morone, who had been the first, and was destined to be the last, president of the Council of Trent, was a prisoner in the Castel Sant'Angelo. The principal charge against both these cardinals was their association with Flaminio. In 1557, too, Carnesecchi was summoned to Rome to face trial for heresy, and Priuli was deprived of the diocese of Brescia. Soon many other friends of Flaminio were being investigated by the Inquisition: Apollonio Merenda, for a long time Pole's chaplain; Donato Rullo; Giles Fuscherat, Bishop of Modena, who heard Flaminio's confession shortly before his death—Paul IV shut him up in the Castel Sant'Angelo—and Vittorio Soranzo, Bishop of Viterbo when Flaminio was there, later Bishop of Bergamo—he was captured by the Chief Inquisitor of Venezia, Michele Ghislieri, later Pius V, imprisoned in the Castel Sant'Angelo, tried, convicted, deprived of his diocese, and executed.[54]

Flaminio's works were accused before the Inquisition, not just the *Beneficio di Cristo* and the *Apology* for it, but also the prose *Paraphrase* of the psalms, the *Exposition* of the psalms, the *Carmina Sacra*, and several Italian letters.[55] Then, in 1559, Paul IV put all Flaminio's works on the Index.[56] After Paul IV's

---

[54] Comba, I, pp. 509–11.
[55] Cuccoli, p. 92.
[56] *Ibid.*, p. 94.

death Beccadelli and Fuscherat, now cleared, were charged with revising the Index. They gave a favourable report on Flaminio's works to the Council of Trent, which removed them from the Index.[57]

Henceforth Flaminio became a minor classic up until the early nineteenth century when humanist Latin was virtually forgotten. He occupied an even more prominent position than before in the third edition of the *Carmina Quinque Illustrium Poetarum* published in 1552. Here the second book of epistles appeared for the first time (Com. IV) and the newly published *Carmina Sacra* for the first time in Italy. Thenceforth his poems were often reprinted, as were his versions of the psalms and his religious songs, the last two particularly in the northern countries. Three major editions of Flaminio's poems were published in the eighteenth century, the two Cominian editions published in Padua in 1729 and 1743, both edited by Mancurti, and the joint edition of Flaminio's and Fracastoro's poems published in Verona in 1747. *Carmina Quinque Illustrium Poetarum* was also reprinted in Bergamo in 1753 and Flaminio's poems were published along with those of his friends and contemporaries Fracastoro, Cotta, Bonfadio, Fumano, Arco, Bembo, Navagero, and Castiglione in Verona in 1740. The second Cominian edition was republished in Prato in 1831.

In England a number of Flaminio's poems were published in an anthology of Italo-Latin poetry published in 1684. Alexander Pope made a second selection in 1740. But Flaminio seems early to have become a school book. A word-for-word translation of Flaminio, that was little more than a crib, was published by one John Norton, aged twelve, in London in 1674 under the title of *The Scholar's Vade Mecum being a translation of Marc Antonio Flaminio*, and a selection of thirty-nine of Flaminio's poems, fourteen epistles and twenty-five pastorals, was published in 1792 for use in Winchester School.[58] The last English edition of Flaminio's poems was published by Archdeacon Wrangham in Chester in 1829.

[57] Cuccoli, p. 95.
[58] *Carmina Quaedam Elegantissima accedunt Mar. Antonii Epistolae Quaedam et Lusus Pastorales* in usum Scholae Wintoniensis.

# BIBLIOGRAPHY

Alberti, Leandro. Descriptio Italiae. Bologna, 1550.
—— De viris illustribus ordinis praedicatorum. Bologna, 1517.
Altamura, A. L'umanesimo nel mezzogiorno d'Italia. Florence, 1941.
Amante, B. Giulia Gonzaga. Bologna, 1896.
Annelli, L. I riformatori nel secolo xvi. Milan, 1891. 2 vols.
Atanagi, D., ed. Delle lettere da diversi re, et principi et cardinali, et altri huomini dotti a Mons. Pietro Bembo. Venice, 1560.
—— De le lettere facete et piacevoli di diversi grandi huomini. Venice, 1561.
—— De le lettere di tredici huomini illustri libri tredici. Rome, 1554.
Bainton, R. H. Bernardo Ochino. Florence, 1940.
Barbarani, E. G. Fracastoro. Verona, 1894.
Beccadelli, L. Monumenti di varia letteratura. Bologna, 1799.
—— Vita Contarini. Brescia, 1746.
—— Vita del Polo. Paris, 1677.
Bellon, E. De Sannazarii vita et operibus. Paris, 1895.
Bembo. P. Epistolae. Paris, 1526.
—— Epistolae italicae. Venice, 1552.
—— Gli Asolani. Venice, 1553.
Benrath, K. Julia Gonzaga. Halle, 1900.
Biadego, G. Marcantonio Flaminio ai servigi di Gianmatteo Giberti vescovo di Verona. Atti del reale istituto veneto. LXV, 2 (1905–6), 209–28.
Boehmer, E. The lives of the twin brothers Juan and Alfonso de Valdes, tr. J. T. Betts. London, 1882.
Boncampagni-Ludovisi, U. Roma nel rinascimento. 5 vols. Albano Laziale, 1928–30.

## BIBLIOGRAPHY

Bonfadio, J., and Fracastoro, G. Carmina. Padua, 1718.
—— Lettere famigliari. Bologna, 1744.
Bonnet, J. Aonio Paleario. Paris, 1863.
—— Olimpia Morata. Paris, 1850.
Bottiglione, G. La lirica latina in Firenze nella 2.ª metà del secolo xv. Annali della reale scuola normale superiore di Pisa. Pisa, 1913.
Brown, G. K. Italy and the reform to 1550. Oxford, 1933.
Brutus, J. M., ed. Epistolae clarorum virorum. Lyons, 1561.
Buchanan, George. Davidis psalmi aliquot latino carmine expressi. Paris, 1546.
Bullock, W. L. Lyric innovations of Giovanni della Casa. PMLA, XLI (1926), 82–90.
Burchard, J. Liber notarum. Città di Castello, n.d.
—— Diarium. Paris, 1883–5.
Camerario, J., ed. Epistolae aliquot Marci Antonii Flaminii de veritate doctrinae eruditae et sanctitate religionis . . . ex italico. Nuremberg, 1571.
Cantimori, D. Atteggiamenti della vita culturale italiana alla riforma. Rivista storica italiana. Napoli, 1936.
—— Eretici italiani del cinquecento. Florence, 1939.
—— Per la storia degli eretici italiani del secolo xvi in Europa. Rome, 1937.
Cantù, C. Eretici d'Italia. Paris, 1866–70. 5 vols.
Capasso, C. Paolo III, Messina, 1926.
Capponi, D. G., ed. Joannis Antonii Flaminii Forocorneliensis epistolae familiares. Bologna, 1744.
Caracciolo, A. Vita Pauli IV. Cologne, 1612.
Cardella, L. Memorie storiche di cardinali. 9 vols. Rome, 1792–7.
Carducci, G. Opere. Bologna, 1889–1905. XV.
—— Studi letterarî. Opere. Bologna, 1889–1905. VIII.
Carrara, E. Storia della poesia pastorale. Milan, 1917.
—— La favola pastorale, Milan, n.d.
Castaldo, G. B. Vita del beato Gaetano Thiene. Modena, 1612.
Castiglione, B. Lettere. Padua, 1769. 2 vols.
—— Lettere. Milan, 1826.
Catharino, Brother Ambrogio (Lancelloto Politi). Compendio d'errori et inganni luterani, contenuti in un libretto, senza nome de l'autore, intitolato, trattato utilissimo del benefitio di Christo crucifisso. Rome, 1544.
Cesareo, G. A. Buffoni, parassiti e cortigiane alla corte di Leone X. Nuova rivista storica, VIII (1923, 79–82.)
Chiminelli, P. Il contributo italiana alla riforma. Rome, 1921.

## BIBLIOGRAPHY

Chiminelli, P. Scritti religiosi. Torino, 1925.
Chiurlo, B. Review of Pasquale Rossi's Marcantonio Flaminio (Vittorio Veneto, 1931). GSLI, CIV (1934), 104–16.
Church, F. The Italian reformers. New York, 1932.
Cian, V. Galanterie italiane. Torino, 1888.
—— Scritti di erudizione. Siena, 1951.
—— Umanesimo e rinascimento. Florence, 1941.
—— Un illustre nunzio pontificio B. Castiglione. Rome, 1951.
Ciccarelli, A. Le vite de' pontefici con le effigie. Rome, 1587.
Cistellini, A. Figure della reforma pretridentina. Brescia, 1948.
Comba, E. I nostri protestanti. Florence, 1895–7. I and II.
—— Storia della riforma in Italia. Florence, 1881. I.
Corrado, S. comment. on Epistolae ad Atticum. Venice, 1544.
Cortese, G. Opera. Padua, 1774.
Corvisieri, C. Compendio dei processi del santo offizio di Roma ... sotto Paolo III, Giulio III, e Paolo IV. Archivio della società romana di storia patria, III (Rome, 1880), 261–90.
—— Documenti inediti sul sacco di Roma. Rome, 1873.
Costa, E. Antologia della lirica latina in Italia nei secoli xv e xvi. Città di Castello, 1888.
—— Marc Antonio Flaminio e il cardinale Alessandro Farnese. GSLI, X (1887), 383–7.
Croce, B. Giovanni di Valdes. Bari, 1938.
—— Poesia populare e poesia d'arte. Bari, 1933.
Cuccoli, E. Marc Antonio Flaminio. Bologna, 1897.
Curtius, E. R. European literature and the latin middle ages. London, 1953.
Dal Canto, Alete. Pietro Carnesecchi. Rome, 1911.
Della Casa, G. Il catalogo de' libri, li quali nuovamente nel mese di maggio nell'anno presente MDXLVIIII sono stati condannati et scomunicati per heretici.
Dolce, L. Lettere di diversi eccellentissimi huomini. Venice, 1559.
—— Osservazioni nella volgare lingua. Venice, 1550.
—— ed. V. Colonna. Rime. Venice, 1559.
Domenichi, L. Facetie. Venice, 1584.
Douglas, R. M. Jacopo Sadoleto. Cambridge, Mass., 1959.
Drei, G. I Farnese. Rome, 1954.
Edward VI, King of England. The literary remains of King Edward VI, ed. J. G. Nichols. London, 1857.
Ellinger, A. Hymnorum ecclesiasticorum. Frankfort, 1578.
Feliciangeli, B. Caterina Cibo. Camerino, 1891.
Ferrai, L. A. Lettere di cortigiane del secolo xvi. Florence, 1884.
Ferrajoli, A. Il ruolo della corte di Leone X, 1514–16. Rome, 1911.

## BIBLIOGRAPHY

Flaminio, G. A. Compendio della volgar grammatica. Bologna, 1520.
—— De educatione et institutione liberorum. Bologna, 1524. Reprinted in Gli scrittori pedagogici del secolo xvi, ed. G. B. Gerini. Torino, 1897.
—— Epistolae familiares. Bologna, 1744.
—— Libri tre de institutione harmonica. Bologna, 1516.
—— Silvarum II. epigrammatum III. Bologna, 1515.
Flaminio, M. A. Actii Synceri Sannazarii odae. Eiusdem elegia de malo punico. Ioannis Cottae carmina. M. Antonii Flaminii carmina. Venice, 1529.
—— Alcune lettere. n.p., n.d.
—— Beneficio di Gesù Cristo crocifisso verso i cristiani. Reprinted by G. Paladino in Opuscoli e lettere di riformatori italiani del '500, vol. I. Bari, 1913.
—— Carminum libri duo. eiusdem paraphrases in triginta psalmos, versibus scripta. Lyons, 1548.
—— Carmina quinque illustrium poetarum. Florence, 1549.
—— Carmina quinque illustrium poetarum. Florence, 1552.
—— Flaminiorum Forocorneliensium carmina. Padua, 1743.
—— and Fracastoro, G. Carmina. Verona, 1740.
—— —— Carmina. Verona, 1747. 2nd edn. (Other editions, 1759, 1782.)
—— Carmina quinque illustrium poetarum. Bergoma, 1753.
—— Carmina quaedam elegantissima accedunt Mar. Antonii epistolae quaedam et lusus pastorales in usum scholae Wintoniensis. Winchester, 1792.
—— Davidis psalmi aliquot latino carmine expressi. Paris, 1546.
—— Davidis... psalmi... Flaminio et Spinula. Basle, 1558.
—— De rebus divinis. Paris, 1550.
—— Doctissimorum nostra aetate italorum epigrammata. Paris, n.d.
—— Epistolae aliquot Marci Antonii Flaminii de veritate doctrinae eruditae et sanctitate religionis. Nuremberg, 1571.
—— Hymni. Frankfurt, 1578.
—— In galli obitum. Amphitheatrum sapientiae socraticae joco-seriae, ed. C. Dornau. Hanover, 1619.
—— In librum psalmorum brevis explanatio. Venice, 1545.
—— In librum psalmorum brevis explanatio... adjectae paraphrases. Paris, 1546. (Other editions, Lyons, 1548; Paris, 1549; Lyons, 1552; Antwerp, 1558; Venice, 1563; Lyons, 1569; Lyons, 1576).
—— Letters: See Atanagi, Lettere... a Bembo, pp. 49$^{r-v}$.
 —————— Lettere facete, I, 304-6.

## BIBLIOGRAPHY

——— Letters: See Atanagi, Lettere 13, pp. 294-358.
Biadego, pp. 209-28.
Camerario.
Costa, GSLI, X, 383-7.
Cuccoli, p. 118, fn 1.
Felicangeli, pp. 231-40.
Paladino, I, 68-89.
Pino, II, 151-6.
and the 1743 ed. of Flaminio's poems, pp. 295-305.

——— Michael Tarchaniotae Marulli neniae. eiusdem epigrammata nunquam alias impressa. M. Antonii Flaminii adulescentis amoenissimi carminum libellus. Fano, 1515.
——— Paraphrasis in duodecimum Aristotelis librum de prima philosophia. Venice, 1536.
——— Paraphrasis in duos et triginta psalmos. Venice, 1538.
——— Vita beati Mauritii pannonii. De viris illustrium ordinis praedicatorum, ed. Leandro Alberti. Bologna, 1517.
Fontana, B. Documenti vaticani contro l'eresia. Archivio della reale società romana di storia patria, XV (Roma, 1892), 71-166; 365-474.
Fracastoro, G., and Bonfadio, J. Carmina. Padua, 1718.
——— and Arco, Nicolo d'. Carmina. Padua, 1739.
——— and Flaminio, M. A. Carmina. Verona, 1740.
——— Opera omnia. Venice, 1555.
——— Opera. Bologna, 1739.
Fuochi, M. Hymnus in Pana di Marc Antonio Flaminio. Atene e Roma (1904).
Gagny, J., ed. Doctissimorum nostra aetate italorum epigrammata. Paris, n.d.
Gasquet, Cardinal F. A history of the venerable English college, Rome. London, 1920.
——— Cardinal Pole and his early friends. London, 1927.
Gerini, G. B. Gli scrittori pedagogici del secolo xvi. Torino, 1897.
Giberti, G. M. Opera. Hostiliae, 1740.
Giordani, G. Della venuta e dimora in Bologna del sommo pontifice Clemente VII per la coronazione di Carlo V imperatore. Bologna, 1842.
——— Vita del conte Andrea Bentivoglio. Bologna, 1840.
Giorgi, E. Le più antiche bucoliche volgari. GSLI, LXVI (1915), 140 ff.
Giovio, P. De vita Leonis decimi pontificis maximi libri quatuor. Florence, 1551.
Giraldi, L. G. De poetis nostrorum temporum, II. Basle, 1580.

## BIBLIOGRAPHY

Giustiniano, P. Trattato di ubidientia... con una pistola del medesimo a Marc Antonio Flaminio. Venice, 1535.
Gnoli, D. Orti letterarî nella Roma di Leone X. Nuova antologia (January 16, 1930).
Graf, A. Attraverso il '500. Torino, 1888.
Grassio, Paris de. Il diario di Leone X. Rome, 1884.
Gruter, J. Delitiae CC italorum poetarum. Frankfort, 1608.
Heep, H. Juan de Valdes. Leipzig, 1909.
Jones, W. P. The pastourelle. Cambridge, Mass., 1931.
Kaminski, D. G. Marcantonio Flaminio ed i chierici regolari. Regnum Dei, II (1946), 5–18.
Laemmer, H. Monumenta vaticana historiam ecclesiasticam saeculi xvi illustrantia. Freiburg im Breisgau, 1861.
Longolio, C. Epistolarum libri ix. Paris, 1526.
Maddison, Carol. Apollo and the nine. London, 1960.
Manuzio, P. Epistolae italicae clarorum virorum. Venice. 1551.
—— Lettere volgare... nobilissimi uomini. Venice, 1542.
Manzoni, G. Estratto del processo di Pietro Carnesecchi. Miscellanea di storia Italiana, X (Torino, 1870).
Minturno, S. Dell'arte poetica. Naples, 1725.
Molza, F. M. Ninfa tiberina. n.p., n.d.
—— Poesie. Milan, 1808.
Morell, T. poems on divine subjects. London, 1732.
Muzio, G. Tre testimoni fedeli. Pesaro, 1555.
Nardella, T. La seconda Roma. Milan, 1927.
Navagero, A. Opera omnia. Padua, 1718.
Niccolai, F. Pier Vettori. Florence, 1912.
Norton, J. The scholar's vade mecum... being a translation of Marc Antonio Flaminio. London, 1674.
Paladino, G. Opuscoli e lettere di riformatori italiani del '500, vol. I. Bari, 1913.
Paleario, A. Opera. Iena, 1728.
Papotti, T. Elogi di illustri imolesi. Imola, 1841.
Partenio, B. Dialogi italiani de imitatione poetica. Venice, 1565.
Paschini, P. Eresia e riforma cattolica al confine orientale d'Italia. Rome, 1951.
—— Roma nel rinascimento. Bologna, 1940.
—— S. Gaetano Thiene. Roma, 1926.
—— Un amico del cardinale Polo: Alvise Priuli. Rome, n.d.
Pastor, L. Storia dei papi. Rome, 1942–51.
Pecchiai, P. Roma nel cinquecento. Bologna, 1948.
Pighi, G. Gianmatteo Giberti vescovo di Verona. Verona, 1900.

## BIBLIOGRAPHY

Pino, B. Della nuova scielta di lettere di diversi nobilissimi huomini. Venice, 1582.
Pole, R. De concilio. Venice, 1562.
—— Epistolae, ed. G. G. Schelhorn. Brescia, 1744-5. 4 vols.
—— Lettere. Brescia, 1548.
—— Letters in Epistolae clarorum virorum, ed. J. M. Brutus, Lyons, 1561.
Politi, Lancelloto. See under Catharino, Brother Ambrogio.
Poliziano, A. Poesie italiane. Milan, 1825.
—— Poesie latine. Florence, 1867.
Pope, A. Selecta poemata italorum qui latine scripserunt. London, 1740. 2 vols.
Pulci, B., etc. Bucoliche.... Florence, 1481.
Ranke, Leopold von. The history of the popes. tr. E. Foster. London, 1906.
Riccio, B. De judicio. Ferrara, 1562.
—— Epistolae. Bologna, 1560.
—— Epistolarum familiarium libri IIII. Ferrara, 1562.
Rodoconachi, E. Courtisanes et bouffons. Paris, 1894.
—— Histoire de Rome: Le pontificat de Jules II et de Léon X et Adrien VI et Clément VII. Paris, 1928-33.
—— La femme italienne à la renaissance. Paris, 1907.
—— La première renaissance. Paris, 1912.
—— Une courtisane vénitienne. Paris, 1894.
—— Vittoria Colonna et la réforme. Versailles, 1892.
Rosalba, G. Le egloghe piscatorie di J. Sannazaro. Naples, 1888.
Roscoe, W. The life and pontificate of Leo X. Liverpool, 1805. 4 vols.
Ruscelli, G. Lettere di diversi autori eccellenti. Venice, 1556.
—— ed. Vittoria Colonna, Rime. Venice, n.d.
Sadoleto, J. Epistolae. Rome, 1760.
—— Opera. Verona, 1738. 4 vols.
Sainati, A. La lirica latina del rinascimento. Pisa 1919.
Sannazaro, J. Arcadia, ed. M. Scherillo. Torino, 1888.
—— Opera omnia. Venice, 1535.
Schenk, W. Reginald Pole. London, 1950.
Scherillo, M. Un poeta romantico del rinascimento, Jacopo Sannazaro. Nuovo antologia (February 1925), 337-47.
Serafino, A. Opere. Venice, 1548.
Serassi, P. A., ed. Lettere di negozii del conte Baldasar Castiglione. Padua, 1769-71. 2 vols.
—— Poesie di Francesco Maria Molza. Milan, 1808.
Shaw, H. N. I grandi riformatori. Florence, 1897.

## BIBLIOGRAPHY

Signorile, A. La ninfa tiberina di F. M. Molza. Bari, 1921.
Tacchi-Venturi, P. Storia della compagnia di Gesù. 2 vols. Rome, 1950–1.
Tallarigo, C. M. G. Pontano e i suoi tempi. Naples, 1874.
Tasso, B. Rime II. Bergamo, 1749.
Taygeto, J. A. Carmina praestantium poetarum. Brescia, 1565.
Tiraboschi, G. Storia della letteratura italiana. Modena, 1772.
Toffanin, G. Il cinquecento. Milan, 1950. 4th edn.
—— L'umanesimo al concilio di Trento. (Vida's De republica.) Bologna, 1955.
Tommasino, G. Tra umanisti e filosofi ... Philalethes. Maddaloni, 1921.
Torraca, F. J. Sannazaro. Naples, 1879.
—— La materia dell'Arcadia. Città di Castello, 1888.
—— Rassegna critica della letteratura italiana. Naples, 1921.
—— Studi di storia letteraria. Florence, 1923.
—— Studi di storia letteraria napoletana. Livorno, 1884.
Ubaldini, G. P. Carmina poetarum nobilium. Milan, 1563.
Valdes, J. de. A commentary on the first book of psalms. London, 1894.
—— A commentary upon Our Lord's sermon on the mount. London, 1882.
—— Alphabeto cristiano. London, 1861.
—— Alphabeto cristiano, ed. B. Croce. Bari, 1938.
—— Dialogo de doctrina cristiana. Coimbra, 1925.
—— Instrucción cristiana para los niños. Bonn, 1883.
—— Le cento et dieci divine considerazioni. Basle, 1550, and ed. E. Cione, Milan, 1944.
—— Lac spirituale. Brunswick, 1864.
Verrepaeus, S. Selectiores epistolae clarorum virorum. Dilingae, 1573.
Vettori, P. Letters in Epistolae clarorum virorum, ed. J. M. Brutus. Lyons, 1561.
Vida, H. De republica, in G. Toffanin, L'umanesimo al concilio di Trento. Bologna, 1955.
Wrangham, Archdeacon, ed. Fifty select poems of Marc Antonio Flaminio imitated by E. W. Barnard. Chester, 1829.
Young, M. The life and times of Aonio Paleario or a history of the Italian reformers in the sixteenth century. London, 1860. 2 vols.
Zabughin, V.
—— Storia del rinascimento cristiano. Milan, 1924.
Zino, P. F., ed. Giberti's opera. Hostiliae, 1740.

# INDEX

Adrian VI, 39, 41–2, 44
Alberti, Leandro, 20, 25, 26, 160
Antonio Mario poems, 25 fn. 4
Arco, Count Nicolò d', 25, 91, 129, 206

Barbarossa, Khaireddin, 80–1
Bassiano, Ulisse, 87, 175 fn. 11, 176–7, 178, 179, 195–7, 201
Beccadelli, Lodovico, 25, 113, 118, 119, 121, 124, 174, 201, 202, 206
Bembo, Pietro, 27, 77, 78, 79, 111, 121, 139, 169, 203, 206
*Beneficio di Cristo*, 143–6, 147, 151, 197–8, 205
Beroaldo, Filippo, jr., 12, 13, 14
Bocchi, Achille, 19, 20, 21, 22, 77
Bologna, 23, 24–5, 26, 41
Buchannan, George, 162, 164–5

Caracciolo, Galeazzo, Marquis of Vico, 110, 141–2, 143
Caraffa, Gianpietro (later Paul IV), 42, 45, 72, 74, 78, 84, 107, 124–6, 137, 142, 194–5, 201–2, 205
*Carmina sacra*, 185–91, 195, 205, 206
Carnesecchi, Pietro, 107, 108, 110, 111, 114, 116, 117, 118, 121, 122–3, 138, 140, 141, 142, 146, 176, 186, 195, 202, 205
Caserta, 98, 103, 111
Castiglione, Count Baldassare, 14, 15, 16, 19, 20, 21, 23, 182, 206
Catullus, 13, 18, 22, 60, 61, 67, 68, 87, 98, 165
Charles V, 25, 39, 44, 45, 76–8, 80, 146
Cibo, Caterina, Duchess of Camerino, 117, 171, 193–4
Clement VII, 42, 43, 44, 71, 74, 75–7, 81, 84, 111
Colonna, Vittoria, 12, 72, 90, 109, 110, 117, 120, 121, 124, 138, 171, 177–8
Contarini, Gaspare, 42, 78, 79, 83, 84, 94, 107, 112, 115, 119, 121, 132, 135–7, 138, 168
Cortese, Gregorio, 78, 79, 83, 84, 85, 94, 107, 112

della Casa, Giovanni, 74, 117, 197

epyllion, 66–7

Farnese, Cardinal Alessandro, 82, 86, 87, 89, 126, 147, 148–50, 152, 159, 160, 164, 169–70, 174, 200
Flaminio, G. A., 1–5, 8, 9, 10, 12, 14, 15, 16, 19, 20, 21, 23, 24, 27–8, 40, 41, 77, 84, 160
'Flaminio', the name, 1, 3
Florimonte, Galeazzo, 74, 75, 97, 103, 121, 132–3, 174, 183–5, 195
Fracastoro, Girolamo, 35, 74, 75, 88, 90, 93, 163, 169, 177, 206

Giberti, Gianmatteo, 42, 43–5, 49, 68, 69, 71, 72, 73–6, 77, 78, 84, 85, 87, 91, 92, 94, 95, 104, 107, 147, 151
Gonzaga, Giulia, 80–2, 109–10, 123–4, 125–6
Goritz, Johannes, 46, 49

Homer, 60, 61, 62, 63, 64, 65
Horace, 13, 14, 17, 18, 19, 55, 60, 86, 96, 148, 160, 165, 166

Inquisition, 107, 116, 121, 125–6, 129, 137–9, 142–3

justification by faith, 78, 107–8, 112, 117, 120, 123, 138, 143–4

Leo X, 5–7, 8, 9, 10, 11, 12, 24, 38, 43, 44
literary groups in Roman gardens, 45–6
Longueil, Christophe de (Cristoforo Longolio), 26, 27, 28, 34, 35, 40, 111
*lusus pastorales*, 29–33, 50–6, 98–103, 111, 182, 183
Lutherans, 28, 39, 44, 72, 78, 84, 108, 112, 113, 115, 116, 122, 123, 137–9, 140–1, 168, 197
Mannerism, 161–2
Marullus, Michael Tarchaniota, 20, 21

215

# INDEX

Molza, Francesco Maria, 26, 40, 47, 48, 49, 77, 177, 182
Morone, Cardinal Giovanni, 116, 121, 129, 140, 142, 173, 174, 205

Naples, 14, 95–8, 107–11, 116, 128, 138
Navagero, Andrea, 29, 54, 182, 206

Ochino, Bernardino, 110, 117, 137–8
Oratory of Divine Love, 42, 78
Ovid, 60, 61, 62

Paleario, Aonio, 139, 140, 203, 204
Pallai, Biagio, 46, 172
Paul III, 76, 78, 82, 84, 85, 94, 152, 200
Petrarch, 18, 32, 50, 68, 100
Pole, Reginald, 27, 28, 78, 83, 84, 85, 93, 107, 116, 117, 119–22, 123, 124–26, 132, 134, 137, 140, 141, 147, 151, 154, 155, 158, 169, 171, 200, 202, 204–5, 205
primitivism, 89, 156–8
Priuli, Luigi, 78, 84, 116, 121, 122, 132, 140, 147, 154, 159, 168, 169, 186, 192–3, 202, 205
Psalms, explanation of, 152–3, 161, 205
Psalms, prose translation of, 79, 93, 94–5, 159–60, 161, 205
Psalms, verse translation of, 159–68, 182
Reform thought in Italy, 107–12, 122–9, 137–9, 141–6, 197
Reform within the Church, 41–2, 78, 85, 105–7, 120
Ricci, Bartolomeo, 28, 130, 132
Rome, 10–12, 26, 38–42, 45–8, 72, 171–3
Ronsard, Pierre de, 52, 65, 67, 173

Sack of Rome, 72
Sadoleto, Jacopo, 25, 42, 45, 73, 107, 121, 139, 182, 203
Sannazaro, Jacopo, 14, 38, 54, 78, 96
Sauli, Stefano, 27, 28–9, 33, 35, 38, 87, 177
Serravalle (Vittorio Veneto), 1, 3, 4, 27–8, 34–5, 50, 69, 147, 202
Sessa Aurunca, 97–8

Tasso, Bernardo, 57, 67, 116
Trent, Council of, 140, 154–5, 159, 168–9, 205, 206

Urbino, 15, 16

Valdes, Juan de, 82, 107–12, 117, 123, 126, 138, 152, 153, 205
Vergerio, Pietro, Paolo, 197–8
Vergil, 18, 56, 60, 62, 92, 96, 103
Vermigli, Peter Martyr, 110, 129, 138–9
Verona, 44, 45, 73–5, 84, 95
Vida, Girolamo, 154–5, 158–9
Viterbo, 119, 121–4

www.ingramcontent.com/pod-product-compliance
Lightning Source LLC
Chambersburg PA
CBHW021404290426
44108CB00010B/375